CISTERCIAN FATHERS SERIES: NUMBER TWENTY-SEVEN

William of St Thierry

Exposition on the Epistle to the Romans

CISTERCIAN FATHERS SERIES: NUMBER TWENTY-SEVEN

Exposition on the Epistle to the Romans

William of St Thierry

Translated by
John Baptist Hasbrouck
Monk of Our Lady of Guadalupe Abbey

Edited, with an introduction, by
John D. Anderson

Cistercian Publications
www.cistercianpublications.org

LITURGICAL PRESS
Collegeville, Minnesota
www.litpress.org

A Cistercian Publications title published by Liturgical Press

Cistercian Publications
Editorial Offices
161 Grosvenor Street
Athens, Ohio 45701
www.cistercianpublications.org

This translation has been made from the Latin edition published by
J. P. Migne in the *Patrologiae cursus completus, series latina*, volume 180,
cols. 547-694 under the title *Expositio in epistolam ad Romanos, Guillelmi
abbatis Sancti Theodorici*.

William of St-Thierry (1085?–1147/8)

© 1980 by Cistercian Publications. © 2008 by Liturgical Press, Collegeville, Minnesota. All rights reserved. No part of this book may be used or reproduced in any manner whatsoever, except brief quotations in reviews, without written permission of Liturgical Press, Saint John's Abbey, PO Box 7500, Collegeville, MN 56321-7500. Printed in the United States of America.

Library of Congress Cataloging-in-Publication Data

Guillaume de Saint-Thierry, 1085 (ca.)–1148?
   Exposition on the Epistle to the Romans.

   (Cistercian Fathers series ; no. 27)
   Translation of Expositio in epistolam ad Romanos.
   Bibliography: p. 301
   Includes index.
   1. Bible. N.T. Romans—Commentaries. I. Anderson, John
      Douglas, 1943– II. Title.
BS2665.G8413   227'.1'07   78-1296
ISBN 0-87907-327-6

DEDICATION

*The editors of Cistercian Publications
dedicate this volume*

to the memory of

TERESA ANN DOYLE OSB
1905-1979

*a gentle woman and a generous scholar
in the great benedictine tradition*

TABLE OF CONTENTS

Introduction 3
Editor's Comment 11

Exposition on the Epistle to the Romans

Preface 15
BOOK ONE
  Chapter One (Romans 1) 19
  Chapter Two (Romans 2:1-2:9) 43
BOOK TWO
  (Romans 2:11-2:29) 53
  Chapter Three (Romans 3) 62
  Chapter Four (Romans 4) 75
BOOK THREE
  Chapter Five (Romans 5) 91
  Chapter Six (Romans 6) 110
BOOK FOUR
  Chapter Seven (Romans 7) 129
  Chapter Eight (Romans 8:2-8:4) 149
BOOK FIVE
  (Romans 8:5-8:39) 157
  Chapter Nine (Romans 9:1-9:21) . . . 182
BOOK SIX
  (Romans 9:22-9:33) 191
  Chapter Ten (Romans 10) 199
  Chapter Eleven (Romans 11) 208
BOOK SEVEN
  Chapter Twelve (Romans 12) 229
  Chapter Thirteen (Romans 13) 237
  Chapter Fourteen (Romans 14) 245
  Chapter Fifteen (Romans 15:1-16:27) . . 255
Scriptural Index 273
Patristic Index 286
Topical Index 291
Bibliography 299
Abbreviations 301

INTRODUCTION

THE EXPOSITION ON ROMANS is a monastic text from start to finish. In it William of St Thierry is not concerned with refutation, dialectic, or scholastic disputation. He deals with something more personal. His task is one of joy and delight. His goal is humility of heart and devotional purity. Fundamental to William's motivation is the centrality of grace in the spiritual life. Only when man is in touch with grace and its radical importance in his existence and in all that he accomplishes can growth occur. William is convinced of this; he hopes to convince us of it.

Throughout the Preface to the *Exposition on Romans* William sings the praises of God's grace. He cites examples from scripture of the efficacy of grace. He cites Paul himself as an example of the sufficiency of grace. Then, and this is to be characteristic of William's style throughout the *Exposition*, he breaks into prayer, 'Lord Jesus, beautiful above the sons of men . . . . ' Several times in the course of the commentary William shifts from narrative to address God directly. In this way he adds a personal, intimate touch to a literary genre which was soon to become settled into the regimented methodology of the schools.

In his treatment of the *Epistle to the Romans* William comments on, or accounts for, almost every word in the epistle. No passage of more than a few words is omitted; and no passage of any importance is left out. What does not occur formally as biblical text is paraphrased or assimilated by the author and used in his introduction to the next section of the biblical text for discussion. The scripture text used by William is essentially what has come to be accepted as the Vulgate text; there are, of course, many inconsequential transpositions of words and synonym substitutions. The biblical text of Paul's *Epistle to the Romans* in the early part of the single extant manuscript of the *Exposition* is likewise fundamentally the Vulgate reading. William does not in general, however, seem to give any special value to this scriptural reading in his presentation of the scriptural text. The variations from the Vulgate text which occur in this text of Paul's epistle do not occur with any regularity in the biblical text presented by William in his commentary.

In the *Exposition on Romans* William manifests a bias for the Greek text as containing superior readings. This he gets from Rufinus' translation of Origen's *Commentary on Romans.* Time and again Rufinus uses expressions like *sicut melius Graecus habet* when introducing a scriptural verse. Rufinus, however, has many more instances of this greek bias than William borrows in his commentary.

Among early cistercian writings William's *Exposition on Romans* is something of an anomaly, for it departs from the object of most cistercian exegesis, the *Song of Songs.*[1] It reflects, perhaps, William's experience at the school of Rheims before he became a benedictine monk, for the *Epistle to Romans* was one of the most popular books for commentary in the schools. There seems to be evidence for only one other twelfth-century commentary on *Romans* by a Cistercian, that attributed to Guerric of Igny by Charles DeVisch in his seventeenth-century catalog of cistercian writers.[2] But this work is not extant and is of very doubtful attribution. In fact, later editors of Guerric do not even mention it.[3]

William's *Exposition on Romans* was written at Signy, William entered this cistercian abbey in 1135 and died there in 1148. During these thirteen years he produced several literary works besides this biblical commentary. Stanley Ceglar has presented arguments for William's writing of the *Exposition* during the period 1135 to the end of 1138.[4] Reprinted in Migne's *Patrologia latina* from Tissier's seventeenth-century edition, the *Exposition on Romans* is extant in a single twelfth-century manuscript from Signy which is now in the library at Charleville: MS 49.

Charleville MS 49 passed from the cistercian abbey of Signy to the municipal library at Charleville at the end of the eighteenth-century amid upheavals caused by the French Revolution and the confiscation of church property. The manuscript is actually two separate manuscripts: an eleventh-century manuscript containing the *Epistles* of Paul and a twelfth-century manuscript of the *Exposition on Romans* of William of St Thierry in several hands. The first part of MS 49 consists of folios A–102 and contains Paul's *Epistles* including the *Epistle to the Laodiceans*. All of these except the *Epistle to Philemon* are annotated with from one to fifty-nine glosses. Some of the glosses are without attribution in the manuscript. Others are attributed to Gregory, Augustine, Basil, Origen, Cassian, Leo, and one is attributed to Plato. The glosses in the eleventh-century section of MS 49 are in three hands: the Signy-hand, the scribal hand responsible for the text itself; the Leo-hand, a hand which accounts for glosses drawn from the works of Leo the Great, e.g., f. 5^r and f. 8^v. William does not use either of these glosses. Finally, there is the William-hand, responsible for only three brief glosses on the *Epistle to the Romans:* f. 1^v identifies a gloss in the Signy-hand as Augustine, *De gratia et libero arbitrio;* f. 10^v adds a missing *sectabantur* to Rom 9:30; and f. 10^v adds a missing *descendet* to Rom 10:7. The William-hand is responsible for extended glosses on others of Paul's Epistles, e.g. f. 60^v, *Ep. to Philippians;* f. 63^r, *Ep. to Colossians*. This hand and the hand of the last forty or so folios of MS 49 share characteristic ligatures and abbreviations and are, in fact, the same hand.

This is the William-hand which accounts for that section of the twelfth-century part of MS 49 beginning at f. 175^r. Déchanet feels that this is William's own hand. His argument for this belief is presented in an article published in 1952.[5] Briefly, the attribution to William of this hand is based on a folio attached to another Charleville MS, 114, containing a passage from William's *Exposition on the Song of Songs*. This single folio Déchanet sees as the only surviving evidence of an early text of the *Exposition on the Song of Songs*. The script on this folio is the same as that in the last folios of MS 49.

The second manuscript, or the second part of MS 49, folios 103–216, is a twelfth-century product. It contains William's *Exposition on Romans* written in at least five hands.[6] A noteworthy feature of this text is the abrupt shift in hands on folio 175^r. At line 13 the hand changes to one which is also responsible for numerous corrections in the earlier sections of the *Exposition*. Déchanet attributes this hand to the author.

The provenance of the eleventh-century portion of MS 49 has not been determined. It may have been brought to Signy by William when he came from St Thierry. No evidence has been presented for its origin. A study of the scriptorium at St Thierry and of the scriptorium at

Signy would help answer this question. The second part of the MS, the text of the *Exposition on Romans*, seems to have originated at Signy and is said to have been written under William's supervision and ultimately to have been completed by the author himself.

The manuscript contains a twelfth-century *ex libris* on the inside of the front cover: *Sancte marie signiaci.* On folio 216v, at the end of the *Exposition on Romans* there is an *ex libris* from the sixteenth century with library markings: *Liber sancte marie signiacensis signatus littera b numero xii.*[7] There is further evidence of a later hand on folios 103–105v and 108r where some hashmarks have been made in the margin next to the text. Also, the chapters in Paul's *Epistles* have been numbered in the eleventh-century portion of the manuscript and in William's *Exposition* as well. Furthermore, the only example of a greek word in greek script is one written above the top line on folio 148r to correct the Latin word *cogitate*, written in small greek capitals, to the corresponding greek word appropriate to Rom 6:11: λογίξεσθε. The script of this greek word is much later than the twelfth century; it is probably from the fourteenth or fifteenth century.

The relationship between the two parts of MS 49 can be established by an examination of the glosses on the *Epistle of Paul to the Romans* and by an examination of the biblical text itself. In over a dozen cases William used these glosses in his *Exposition on Romans*. The exact references can be found in the notes to the translation given in this volume. William's biblical text also reveals some use of the text of Paul's *Epistle to the Romans* in the eleventh-century portion of MS 49. An interesting variation from the Vulgate text, which William's biblical text tends to parallel, occurs in Rom 2:15, where part of the verse is in the genitive case rather than the ablative. William says that the *Latinus interpres* at this point is following greek usage which lacks the ablative case and uses the genitive for these words.[8] The use of the expression 'the Latin translator' here refers to the biblical text in the early part of MS 49, folio 2v. Origen's *Commentary on Romans* has the ablative for these words for Rom 2:15 at the point of discussion of this verse (PG 14:892). Although the genitive is used in the verse when it occurs elsewhere in the commentary (PG 14:1138), there is a marked preference for the use of the ablative in this verse in Origen's *Commentary*, one of William's chief sources.

Furthermore, the William-hand is evident in two corrections of the scripture text: f. 10v *sectabantur* in Rom 9:30, and *descendet* in Rom 10:7. Also, on f. 1v the William-hand identifies another gloss as that of Augustine. In Book One in his discussion of Rom 1:20-21 William uses this gloss, which Florus of Lyons refers to in his *Exposition on Paul's*

Epistles (PL 119:282).

In his Preface to the *Exposition on Romans*, William tells us which authors he drew from for his commentary. He names Augustine, Ambrose, and Origen. The *Commentary on Paul's Epistle to the Romans* of Origen was used in Rufinus' translation, a manuscript of which exists today in the Charleville library and which came there from Signy. William says he drew on the works of the Fathers, especially the three he names. In addition, he acknowledges the use of some unnamed masters of his own time whose orthodoxy he measures by the yardstick of the teachings of the Fathers.

The widespread use of Origen and of Augustine is obvious from the notes to the translation in this volume. However, two considerations are worth noting. First, that the use of Origen as a monastic authority is sanctified by a centuries-long tradition in the West. Second, Augustine provides source material primarily through the intermediary of the *Exposition on Paul's Epistles* of Florus of Lyons, a ninth-century author whose works tended to be collections of passages from various earlier authors.

Rufinus' translation of Origen's *Commentary on Romans* dates from the fifth century; its use was commonplace in medieval exegesis of *Romans*. For example, Rhabanus Maurus and Sedulius Scotus in the ninth century both used Rufinus' translation in their commentaries on *Romans*. Origen was also used by Anselm of Laon in the early twelfth-century in the *Glossa ordinaria*. In the middle of the century Origen was a source for the commentaries on Paul's *Epistle* by Peter Abelard and Peter Lombard.

Origen's presence in the monastic world is especially well-documented. The *Homiliary* of Paul the Deacon, commissioned by Charlemagne, contains six readings attributed to Origen—all of them apocryphal. These readings formed part of the Matins lections in the West from the ninth century until the reform of Pius V in the sixteenth century. The earliest known cistercian lectionary, the *Breviary* of Stephan Harding dating from about 1130, contains some of these Origen readings. The works of Origen were used by Cassiodorus, Gregory the Great, Alcuin, Sedulius Scotus, Rhabanus Maurus, Amalarius of Metz, John Scotus Erigena, Notker Balbulus, Peter Lombard, Bernard of Clairvaux, William of St Thierry, Peter Abelard and Hugh, Andrew, and Richard of St Victor. Benedict of Aniane, the great monastic legislator and reformer of the Carolingian age, praises Origen as a model for monks. Origen is represented in most of the libraries whose twelfth-century collections can be reassembled. In brief, Origen was part of the tradition of spirituality in the West, especially the tradition of monastic spirituality.

Another point of importance regarding Origen is the peculiar nature of Rufinus' technique of translation. Rufinus altered what he read to make it conform to his own western point of view. This was also the approach of Jerome and Hilary of Poitiers, among others, when they rendered greek texts into Latin. There is no point inquiring into the accuracy of Rufinus' renderings of the greek text. He was not, strictly speaking, translating. He was trying to provide latin versions of greek writings for the spiritual instruction and edification of his readers. Therefore, when William of St Thierry confesses that he used Origen in his *Exposition on Romans* he must be understood with significant qualifications. William used Origen, bowdlerized, as it were, for a western audience. Furthermore, William adapted the text of the Origen-Rufinus *Commentary* to his own purposes.

We must remember that translations of greek theological works into Latin were scattered about the monastic libraries of Europe. There was no library which possessed all the available latin translations and under these conditions no western biblical commentator could systematically have mastered the thought of the Greek Fathers. In his *Exposition on Romans*, therefore, William was not synthesizing two great systems of theological thought, that of Origen and that of Augustine, as has been suggested by Bouyer, but rather was using traditional monastic sources for the exegesis of Paul's *Epistle to the Romans*.

The second area of consideration is William's use of Augustine through the collection of various augustinian passages put together by Florus of Lyons. This collection was compiled between 840 and 850. Florus' *Exposition on Paul's Epistles* was very popular in the twelfth century. Manuscripts from twelfth-century France are especially numerous. The Cistercians had a special fondness for this collection of Augustine's comments on Paul. Clairvaux had a copy in the twelfth century. Rheims had several manuscripts of Florus' work. St Thierry had two copies of the *Exposition on Paul's Epistles* in the twelfth century.

This is an area of indebtedness to a source for William of St Thierry which has been ignored. This is possibly because Déchanet said he took a great deal of trouble to examine William's possible use of Florus—with little to show for the effort.[9] Be that as it may, the notes for the translation in this volume are clear evidence of William's use of Florus.[10]

The third person William names as a source is Ambrose. The degree of his indebtedness to this author has eluded discovery thus far. Other sources used by William are Bede, Horace, Plato, Cicero, Isidore, Cassian, and Gregory the Great. No contemporary sources have been found to date.

The Bible constitutes a major source for William's language and expression. There are over two hundred instances of William's use of passages from the New Testament, either in direct quotation or in allusion. Likewise, over two hundred citations of the Old Testament occur, almost a hundred from the Psalms alone.

Finally, a few words need to be said about the *Glossa ordinaria*, that complex set of glosses and commentary on the scriptures which was initially the work of Anselm of Laon and his followers during the first quarter of the twelfth century. If William had studied at Laon, as has been hypothesized by some (with no convincing evidence), one would expect some similarities between his *Exposition on Romans* and that section of the *Glossa ordinaria* which covers *Romans*. This is an especially tantalizing area of inquiry because Anselm of Laon himself seems to have been responsible for that section of the *Glossa*.[11]

There are some glosses on the text of *Romans* in the eleventh-century section of MS 49 which do show some affinity to the *Glossa*. These are in the Signy-hand responsible for the biblical text itself. From an examination of MS 49 and a comparison with the 1495 printed edition of the *Glossa*, now in the Library of Congress, it is clear that the glosses on *Romans* in MS 49, especially a lengthy marginal gloss on f. A^v and the interlinear glosses on the same folio are the same as those contained in the *Glossa*. However, the glosses in MS 49 do not signal a source for William's *Exposition on Romans*. For those passages which are common to the printed edition of the *Glossa* and William's *Exposition* are also found in Florus of Lyon's collection of passages from Augustine. Thus, while the glosses in MS 49 are related to the contents of the *Glossa ordinaria*, there is nothing to suggest that William used that work being done by Anselm of Laon at about the same time he was writing his own *Exposition on Romans*.

In point of fact, the assertions that William is indebted to Anselm of Laon or that his technique of exegesis is that of the school of Laon, while totally unproven, might possibly be open to substantiation. But if one were interested in proving this unsubstantiated hypothesis he might do well to examine the movement of anselmian teaching from Laon to Rheims in the person of Anselm's student Alberic of Rheims, who taught at Rheims from 1118 to 1136, the same period during which William was at St Nicaise in Rheims and at St Thierry just outside the city.

JOHN D. ANDERSON

NOTES

1. Joachim of Flora, while not representative of cistercian exegetes, has extant works on the *Apocalypse*. The *Commentary on Ruth* ascribed to Isaac of Stella is of very doubtful authenticity.
2. *Bibliotheca scriptorum sacri ordinis Cisterciensis* (Cologne, 1655) p. 131.
3. CF 8, pp. xviii-xix. Also, the *Commentary on Romans* attributed to Gilbert of Hoyland by DeVisch, *Bibliotheca*, p. 126, is spurious; see F. Stegmüller, *Repertorium biblicum medii aevi* (Madrid, 1950) No. 2497.
4. *William of St. Thierry, the Chronology of His Life With a Study of His Treatise On the Nature of Love, His Authorship of the Brevis commentatio, the In Lacu, and the Reply to Cardinal Matthew* (Ann Arbor: University Microfilms, 1971) p. 190.
5. 'Un recueil singulier d'opuscules de Guillaume de Saint-Thierry: Charleville 114', *Scriptorium* 6 (1952) p. 201 n. 17.
6. The twelfth-century section of MS 49 consists of sixteen gatherings some of which contain hands peculiar to them. The first gathering, fol. 103^v-104^v, contains the Preface in a hand which does not occur elsewhere in the MS. A second hand occurs in the second and third gatherings: fols. 105^r-112^v; 113^r-114^v. These two gatherings may contain different, but similar, hands. The third hand occurs in gatherings four through nine. On fol. 160^v a fourth hand occurs which runs until fol. 175^r where the fifth hand, the William-hand, takes over.
7. The date of the second *ex libris* is given in C. Samaran and R. Marichal, *Catalogue des manuscrits en écriture latine* Vol. 5, p. 43.
8. Such grammatical discussions are common in medieval commentaries on Scripture and should not be construed as evidence for a knowledge of Greek on the part of the author. They are part of the common stock of exegesis passed on from one generation of commentators to another.
9. CS 10, p. 36 n. 94.
10. Further work to be done on this point can be helped by the Appendix on pp. 168-186 of C. Charlier's article, 'La compilation augustinienne de Florus sur l'apôtre', *Revue bénédictine* 57 (1947). This Appendix lists the works of Augustine and the chapter and verse in Paul's epistles they are referred to by Florus.
11. B. Smalley, *The Study of the Bible in the Middle Ages* (Oxford: Blackwell; Notre Dame, 1964) p. 60.

EDITOR'S COMMENT

For this translation the Migne text has been used. A careful reading of MS 49 was then used in the editing of this translation to correct for the errors, additions, and deletions in Migne's text. There is need for a study of Migne's text as a possible witness to a manuscript different from Charleville MS 49. The setting off of the biblical text for commentary as well as the numbering of chapters and verses is a later addition to the text as it occurs in MS 49.

Greek words are presented in the text in the form in which they occur in the manuscript. In each instance clarification can be found in the notes concerning what greek word is meant and its source.

Finally, thanks must go to: Ms Rozanne Elder for her continual assistance; Sr Hildegarde Chabol of Saint-Thierry for assisting in the obtaining of Charleville MS 49; Mr R. Bruce Miller, Head of Acquisitions, Library of the Catholic University of America, for his scholarly assistance and constant support.

WILLIAM OF SAINT THIERRY
Monk of Signy

EXPOSITION ON THE EPISTLE TO THE ROMANS

preface

WE HAVE BEGUN Paul's *Epistle to the Romans,* complicated as it is by a broad array of difficult questions, not to explain it, which is beyond our ability, but to weave a continuous commentary that is not original, but which combines certain opinions and statements of the holy fathers, especially blessed Augustine. These have been gathered from their books and tracts for our modest work by omitting the troublesome questions in them.[1] The resulting commentary should be much more acceptable to the readers since it is not founded on novelty or vain presumption but is recommended by the profound authority[2] of outstanding teachers·such as blessed Augustine, as I have said, and also Ambrose, Origen, and some other learned men, even some masters of our own day, who, we are certain, have not in any way transgressed the limits set by our Fathers. Therefore, no one should accuse us of theft, since we have given ourselves away. As in the poet's fable[3] we have festively clothed our little bird in the plumes and colors of other birds, so that if these should come and each one carry off what he recognizes as his own, our little crow would be naked or even nonexistent.

The joy of contemplating the grace of God and the glory of God, which must be preached to all, have brought me to this task. The apostle Paul was a stout-hearted champion of God's glory throughout this whole epistle, and defended it with apostolic authority and prudence against the Jews; the holy fathers everywhere defended it against heretics, and we desire it to be inscribed in our hearts in order to acquire a disposition of total humility and to achieve purity of devotion. Those who completely devote themselves to divine worship should know that piety is the worship of God, as Scripture says;[4] but there is no piety without thanksgiving and no thanksgiving without an acknowledgement of grace. By meditating frequently on this they become the blessed who are poor in spirit,* to whom the kingdom of heaven belongs and whose spirit is believed to be totally with God. For grace predestined us before we existed, when we were nothing; when we turned away, it called us and when we turned back, it justified us; and it will glorify us when we are justified if we are not ungrateful. Grace accomplishes good in us so we may will; it cooperates with us when we do will; and without it we can neither will nor accomplish any good. Just as we were created by God from no subsisting elements so that we might be something among his creatures, so by grace we have been created in good works by no merits of our own.* And therefore if we merit anything, it is a grace, and what we merit is grace for grace. Indeed, to bear the fruit of a grace received is an increase of grace, just as to have received grace in the first place is a grace. Grace goes before us so we can pray; it helps us while we pray; and it gives us what we pray for. The Virgin was filled with grace so she could become the Mother of God;* he who was born of the Virgin was found to be full of grace.* Noah, Abraham, Moses and the rest of the holy fathers are said to have found grace with God, and when the apostle Paul sought something

Mt 5:3

Cf. Eph 2:10

Lk 1:28
Jn 1:14

2 Cor 12:9	else, he was told that grace would suffice.*

Lord Jesus, beautiful above the sons of men, when you came by a special privilege grace was poured forth on your lips; this was the oil of gladness with which you appeared anointed above your fellows.* For this reason the young maidens loved you, running after the odor of your ointments.* Anticipated by grace, men saw grace in your face. Leaving the tax office, even the publican tax collector followed after you;* and Peter and Andrew, James and John left both their nets and their father and followed you.* Even today grace makes something in your words resonate in the ears of those before whom it goes, which does not touch the ears of the rest. Grace invokes those things that are not, as though they were,* and sets them in accord with the humble because they are brothers. It puts an end to the shame which they felt for you; it cheers the hearts of the humble and makes their countenances pleasing because they are as they were created to be, and they have not been taken captive in a strange land.* In this life you freely give whatever you give us, and you receive from us nothing that you have not given first. Even when you wish to be loved by us gratuitously, you count it as gratuitous in us that we love you for your own sake, since you, Omnipotent one, can give us nothing greater according to the merit of your love than that we love you. Moreover you redeem our souls from the [pleasures] and iniquities of our outrages and crimes and make our names honorable in your sight* so that we may be called, and may be, sons of your grace, as though we loved you freely. You first forgave us our many great sins to make us worthy of your love. But grace is yours and comes to us from you, and therefore to you alone be glory, O Lord our God. If anyone glories, let him glory only in you. For even faith itself cannot be in us if it is not from you, and without faith no good work comes to pass in man, for all that is not of faith is sin.*

Margin references:
- Ps 44:2,8
- Sg 1:2-3
- Mt 9:9
- Mt 4:18
- Rm 4:17
- Ps 136:3-4 [PL: are taken away to other purposes.]
- [PL: usuries]
- Ps 71:14
- Rom 14:23

NOTES

1. *Questio* as a technical theological term received precise definition as scholasticism developed and incorporated 'questions' in its methodology. See Chenu, *Nature, Man, and Society in the Twelfth Century* (Chicago, 1968) p. 294.

2. *Novitas* and *vanitatis praesumptio*, on the one hand, and *auctoritas*, on the other, delineate the polarity in William's view of the theological controversy in his day. Cf. the juxtaposition of *superba curiositas* and *humilis pietas* at Rom 1:24 below.

3. Horace, *Ep.* 1.3.19

4. This equation of piety and the worship of God occurs several times in William's works. See below at Rom 1.18 where William attributes it to Job. William's source here is Augustine, *On Spirit and Letter 11.18;* PL 44:211. Also, see Aug., *City of God 4.23; 10.1;* PL 41:130, 278-79.

BOOK ONE

CHAPTER ONE

Rm 1:1	VERSE ONE. **Paul, the servant of Christ Jesus** You are great, Lord, and exalted; you look down on the humble, and the proud you know from afar. You knew Saul who derived the form of his name and his persecution from a proud king and persecutor; but you did not know him from afar. You humbled him like
Ps 88:11	the wounded proud man;* with the arm of your power and the spirit of your grace you changed Saul
Ac 9	to Paul,* a young Benjamin penetrating the heavens
Ps 67:28	in ecstasy* and hearing in God's paradise secret
2 Cor 12:4	words which it is not lawful for a man to utter.* At first he was a ravenous wolf but at evening time he
Gn 49:27	divided the prey.* From that place he brought us back something which was lawful for a man to utter, but which no one can fully understand unless he possesses something more than humanity. He was called Saul in Hebrew, Saulus in Latin, as if Saülus, just as Jacob becomes Jacobus and Joseph becomes Josephus, and so forth. When he was selected by you to be a chosen vessel to preach your grace to the Gentiles, he preferred to be called Paul rather than

Saul, from the word *paululus* or little, that is, a humble, quiet man on whom the Holy Spirit rests, so that by his very name he might confound the pride of those who presumed to ascribe your grace to their own merits.[1] This was for his own humility. As for your glory, when he had brought Paul the proconsul of Asia under your gentle yoke* and had made him a provincial of your kingdom, then he also preferred to be called Paul rather than Saul as a sign of so great a victory.* For the enemy is more solidly defeated in him over whom he has a greater hold. And the ancient enemy holds a greater number of the proud by reason of their nobility, and still more of them by reason of authority.[2]

Cf. Mt 11:30

Ac 13:9

Servant of Christ Jesus The profession of this servitude* is one of humility, of glory and of outstanding authority, since he professes, as if glorying, that he is the servant of the one who said, 'It is a great thing for you to be called my servant.'* He served him in the gospel of his Son, as he himself said.*

PL: servant

Cf. Is 49:6
Rm 1:9

Of Christ Jesus 'Jesus' is a proper name, and 'Christ' is the name of the mystery.[3] It means the same as Messiah. In the name of Christ Jesus therefore is understood the power of a Saviour King, for only from a Saviour King can salvation be hoped for.

Called to be an apostle He was called through grace, for no one should take the honor to himself unless he is called by God, as Aaron was.*

Cf. Heb 5:4

Apostle An apostle is said to be 'sent' or rather 'sent back', that is, sent personally to call those who were left behind until now. Of them the prophet said, 'You will put them behind you.'* They are truly behind and in back who are given over to this world which should be left behind.

Ps 20:13

Set apart for the gospel of God Note that he chose to express 'set apart' by the very word by which God set him apart saying, 'Set apart for me Paul and Barnabas for the work for which I have received them.'* The work for which he was received is the gospel.

Ac 13:2

Rm 1:2

VERSE TWO **Which he had formerly promised through his prophets** It began with the prophets and was brought to an end with the apostles.

Rm 1:3

VERSE THREE **In the holy scriptures,** put forth by the Holy Spirit as a fixed and lasting record of all things.
  Concerning his Son, who was born of him eternally, before the daystar and before all time.* He alone has always existed as God born of God, but in time he was made man for him, that is, by the will and disposition of the Father, since his honor and goodness demanded this. The Son of God was made man, in that he who was made was assumed into the unity of person by the Son of God, who was not made but born, so that the same one is the Son of God who is the son of man, born of God the Father according to his divinity, and **made of the seed of David according to the flesh.** From the seed of David because the promise was made even more manifestly to David than to Abraham.

Cf. Ps 109:3

Rm 1:4

VERSE FOUR **He was predestined the Son of God in power.** The Saviour appeared to men as an outstanding light of predestination and grace,[4] since the same grace works to make every man a Christian from the very beginning of his faith, as made that man into Christ from his beginning. Jesus is therefore predestined and will be the son of David according to the flesh, and yet the Son of God in power. In him was predestined such a high and lofty elevation of human nature that it could not be raised higher,[5] just as there was nowhere lower that the Divinity could descend for us. From the point where this man began to be, the Son of God also began to be. According to the greek version, he was not predestined, but destined, since he was always God and came in power; that is, in that which he was.[6] For Christ is the power of God and the wisdom of God.* Christ is predestined, or destined towards power; that is, without any hindrance from sin either contracted at his origin[7] or committed by his will.[8] This predestination of his is his glory, which he who was born in the world as man had with the Father

1 Cor 1:24

'before the world was made'.* Just as he is predestined to be our head, so we are predestined in him to be his members.⁹

According to the Spirit of holiness He was predestined to be born according to the Spirit of holiness, about whose mother it was said to Joseph, 'That which is conceived in her is of the Holy Spirit'.* And to the mother herself it was said, 'The Holy Spirit shall come upon you, and the power of the Most High shall overshadow you.'* Although flesh was truly born of flesh, the conception of his flesh was completely spiritual. The love of God and the Spirit of holiness accomplished in her what sinful concupiscence and carnal love usually achieve in others, infecting them all with the disease of original sin. On this point however a scandal of faith about Christ must be avoided by christian piety lest it be said or believed that he is the Son of the Holy Spirit because he is conceived of the Holy Spirit. Mary conceived of the Holy Spirit, not because she received the seed of birth from the substance of the Holy Spirit but because through the operation of the Holy Spirit her nature ministered its substance to the divine birth. Because love of the Holy Spirit burned in her holy soul in a singular way, the power of that same Spirit worked marvels in her flesh.

The text continues: **from the resurrection of the dead of our Lord Jesus Christ.** This phrase can be understood as applying to the resurrection of those dead whom Christ resuscitated,* or else those whom he wished to have as witnesses and associates of his own resurrection,* so as to manifest clearly that he was the Son of God. But even if that phrase 'from the resurrection of the dead of Jesus Christ'* is read in such a way that Paul is one of those included in the resurrection of the dead of Jesus Christ our Lord, that is, one of those for whose life Jesus Christ our Lord died so that he might raise them from the death of the soul, it should not seem absurd because it is not unusual in Scripture. Thus you have, 'Daniel, one of the children of the captivity of Judah.'* But since he had written the phrase 'Paul, servant of

Christ Jesus' shortly before, why does he repeat the words 'of Jesus Christ our Lord'? Such repetition is found frequently in Scripture, especially in the older books. For instance, 'And Moses did what the Lord commanded Moses.'*[10] A more plausible explanation is that the name of Jesus tasted sweet to Paul's mouth because love of him burned in his heart, and it was pleasant for him to sprinkle his sayings and writings which were about Jesus with the frequent mention of his name. The same holds true for the pronouns referring to Jesus, such as 'in whom, through whom, in him, through him'. Everywhere Paul uses them so frequently and superfluously that sometimes they are wearisome to the reader unless he takes into account the affection of the writer.

Ex 40:21

VERSE FIVE Through whom we have received grace and apostleship. Through whom as a reconciler for our sins we have received grace, that is, the remission of those sins; and through whom as through wisdom, with contempt of present things, the grace of future things is savory to us. He says, 'Through whom we have received grace and apostleship,' grace to be patient in our labors, and apostleship to give authority to our preaching;[11] grace to be persuasive when we must be persuasive and apostleship to coerce those who must be coerced.

Rm 1:5

To bring about the obedience of faith among all nations Such was the grace that the apostles received that the gentile nations which were outside God's covenant and Israel's commonwealth* not only received the faith and believed the preachers, but also undertook a new mode of life and a new pattern of religious behavior out of reverence for the name of Christ.[12]

Cf. Eph 2:12

VERSE SEVEN To all who are at Rome, beloved of God and called to be saints They are not first called to be saints and then loved for their sanctity, but they are first freely loved and then called to be saints, that is, called to be holy, so that grace may be grace.* 'Called to be saints,' he says. By common

Rm 1:7

Cf. Rm 11:6

custom a carpenter's apprentice, although still new, is already called a carpenter, and the same holds for apprentices of other trades. So whoever is called and has enlisted in the pursuit of holiness is rightly called holy now.¹³ Therefore the prophet says confidently, 'For I am holy'.* Paul who is called to be an apostle writes to the disciples called to be holy, for just as Paul was called by grace to be an apostle of Christ, so everyone of them is called by the same grace to be a Christian, and to be loved and holy.

Ps 85:2

Grace to you and peace from God our Father and from the Lord Jesus Christ The grace of God is that by which our sins are forgiven, so that we may be reconciled with God; peace is that by which we are reconciled. Similarly we say 'the law and the prophets', although the prophets are contained within the law. Both remission and peace pertain to the general grace of God. This apostolic blessing of grace and peace should be understood as applying to the whole Church; it should not be thought of as less powerful than the blessings of Abraham, Isaac and Jacob over their children, since the Apostle asserts the same thing confidently about himself, saying, 'Do you seek a proof that Christ is speaking in me?'* Again he says, 'I think that I also have the spirit of God.'* It is right to believe that the churches flourish even today by this apostolic blessing. In them is found the peace of God, and, without doubt, grace also. Otherwise, grace and salvation are far removed from sinners, and the preacher's peace returns to him, as the Lord said to the disciples in the gospel. 'In whatever house you enter, say, "Peace be to this house". And if a son of peace be there, your peace will rest on him. But if not, it will return to you again.'*¹⁴

2 Cor 13:3

1 Cor 7:40

Lk 10:5-6

Rm 1:8

VERSE EIGHT **First I give thanks to my God** The preacher of grace selected an excellent beginning by grace, for God is first to be adored and then entreated. So the psalmist says, 'Praising I will call upon the Lord.'* Thus the preacher of grace first gives grateful thanks to him from whom all grace

Ps 17:4

is hoped for and received, and then in due order grace itself is preached. A grateful awareness of his gifts on the part of the receiver and a humble, pious understanding of the divine goodness is pleasing to the most good God. And the sacrifice of charity in an expression of congratulations to a brother over his progress toward God pleases God greatly. Just as no sin is greater in God's sight than ingratitude for grace, so for the faithful soul, accustomed to divine graces, nothing is sweeter or more pleasant than giving thanks for his own progress or for that of his neighbor. We give thanks on our behalf when we faithfully think that the grace we have received we have freely received from God, and by thinking this we excite ourselves with greater devotion and humility to the love of the giver; or when we joyfully return to God in actual good works the faculty of performing good works which we have freely received in our affections. We give thanks for our neighbor when we rejoice that we receive grace in him whom we love in God. Whoever, therefore, always tries to please the Lord in these matters, and always merits receiving greater gifts in himself, is both worthy and suitable to intervene also on others' behalf.

'First I give thanks to my God,' says our author. The great confidence of the man and the great sense of piety to call his own the Lord God of all things! Such he is, however. Whoever says 'my God' with sweet and pious affection and with sure and trusting charity speaks securely because he has made the God to whom he belongs his own; and before him to whom he makes an offering he confidently places whatever he offers, and he is always in the presence of God who is always present to him. No one can say this whose god is his belly or anything else which he loves in the place of God or together with God but not, however, for God's sake. God alone is to be loved, and he does not at all allow his love to be stained by strange loves, since he alone suffices for the lover. The Lord God of all things is properly the God of that man to whom he is pleasing in himself and for himself; his mind perseveres in all his judgments with his will fixed in this. A quiet will is a thing of pleasure for the mind. This saying is especially appropriate to the love of God. Short of him, beyond him, outside of him nothing is to be loved except what is loved for him and in him. Whoever does not want to pass away with passing things has to fix his steps on something stable. But that blessed man to whom the Lord his God belongs becomes in turn a man of God when he imitates the Apostle who served God with his spirit in the gospel of his Son,* *Cf. Rm 1:9* and serves in the things of God with his own spirit and with the Holy Spirit. This is what the bride says of the bridegroom in the Song of Songs, 'My beloved is mine and I am his; he shall abide between my breasts.'* *Sg 2:16, 1:12*

I give thanks to my God through Jesus Christ for all of you So the Apostle, the great preacher of grace, judges that thanks are to be returned always to the Lord God of his heart for all things, and that this thanks is to pass through Jesus the High Priest and the mediator of God and men. In this way thanksgiving is to be returned through him, through whom gifts of grace come to us from God in the first place. Note that the Apostle writing to various people gives thanks in some places for all of them; in other places he gives thanks, but not for all of them; and in other places he does not give thanks at all. When he gives thanks for all, he does not load them with blame and reproach; when he gives thanks but not for all as in the letters to the Corinthians and to the Colossians,* *1 Cor 1:4, Col 1:3* he intimates that there is something the matter with them which is reprehensible; but when he does not give thanks at all, he shows there is something seriously wrong with them which is contrary to thanksgiving.[15]

Because your faith is spoken of in the whole world Your faith, he says, is the catholic faith of all in the whole world, because the form and example of your faith is for the instruction of the whole world. Perhaps the Apostle already foresaw in spirit that Rome, which was the seat of the earthly empire, would be the first seat of the christian priesthood. From it as from a spring would flow out that which would be preached and believed for salvation throughout the world. Therefore he not only gives thanks but also prays in regard to future things, and says the following:

Rm 1:9

VERSE NINE. **For God is my witness, whom I serve with my spirit in the gospel of his Son, that without ceasing I make mention of you always in my prayers** Paul was not doing wrong, because he was using his oath well. Oaths are not good, for the Lord says, 'Let your speech be yes, yes or no, no; that which is over and above these comes from evil.'*

Mt 5:37

Still an oath is necessary to persuade another of that about which it is useful to be persuaded, but the evil comes from the one to whom the oath is given. The oath is caused by his infirmity, which is evil, because for him there is no hope or possibility of persuading in any other way. The greatest oath is that by which God is called to witness what is said, and in this the greatest care must be taken by the one who swears lest he take the name of the Lord our God in vain, violating the command of the law.*

Ex 20:7

God is my witness, whom I serve with my spirit This service is free because it is one of love and piety. I serve with my spirit, he says, because I act willingly, not under the impulse of fear nor with the hope of reward, but with an inner knowledge of justice and with love of truth.

In the gospel of his Son What could be more acceptable, what more delightful and pleasant to this faithful servant and vessel of election than to serve God in the gospel of his Son? The text continues:

Rm 1:10

VERSE TEN. **Without ceasing I make mention of you in my prayers** I make mention of you in my prayers always and without ceasing, that is, in my prayers which I make always and without ceasing. Certainly he fulfilled what he enjoined on his disciples when he said, 'Pray without ceasing'.*

1 Th 5:17

Asking that somehow by God's will I may now at

last have a prosperous journey and come to you
Note that setting out on the work of the gospel, a
holy work, he nevertheless waits until he has im-
plored with prayers not only that the journey be
prosperous for him but that it be prosperous according to the will of God, for the journey of him who
journeys according to the will of God [does not
always prosper]. Indeed, there is prosperity for a
journey in accordance with the will of God when the
cause is similar to the cause which he offers saying:[16]

[PL: always prospers]

Rm 1:11-12 VERSES 11-12. **For I long to see you, that I may
impart to you some spiritual grace to strengthen
you, that is to say, that I may be consoled together
in you, by that which is common to us both, your
faith and mine.** First of all we should know that it is
an apostolic work to long for the brothers and to
visit them, but only for the giving or receiving of
some spiritual grace. Otherwise, it is not commend-
able to make the circuit of the brothers.[17] Some
grace is spiritual and some grace is not. For instance,
virginity is a spiritual grace and marriage is not
spiritual, but both are gifts from God.[18] But the
most spiritual of graces are the charisms of spiritual
understanding, either about moral or mystical matters,
and they should be compared spiritually with
spiritual things.* The Apostle wishes spiritual gifts to
be given to those whom he urges on to true perfection. When it is achieved he himself receives consolation seeing his work progress firmly and steadfastly
in the improvement of his disciples; they are consoled by sharing the apostolic grace.[19] Mutual edification of faith cannot fail to occur when the disciples
see in the master what they should imitate, and the
master is encouraged to greater labors for the gospel
by seeing his disciples' progress. He does not wish
the brothers to be ignorant of his solicitude in their
regard, for he wants the awareness of the kindness of
their teacher to prepare in their hearts a place for the
things to be taught.

Cf. 1 Cor 2:13

Rm 1:13 VERSE THIRTEEN. **But I have been hindered up**

to now Hindered by whom? If we say 'by God', it is certainly not unworthy of God to dispose of his servants' acts, for he knows on which city the rain of the word of God should fall, and on which it should not. Therefore we find in the Acts of the Apostles, 'We wished to go into Bithynia but the Spirit of Jesus Forbade us.'* If we say that Paul was hindered by Satan, as he himself clearly says elsewhere,* God sometimes permits this in order to put his servants' perseverance to the test. But be assured that Satan cannot in any way know or disturb a holy intention or a holy counsel that is stirring in one's heart, unless he becomes aware of it from external signs. But what is shown forth through outward signs he can block, only if God permits.

Ac 16:7

1 Th 2:18

That I may have some fruit among you also, as well as among the other Gentiles Everywhere the Apostle managed the Lord's money, and in every case he took in profits. He sowed everywhere, and on every side he reaped. 'In order that I might have some fruit among you.' We should not overlook the fact that often he seems to use the word 'fruit' in the singular when it refers to some good, but in the plural when he speaks about the works of the flesh, which he condemns. He says elsewhere, 'The fruit of the Spirit is charity, joy, peace, etc.,'* but when speaking about the fruits of the flesh he says, 'They are manifest, being fornication, uncleanness, etc.'* The reason for this is that, as even the heathen philosophers say, all the virtues are one virtue and whoever perfectly possesses one of them possesses all of them; but the vices are at odds even with one another. The text continues:

Gal 5:22

Gal 5:19

Rm 1:14

VERSE FOURTEEN. **To the Greeks and to the barbarians, to the wise and to the unwise I am a debtor** Charity cannot be compressed or restricted. It is indebted to everyone and gives itself to everyone. It does not shun greek wisdom or barbarian folly. It thinks no one should be abandoned. While it speaks to some who are wise, to others who are unwise it protests that it knows nothing but Christ Jesus and him crucified.* Some it teaches by means of the law and

1 Cor 2:2

the prophets, others it persuades by signs and wonders. Therefore when Timothy was sick, Paul did not use his power of working cures but gave him medical advice.* Trophimus he left sick at Miletus,† but he cured the father of Publius, suffering from dysentery and fever, with only a word and a prayer,* and he restored to life and health Eutychus who had fallen from the window of an upper room.* Signs are needed nor for believers, but unbelievers, not for the wise but for the unwise. And he continues most willingly.

*1 Tim 5:23
†2 Tim 4:20
Ac 28:8
Ac 20:10

Rm 1:15

VERSE FIFTEEN. **So as much as in me, I am ready to preach the gospel to you also who are at Rome** He means either, 'I owe it to you at Rome to preach the gospel, and this I am eager to do', or else, 'As much as is in me, I am ready to preach to you'. It is as if he had said, 'You who are at Rome are not among the unwise.' The wise man was eager to speak to the wise, but in regard to the unwise he felt as he wrote elsewhere, 'If I do this unwillingly, a commission is entrusted to me, and woe to me if I do not preach the gospel.'* One who preaches the good news must speak to all, both wise and unwise, but Paul is eager to preach to those of whom it is written, 'Blessed is he who speaks in the ear of the hearer'.*

1 Cor 9:17

Source unknown

Now for a brief recapitulation of what has been said: after the Apostle has begun to speak, not in the learned and persuasive words of human wisdom, but in simplicity, as his God-given mission to the Romans for the gospel recommended, for his own sake, for the sake of God and of his mission, after he had made his entrance into the city of Rome, as it were, by his letter with its fullness of Christ's blessing, he saluted it with peace, as the Lord taught,* and he prepared a welcome for himself among his hearers by his pious and solicitous affection and by the work of his prayers, and then he set out to preach the gospel to them. He saw that worldly wisdom was flowing [together as if for his audience both] from the Jews and from the Roman Gentiles, and that they rested on his peace with which he had saluted them, and so he began saying:

Cf. Mt 10:12

[PL omits]

Rm 1:16	**VERSE SIXTEEN. For I am not ashamed of the gospel of God** He knew that shame for the Crucified was going to be cast up as an obstacle from the very beginning, for it was a stumbling-block to the Jews and foolishness to the Gentiles. But no confusion could exist in a conscience that was already healthy, and no shame in a mind so free.
	For it is the power of God for salvation to everyone who believes Therefore he wrote to the Corinthians, 'But we preach Christ crucified, to the Jews indeed a stumbling-block and to the Gentiles foolishness, but to those who are called, both Jews and Greeks, Christ is the power of God and the wisdom
1 Cor 1:23-24	of God.'* He was not blushing as though ashamed of Christ's cross, nor as teaching one thing and living differently, nor as failing in the power of working miracles. 'It is the power of God for salvation to everyone who believes,' he said, giving it to be understood that it is also the power of God for damnation to those who disbelieve. God's power shows itself also in damnation. In this regard it is written, 'Destroy
Ps 58:12	them in your power'.* It is from these distinctions of power that the right hand and left hand of God take their names.
	To Jew first and to Greek First to Jew and then to Greek, that is, to the Gentiles, 'for salvation is of
Jn 4:22	the Jews'.* The Greeks first gave the human race two names, saying that every man was either a Greek or a barbarian, so that whoever was not a Greek was a barbarian. But Paul makes a much truer distinction, placing Jews first, then Greeks and finally barbarians. Since the Greeks preferred themselves to others because they used laws, the Apostle rightly sets the Jews before the Greeks, because they had previously received all their laws from God. Now he proceeds to treat that power which works for salvation, saying:[20]
Rm 1:17	**VERSE SEVENTEEN. For the justice of God is revealed in the gospel, from faith to faith, as it is written: the just man lives by faith** This justice which justifies believers is faith. Veiled in the Old Testament, it is revealed in the gospel. It is called justice because it justifies those whom it encompasses.

It is God's justice because faith itself is from grace. This faith and this justice progress or move from the faith of those who announce the good news to the faith of those who obey it, from the faith of the Old Testament to the faith of the New, from the faith by which one serves God to the faith by which one enjoys him, from faith in the image in this world to faith in the present reality of the next world, from faith in words by which we believe to faith in that which we shall obtain in eternity. The justice of God is revealed in the gospel, because neither barbarian nor Scythian, no one at all, is excluded from the kingdom of God; the gate of grace lies open equally to all.

As it is written: the just man lives by faith The prophet Habakkuk was right in saying, 'The just man lives by faith',* because faith causes us to understand by believing, and because it is from God and not from ourselves that we believe well and also live well. Neither does right living belong to us as our own unless, when we believe and pray, he helps us who has given the faith by which we believe we must be helped by him. Let heretical pride blush on this point for claiming for itself the first fruits of a good work, while a man claims for himself the beginning of good will as though it were his through his own efforts.

Hab 2:4

Rm 1:18

VERSE EIGHTEEN. **For the wrath of God is revealed from heaven** Having recommended the piety of faith in the revelation of the gospel by which we are made just and pleasing to God, and having recommended also the power of God for the salvation of every believer, from this point the author seems to turn to the converse: God's power in condemning nonbelievers. In the gospel is revealed not only the justice and glorification of believers but also the injustice and wrath of the unbelievers, which is their just condemnation. In man wrath is a movement of the soul toward vengeance; but in God it is the just execution of vengeance. 'Who knows how to number his wrath according to the fear of him?'* Indeed,

Ps 89:11

[PL omits]	the wrath of God means the empty and seductive pleasure of the wicked, bodily affliction and trouble, interior blindness of mind, the sting of [an evil] conscience in sin, the severe judgment of eternal punishment and sometimes even the very illumination of the mind of those who are committing abuse, like the heathen philosophers and the wise men of this world. About them, the author adds **against all the ungodliness and injustice of those men who hinder the truth of God in injustice.** Men of this sort would have been much better off never having known the truth of God, rather than having hindered it in injustice. 'Against all the ungodliness and injustice', namely, of the Jews who have the law and of the Greeks who do not. For whoever sins against the worship of God is impious, as is written in Job, 'Piety is the worship of God'.²¹ Injustice proceeds from impiety when what is owed to God is given to a creature. They are also unjust who sin against faith by which the just man lives. The Apostle carefully calls them men as he does some others in another place, as
[PL: approving] 1 Cor 3:4	though [reproaching] them, 'Are you not men?'* But how do those men get knowledge of the truth since God has not given them the law?
Rm 1:19	VERSE NINETEEN. **Because that which is known of God is manifest in them** It is manifest not only to them but in them, that is, through the natural intelligence which is in them. The text continues: **For God has manifested it to them.** How has he manifested it?
Rm 1:20	VERSE TWENTY. **From the creation of the world the invisible things of God have been clearly perceived in the things that have been made; this includes his eternal power and divinity** Why has he manifested them? **So they are without excuse** Why are they guilty then?
Rm 1:21-22	VERSES TWENTY-ONE AND TWENTY-TWO. **Because when they knew God, they did not glorify him as God or give thanks.** But what did they do? **They became vain and futile in their thoughts.** Not

without punishment. **Their foolish heart was darkened** and they lost through pride what they had perceived through curiosity. This blindness or darkness of heart is a sin and both the punishment of a former sin and the cause of a subsequent sin. What sin? The sin of pride. They became proud, **professing themselves to be wise.** It is usual for proud men to be close to folly. Although not every fool is proud, every proud man is shown to be a fool. But, to repeat, pride is both the punishment of a preceding sin and the cause of a subsequent sin. What sin? Foolishness. **For professing themselves to be wise, they became fools** And foolishness is the punishment of a preceding sin and the cause of a subsequent sin. Which one? Idolatry. So he continues:

Rm 1:23

VERSE TWENTY-THREE. **And they exchanged the glory of the incorruptible God for the likeness of a corruptible image,** first **of a man,** then **of birds,** then **of fourfooted beasts,** and last of all, **of creeping things.** Again, idolatry has become the cause of subsequent uncleanness.

Rm 1:24

VERSE TWENTY-FOUR. **Therefore God gave them up to the desires of their heart, to uncleanness** Just as in the gospel the increase of the justice of God is revealed in many graces from faith to faith, similarly the failure of impiety and injustice is revealed unto damnation and death. 'God gave them up to the desires of their hearts,' says the text. How did he give them up? As the psalmist says, 'He let them go according to the desires of their heart so

Ps 80:13

that they should go after their own inventions.'* 'To give them up' is the same as 'to let them go', that is, not to enlighten the blind, not to correct the erring, not to help the infirm. 'He gave them up to the desires of their hearts.' Apostle and psalmist say the same thing. Their heart is a heart left to itself, blinded by itself, not enlightened by grace, in which the fool

Ps 13:1

finally says, 'There is no God.'* Their inventions were devised according to the desires of their hearts which they did not wish to conquer, but rather to fulfill. Therefore they are said to be given up to the desires of their hearts. And what were the desires of their hearts? Uncleanness in desire exceeding human decency and in action exceeding human custom to such an extent that they afflicted their bodies by that unsuitableness, with natural repugnance and the reproaches of nature against them, and they attempted by a kind of violence to make their bodies more suitable for vice.

But because the above has been said to show the sequence of events through the text, let us return for a while to an earlier part. 'The wrath of God is revealed against all the ungodliness and injustice of those men who hinder the truth of God in injustice, because that which is known of God is manifest in them. For God has manifested it to them.'* The author is here dealing with the philosophers of this world, great men of great energy and remarkable genius, who were able to evaluate creation and through creation the Creator. They would be truly praiseworthy except that they were justly struck down by the prophet's words, 'I girded you but you have not known me.'* They were able to see that God was some kind of eternal life, immutable, intelligible, intelligent, wise and making others wise, a fixed, stable and unwavering truth in which 'whatever is made is life';* and in which all the reasons of things and of creatures are eternally disposed or temporally in action. These philosophers, whose reputation exceeds that of the rest, rightly saw that God was not a body and therefore they transcended all bodies in their search for God. They saw that whatever is mutable is not the supreme God and therefore they transcended every mind and every mutable spirit in their search for the supreme God. In addition, they saw that every species in whatever mutable substance it is what it is and in whatever way it is, and whatever its nature, cannot be except through him who truly is because he is unchangeable. And consequently they saw that the entirety of the whole world from heaven to earth and whatever objects are in them, or whatever life, cannot be except

Rm 1:18-19

Is 45:5

Jn 1:3-4

through him who simply is, and for whom that which is to be is to live and to understand and to be happy. They understood from his immutability and simplicity that he had made all these mutable things, and that he could have been made by no one. They reached the conclusion that whatever exists is either body or life, and that life is something better than body, and that the sensible pertains to the body and the intelligible belongs to life. As a result they preferred the intelligible to the sensible. By 'sensible' we mean that which can be sensed by the sight, touch or any other bodily sense, and by 'intelligible' that which can be understood by a glance of the mind. There is no bodily beauty whether in the state of the body, such as a figure, or in the movement of the body, as in a song, which the mind cannot judge, and this the mind could not do unless it were better than the body. The mind is an entity without bulky quantity, without noisy sound, without time or place. But still it is changeable, because otherwise one mind would not be better than another, nor could it judge the sensible, now more skillfully, now less so. Therefore these talented and learned men easily deduced that the first form was not in those things where change was apparent. And when they saw that in viewing these things the body and soul were perceived in varying degrees of beauty (they would not exist at all if they could lack form completely), they saw there was something in which prime and unchanging form existed. Therefore they rightly believed that it was not comparable to those and was some kind of principle of things, and that it was itself unmade and all things that were made were made from it. That which is known of God was manifested to them by God; his invisible aspects are clearly seen from the things that are made, including his eternal power which rules and contains all things, and his divinity which fills all things.[22]

The heathen philosophers and wise men of this world saw these things about God, but they saw them from afar. They sought the way but lost it because they were unwilling to be humble. They sought God with a proud curiosity when they should have sought him with humble piety.²³ They thought he was to be found in the realm of reason and in the recesses of occult knowledge, whereas he is to be found only in the kingdom of charity and in the radiant seat of wisdom, a wisdom not in long-winded talk but in perfect charity 'from a pure heart, a good conscience and an unfeigned faith'.* [*1 Tim 1:5*] Although some of them found life itself to some degree under the guidance of reason, still they failed in that regard because they relied on themselves. Therefore, the most famous of them, Plato, said, 'We must flee to our bright fatherland, where God is father and where truth shines forth'. What ship shall we take? What sort of trip? Likeness is the key.²⁴ Insofar as we are unlike God, we are far from him. We approach him to the degree that we become like him.²⁵ Upon these men then is the wrath of God revealed, because as we read in the Book of Wisdom, 'They are not to be pardoned; for if they were able to know so much as to make a judgment of the world, how did they not more easily discover the Lord of the world'* [*Wis 13:8-9*] in order to glorify him?

Therefore 'the wrath of God is revealed from heaven against all their ungodliness and injustice,'* [*Rm 1:18*] for in the preaching of the gospel it is announced that he will come to them from heaven, that is, the judge of the ungodly and the unjust who have, as the prophet says, 'changed the glory of God into an idol',* [*Jer 2:11*] adoring the likeness of men and birds and fourfooted beasts and creeping things.* [*Rm 1:23*] They would have done better adoring these if these were at least alive; but proclaiming themselves to be wise, they became exceedingly stupid.

'Those men who hinder the truth of God in injustice.'* [*Rm 1:18*] The truth of God among men consists in a true and natural knowledge of the Godhead, namely, that God truly exists and cares for human affairs; that he who created, disposes and rules whatever he has created; and that no man can doubt that human reason is in God's care and possession, least of all those men who profess philosophy, which is the knowledge of human and divine affairs.²⁶ A man hinders this truth in injustice if he hinders it in idolatry. Idolatry is injustice because it is absolutely contrary to the justice of faith. Men who worship idols hinder in injustice a reluctant and unwilling truth while human nature itself, inherent in man's rational consciousness, cries out in contradiction, rebuking the falsity of this religion, 'for what is known of God is manifest in them: God has manifested it to them'.* [Rm 1:19]

God has shown them what is known of God and what human reason can attain through nature, not what charity can attain through grace, for he gives them through nature a reason capable of sublime understanding, but he gives understanding itself through grace. Through the visible attributes of visible creatures he has shown them his invisible attributes; through visible creation, the invisible power of the Creator; through the visible order of things, invisible wisdom; through visible benefits, the goodness of grace or invisible charity, or as the Apostle says, 'eternal power and divinity'.* [Rm 1:20] The eternal power and wisdom of God is he of whom the Apostle said elsewhere, 'But we preach Christ crucified, to the Jews indeed a stumbling-block, and to the Gentiles foolishness; but to those who are called, both Jews and Greeks, Christ is the power of God and the wisdom of God.'* [1 Cor 1:23-24] But divinity is the Holy Spirit, the divinity of the Father and the Son, who is understood to be their love and their goodness; he is even the divinity common to both, and whatever is common to all three of them is certainly common to them both.²⁷

[Rm 1:20-21] VERSES TWENTY AND TWENTY-ONE. From the creation of the world the invisible things of God have been clearly perceived in the things that have been made; this includes his eternal power and divinity, so they are without excuse, because although they knew God, they did not glorify him as God, or give thanks, but became vain in their thoughts, and their foolish heart was darkened. God is invisible substance, or intelligible essence, a light illuminating

and pouring itself over those who turn toward it, but
striking and confounding those who turn away from
it. God is splendor to him who seeks him, and a heat
from which no one can hide himself. He is the beauty
which seizes every reasonable mind to contemplate
the love of truth, and which rebukes the sluggish and
the vain with a knowledge of their vanity. Since the
unstable motion of changeable things is kept from
being thrown into disarray by God's eternal, im-
movable laws, and is constantly being recalled to a
semblance of stability by the restraints of the revolv-
ing ages, motion shows that it derives its natural
origin from immobile and immutable eternity, in
keeping with its condition as a creature. Insensible
and irrational things are moved by their natural
condition only, and are set in their order by the
power, wisdom and goodness of the Creator. Rational
man, however, is left to the choice of his own will and
the judgment of the reason he has received with the
result that, if by prevenient grace he wills to go where
he is led by the power of reason, he is held fast there
by love and is formed by a growth of piety, by the
beauty of justice and by everlasting happiness and by
the fullness of God's justice, to the fullness of his
everlasting happiness. He is grateful to God his
gratuitous enlightener and his helper and he glorifies
God in himself. Such are the men who, when they
know God, give him thanks and glorify him. But the
wise men of this world did not do this, of whom the
Apostle says that they became 'vain in their thoughts,
professing themselves to be wise' by themselves, and
so they were deserted by grace and were cast away
from the face of the knowledge of God, and 'their
foolish heart was darkened'. What they had learned

[PL omits] [through vanity] they lost through curiosity, as has
Above, Rm 1: been said before.* They became so foolish and
21-22 unwise that they said in their hearts, hearts silly and
Ps 13:1 totally abandoned by grace, 'There is no God'.* And
Above, Rm 1:23 as already mentioned above,* they exchanged the
glory of the incorruptible God for the likeness of the
image of a corruptible man, of birds, of fourfooted
beasts, and of creeping things. 'Therefore God gave

them up to the desires of their heart.'* Augustine says in his book *On Grace and Free Will*, 'This shows clearly that God works in men's hearts to incline their wills wherever he wills, either to good according to his mercy, or to evil according to their merits, and with his judgment sometimes open and sometimes secret, but always just, he deserts them.'[28]

The question is asked in regard to one who is handed over, although he is handed over to his concupiscences for his sins, whether his being under concupiscence is justly imputed to him. The same question could be asked about a man put in jail for his crimes, for no one could rightly attribute to him his being in darkness, because he is there unwillingly, though justly.[29] But as the same Apostle says, man is said to be spirit and soul and body.* Between the spirit and the flesh exists that familiar quarrel that everyone knows so well. The man whom grace does not draw is associated with the flesh and made one with it, and of that man it is said, 'My spirit will not remain in him, because he is flesh.'* The man whom grace attracts is associated with the Spirit and is made one spirit with him, and it is said to him, 'You, however, are not in the flesh, but in the Spirit.'*[30] To be drawn or not to be drawn is the same as to be handed over or not to be handed over. Why this man is drawn and that one is not—these are the Son's secrets. Do not try to seek the answer to these questions if you do not wish to err. If you are not drawn, pray that you may be; and if you pray faithfully now, you will be drawn and not handed over. In those who are drawn and not handed over, it is the grace of God alone at work; in those who are handed over and are not drawn, God's blameless justice is at work.[31]

To whom are they handed over? To unclean devils suggesting unclean desires, so that they might glory in the fulfillment of these suggestions and in the damnation of those who fulfill them as in their own work. It is clear that men of this sort are completely handed over to Satan by the judgment of God for the destruction of their flesh and spirit, unless God's swift mercy intervenes. For this reason the ancient canons rate such men among the possessed and have them prayed for like demoniacs.³²

PL adds: of Scripture [PL omits]

This whole passage* swarming with sordid vices and [presenting CHACENFATON of impurity] seems better passed over than read,³³ but the Apostle was not ashamed or reluctant to write this passage most prudently in order to humble the proud and warn them about where contempt of God leads.* Avarice leads its adherents to the same end, for it serves the creature rather than the Creator as long as it loves money more than God.* These pass such a judgment in regard to the veneration of the Godhead, for they prefer the foul images of animals to him, and they even use the same judgment concerning themselves when they live like irrational beasts adoring their images, and throwing away God's image. And this is the reward which, as is fitting, they receive for themselves from the just judgment of God.* And why?

Rm 1:26-27

Cf. Eph 5:5

Cf. Rm 1:27

Rm 1:25, 28

VERSES TWENTY-FIVE AND TWENTY-EIGHT. **Because they changed the truth of a creature of God into a lie, calling the work of their hands God. And since they did not like to have God in their knowledge, God delivered them up to a reprobate sense,** so that those who had tampered with the notion of God should prove reprobate in their own mind. They should be reckoned to have God in their knowledge who know that his presence is everywhere, and who are either unwilling, or do not dare, to sin in his presence. Therefore the repentent prophet wept saying, 'For I have sinned before you'.*

Ps 50:6

Rm 1:29

VERSE TWENTY-NINE. **Filled with all iniquity,** that is, in all these iniquitous parts. **Malice** Malice is the font and the refuse, and as it were, the mother of all evils. It is written, 'Wisdom hates malice'. Indeed, wisdom is hostile to malice because just as good relishes wisdom in its thought, so evil relishes malice. **Worthlessness** He is worthless who cannot do all that the malice of his heart suggests. **Envy** This is hatred for the good fortune of another although it cannot cause any harm. Things which are obvious ought to be passed over, except that which should not be bypassed: that he joins together gossips and slanderers whom God has pronounced equally hateful. But he placed the foolish and the faithless last, because all these things which they initiate lead to a kind of foolishness of heart and a foolish disarray of morals, to such an extent that falling into a kind of natural stupor they have no loyalty for any neighbor, or even any faith in whatever agreements they have made, and no mercy for anyone in need. There is clear proof in its own nature of how contrary this is to the law of nature. For three states are found in the body: stupor, immortality, and health. Health has no sickness, although when it is afflicted it is sorrowful. Stupor does not sorrow, it lacks a sense of sorrow; the worse it is the more insensible. Again, immortality does not sorrow when every corruption has been removed. Therefore there is no sorrow in an immortal body, none in a stupified body; and still the health of a sorrowing man is closer to immortality than the stupor of one who does not feel. Thus the soul of the wise man, existing not without affection, says of the feeling of health, 'Who is weak and I am not weak? Who is scandalized and I am not furious?'*[34] — 2 Cor 11:29

All these evils which have been enumerated flow as a deadly river from the fountain of pride in which they called themselves wise but became stupid, and its terrible flow must be fled from and avoided. For along this river all reprobates sweetly set their sails for hell, and make for the three ports of their pleasure, and in each they suffer its peculiar betrayals. Now here the word 'betrayal' is used in as much as this is, for God who hands man over, the sentence of a just judge and for him who is handed over it is the trick of deceitful sin. First, the proud and the idolaters are handed over in the desires of their hearts to uncleanness. Second, those who are, as it were, wiser and progressing in evil, and who think that sacrifice should be made not only to idols but to the nature of things, are handed over to base passions and are steeped in graver disgraces. Third, they who cast aside the knowledge of God are handed over to a reprobate frame of mind; they are drowned in a well of wickedness and hopeless destruction. Through the judgment of eternal death the pit opens its mouth under them. The Apostle judges and says:

Rm 1:32

VERSE THIRTY-TWO. **Those who do such things are worthy of death.** 'Do,' he says, not 'did'. Those who did such things and no longer do, but rather repent, are worthy of life. Note that in the first and second place pride suffers such punishments as are not something they could be proud of, if they had any wisdom. In the third place they completely clothe themselves with folly so that the more proud they are, the less they have to be proud of. Pride and folly are close sisters, except that folly is more willingly tolerated because it is found sometimes without pride; pride, however, never exists without folly.

Although they knew the justice of God, they did not understand that they who do such things are worthy of death. They were an eye to themselves and therefore they perceived, but they could not be a light to themselves, and therefore they did not understand. They had their natural reason from God, but they impudently attributed it to themselves and did not seek the help of grace. Therefore they could not understand what would have been very profitable for them to understand, namely, that death is due 'not only to those who do such things, but also to those who agree with those who do them'.* To agree with a sinner is to have the same affection for sin as he does, or else it is to foster the error and keep silent when one could censure.

Rm 1:32

CHAPTER TWO

Rm 2:1

VERSE ONE. **Therefore you are inexcusable, O man, whoever you are, when you judge another.**

This outstanding teacher endowed with wonderful prudence in the ways of the gospel, this Apostle of the Gentiles who knew how to become all things to all men, was always careful to build up and honor his own ministry. After he strongly repressed and humbled part of the Gentiles for their former way of life, because it was necessary, he now turns the scourges of his rebukes on the Jews so as not to increase their aggressive battering of the Gentiles. The result of his action was to be that those who had been equally chastised should be equally united and consoled in the sweet peace of Christ. And although he could have rightly imputed to them the same filth of idolatry and uncleanness as he had to the Gentiles, for the prophetic books are full of it; nevertheless, he prudently spared them, lest when questions about the law arose, which he did not doubt would be most painful to them, their patience would grow weary and sink under the load if it were too burdensome. On the contrary, turning from species to genus, he modestly makes a public correction of them all, so that some may benefit by the correction of others, and yet others not fail in patience, as we have said.

Because all are worthy of death, both those who do and those who consent, 'therefore you are inexcusable, O man'. He is inexcusable because the truth is not hidden from him and yet he continues in wickedness. O man, put in a place of honor, you have God's law and judge according to God's law, and with him every man is a sinner either from guilt of origin or by the addition of his own will, and this whether he knows it or not. For, ignorance in those who refuse to understand is without doubt a sin; and in those who cannot understand, it is punishment for sins. Therefore you, O man, who judge according to the law, are inexcusable, but so are you, every man, although you neither know the law nor judge, you are none the less inexcusable. God does not admit excuses because he knows that he made man right* and also gave him the precept of obedience, and the testimony of his conscience according to the natural law. Neither man therefore has a just excuse, and each is

Cf. Qo 7:30

justly condemned. If they are inexcusable who could not understand the invisible things of God from the creation of the world through the things that have been made, how much more inexcusable are those who are instructed in his law and trust themselves to be guides for the blind and a light for those in darkness? To them, indeed, are these words particularly addressed: 'O man, you are not a spirit. You try to excuse yourself with human pride, thinking like a man and judging like a man.' **In passing judgment on another, you condemn yourself. For you do the same things which you judge.** The world is full of men who judge other men or even punish the acts which they commit. When they judge others, they pass sentence on themselves.

Rm 2:2

VERSE TWO. **For we know that the judgment of God is true, against those who do such things.** Sometimes things that look bad are done with a good motive, and things that look good are done with a bad motive; but other acts are done with the agreement of the doer's mind, whether they appear to be done for good or evil. True judgment belongs to God alone, who knows how to judge the heart.

Rm 2:3

VERSE THREE. **Do you think, O man, who judge those who do such things and yet do them yourself, that you shall escape the judgment of God?**

Ps 67:2

'Let them who hate him flee before his face.'* Those who love God do not flee his judgments but seek them, because they are confident that they will be justified in them. But those who flee them cannot escape them. The text continues:

Rm 2:4

VERSE FOUR. **Do you despise the riches of his goodness and of his patience and long-suffering?** He has now disquieted the despiser; therefore he adds the cause of this patience, saying: **Do you not know that God's kindness leads you to repentance?** The goodness of God is inconceivably rich, because just as he makes his sun to rise, so he does not cease pouring his other goods over the good and bad alike. But the patience of God is directed toward those who despise him, and his long-suffering toward those who fail more through weakness than through deliberation. While sinners persevere in wickedness, God perseveres in patience, punishing a few sins in this world lest belief in divine providence be abandoned, but reserving many things for the final scrutiny, so that the future judgment be given some value.[35] But the mind conscious of itself in evil is already completely subject to punishment, although it believes that God will not judge because it seems to be suffering no punishment at present.[36] This is the reprobate mind itself. This is blindness and hardness of heart. This is the darkness by which the sinner is kept away from the inner light of God, not completely however, while he is in this life. There is also an outer darkness which is understood to pertain rather to the day of judgment, so that he is wholly outside of God who does not will to be corrected while he has time.[37] What does it mean to be wholly outside of God, except supreme blindness? God dwells in inaccessible light,* into which they enter who hear the words, 'Enter into the joy of your Lord'.* 'Do you not know that God's kindness leads you to repentance?' This holds as long as it is the time of mercy. Do you want to hear about the time of judgment?

Cf. 1 Tim 6:16

Mt 25:21

Rm 2:5

VERSE FIVE. According to your hardness and your impenitent heart you treasure up for yourself wrath in the day of wrath and revelation of the just judgment of God Two sorts of men sin stubbornly. One promises himself God's mercy; the other despairs because of the enormity of his sins. Because of those who toy with delays in hope of mercy God has made the final day uncertain; for those who are in danger of despair he has made it a harbor of kindness. Both one and the other lay up for themselves treasures of wrath in the day of wrath, unless they quickly repent. A treasure is where various kinds of riches are hidden away, bit by bit, so that at one time a whole pile can be uncovered. Three treasures are found in Scripture: a treasure on earth, a treasure in heaven, and the one which is called a treasure of wrath. The man who with an impenitent heart collects his acts in the treasure of wrath is called hard; the one who lays up his treasures on earth is called a fool. 'You fool,' he says, 'this night they require your soul from you.'* The wise man, however, is rich toward God* and whatever he does he makes worthy of the kingdom of heaven. The carnal man lays up treasures on earth; the animal man lays up treasures in wrath; and the spiritual man lays up treasures in heaven. The day of wrath is the day of judgment when to each one will be faithfully offered the person, the object, or the place where he has laid up treasures.[38]

    The judge will take note not so much of your abilities as of your will, which he will crown. You willed but, perhaps, could not carry out your will; he will take note of you as though you did what you willed, and of you also it is said, 'To each one according to his works'.* Glory and punishment there will vary as much as diversity of merits here, but God forbid that some venial sins block the just man from eternal life, for this life can scarcely, or even never, pass without them. Similarly a few good works will not help the impious, for it is most difficult to find a life, even of the worst of men, lacking them.

    ·But when wretched men in this life hear 'eternal fire', they promise themselves purgatory in the next life. They say, 'Many will be saved there, as it were, by fire'. The hope of desperate men! First they should know that nothing in this life can be thought of that is harsher than that fire. Then, as the Apostle testifies, he will be saved there by fire who does not build with gold, silver, or precious stones upon Christ the foundation, but with wood, hay and stubble.* He does not refuse to receive the foundation, nor does he reject it after he has received it, and he prefers it to all the carnal delights by which he is held captive or to which he succumbs, when it comes to the critical moment when he must desert either them or Christ. If he does not prefer Christ then he does not have the foundation. For, indeed, the foundation comes before all the subsequent parts of the structure. And

Lk 12:20
Cf. Lk 12:21

Rm 2:6

Cf. 1 Cor 3:12

ignorance of Christ or of good does not excuse anyone from burning in eternal fire, unless he did not believe because he had never heard, and then perhaps he will burn less.

Rm 2:6-7 VERSES SIX AND SEVEN. These things are said in the meantime about the day of wrath, in which God **renders to every man according to his works. To those who according to patience in good works seek glory and honor and incorruption, eternal life.** This is what he says, and this is the order of the following thought. To those who seek glory and honor and incorruption, according to patience in good work, eternal life will be given by God, not only to the Jews, to whom the words of God seem entrusted, but also to the Greeks. The reason is that God's judgment is just, and he is God of the Gentiles as well as of the Jews. On those who through contentiousness of mind and wickedness of soul do not believe the truth but pursue evil, wrath and indignation, trouble and anguish [are] poured, and not only on the Gentiles but on the Jews as well, 'for there is no respect of persons with God.'*

[PL: will be]

Rm 2:11

This is what the text says in the order of its words, but now let us look at the inner sense of the text. He says glory and honor belong to those who bring forth fruit in patience,* that is, 'according to patience in good work'.[39] This glory of incorruption and immortality will exist in the resurrection and will be blessed happiness in both body and soul. The honor is that which man had before he was 'compared to senseless beasts, and became like them,'* namely when he was overflowing with the delights of God's paradise and enjoyed the continuous vision and conversation of God. These things will be rendered in eternal life to those who seek eternal life. About this very life he says, 'This is eternal life, that they may know you the one true God, and Jesus Christ whom you have sent.'* To those who seek God for God's own sake, he will be eternal life, and honor, and glory; he will be all in all.

Lk 8:15

Ps 48:13,21

Jn 17:3

Rm 2:8-9

VERSES EIGHT AND NINE. To those who are contentious and do not obey the truth, but give credit to iniquity, wrath and indignation, and so forth. Understand, prudent reader, what is set before you and notice that to those who perform well, God is said to render glory, honor and eternal life, but that anger and indignation, anguish and trouble await the reprobate. And it is not said that these things are to be rendered by God, for what is good we receive from God, but evils we bring on ourselves.[40]

'To those who are contentious,' he says. Contention is what makes heresies, and raises up schisms and scandals; it causes disobedience to the truth, and gives credence to evil.[41] On them, therefore, anger and indignation, trouble and anguish. Anger is torment inflicted on the soul by the consciousness of sin. By indignation is understood a certain swelling of anger, as though it were a wound, and a kind of widespread disturbance, so that if we say that anger is a kind of severe wound, then its swelling distention is called the wound's indignation.[42] Tribulation is that which does not give us spaciousness, about which the psalm says, 'In tribulation you have given me spaciousness.'* Rather, tribulation causes a narrowness which is the opposite of spaciousness, which is to act well by the grace of God with a cheerful will.

Ps 4:2

To the Jew first, who knew the will of God but did not act accordingly; therefore, he shall be beaten with many blows.* **Then to the Greek,** who will perhaps be beaten with few blows, because he was ignorant. There is a difference between having known God and* having known his will. A Gentile could know God through the creation of the world, but the will of God is known by the law and the prophets.[43]

Cf. Lk 12:47-48

PL adds: not

NOTES

1. For the discussion of Paul's name see Augustine, *Enarr. on Ps 72;* PL 36:916. William's discussion here is typical of that found in earlier commentaries on *Romans.*.
2. The previous three sentences are from Augustine, *Conf. 8.4;* PL 32:753. Florus of Lyons refers to this passage in his *Exposition on Paul's Letters,* one of William's chief sources: PL 119:279.
3. This sentence is from Augustine, *Third Sermon On The Epistle of John, Chapter 2;* PL 35:2000. Florus refers to this passage: PL 119:279.
4. This first part of the sentence is Augustine, *Predestination of Saints;* PL 44:981 = Florus; PL 119:280.
5. The previous sentence and this one up to here are Augustine, *Predestination of Saints;* PL 44:983 = Florus; PL 119:280.
6. The reference is to Origen, *On Romans;* PG 14:849, where *destinatus* is said to be better than *praedestinatus* for this verse.
7. The concept of original sin is referred to by William with a variety of expressions throughout this work, e.g., Rm 5:14: *peccatum originale;* Rm 7:15: *pestis illa generalis ab Adam; inevitabile contagium;* Rm 7:19: *domesticus inimicus.*
8. The expression 'either contracted at his origin or committed by his will' is Augustine, *On the Gift of Perseverance;* PL 45:1034. See also Florus, PL 119:280.
9. This sentence is from Augustine, *Gift of Perseverance*, PL 45: 1034. Also see Florus, PL 119:280.
10. The last two sentences are Augustine, *Enarr. on Ps 67*, PL 36: 820. Also Florus, PL 119:280.
11. The sentence to this point is Origen, *On Roms;* PG 14:852.
12. This paragraph is from Origen, *On Roms;* PG 14:853.
13. These two sentences are based on a gloss in MS 49, fol. Aᵛ, attributed by the MS to Origen.
14. From 'This apostolic blessing . . . ' down to here is taken from Origen, *On Roms;* PG 14:853.
15. For William's discussion of giving thanks for some and for all see Origen, *On Roms*, PG 14:854.
16. This paragraph is based on Origen, *On Roms*, PG 14:857.
17. Cf. *Rule of St Benedict, Chapter 1* on the kinds of monks.
18. The previous sentences are based on Origen, *On Roms,* PG 14:857.
19. This sentence is from Origen, *On Roms,* PG 14:555.

20. This paragraph is a direct quotation from Origen, *On Roms*, PG 14:861.

21. This is not Job. William continually refers it to Job throughout his works. See Augustine, *On Spirit and Letter 11.18;* PL 44:211.

22. 'These philosophers whose reputation exceeds . . . ' down to here is a long passage from Augustine, *City of God 8.6;* PL 41:231. Florus refers to this passage, PL 119:281.

23. William juxtaposes *curiositas* and *pietas* in *Enigma fidei*, CF 9:74.

24. The previous four sentences occur as a gloss on Rm 1:18 of pauline text in MS 49, fol. 1ʳ. Also see CF 6, pp. xlvii–xlviii, where Déchanet discusses the contribution of Plotinus to William's thought. This discussion must be qualified by CF 6, p. 52 n. 7 and Stanley Ceglar's remarks on the augustinian source for William's use of Plato: Ceglar, *William of St. Thierry, the Chronology of his Life* (Washington, D.C., 1971) pp. 275-277. Compare Plotinus, *Enneads*, 1.6.8.

25. Cf. *Enigma of Faith*, CF 9:38-39. In *Enigma* and here William uses Augustine, *Letter 92;* PL 33:319.

26. This definition of philosophy is commonplace. It is taken from Cicero, *De officiis* 2.25, who attributes it to 'ancient philosophers'. The definition appears in Augustine, Boethius, Isidore, Abelard, among others.

27. This sentence is borrowed from Augustine, *Trinity 5.11* and *6.5;* PL 42:919, 927-8. William uses this again in *Enigma*, CF 9:114-115.

28. This passage is from Augustine, *Grace and Free Will 21.43;* PL 44:909. Also Florus, PL 119:282. It also occurs on fol. 1ᵛ of MS 49 as a gloss.

29. This paragraph to here is from Origen, *On Roms*, PG 14:865.

30. From 'But as the same Apostle says . . . ' down to here is Origen, *On Roms;* PG 14:866.

31. This sentence occurs in MS 49, fol. 115ʳ, as a gloss of an unidentified authorship to the pauline text. Compare Augustine, *On the Gospel of John* 26.2; PL 35:1607.

32. William's reference here is uncertain, but for *energumenos* see Cassian, *Conferences 7.12;* PL 46:681-2. Also, see Mansi, *Sacrorum conciliorum nova et amplissima collectio* (Florence 1758-98) Vol. 2, p. 10, Canon 29, Council of Elvira; Vol. 6, 438, Canon 14, Council of Orange.

33. The awkward English renders an equally awkward Latin where the greek adjective κακέμφατον functions as a noun in the sentence. In MS 49, fol. 115ʳ, the Greek word appears in small roman capitals. The word is twice altered: the scribe writing the text in the MS adds above the line an 'h' after the initial 'c'. A second hand, the so-called William-hand of the latter part of MS 49, changes the end of

word to '-ton'. Migne's text presents a misspelling in Greek script for this word: κακεύφατον. The source for this greek term is Quintillian. The word also occurs in Isidore, *Etymologies*, 1.34.5.

34. 'For three states are found in the body . . . ' down to here this paragraph is from Augustine, *Enarr. on Ps 55;* PL 36:650–651. Florus refers to this, PL 119:283.

35. This sentence is from Augustine, *Letter 153;* PL 33:655. Florus refers to this in PL 119:283.

36. This sentence is from Augustine, *Enarr. on Ps 9;* PL 36:126. Florus refers to it, PL 119:283.

37. 'outer darkness': cf. *Enigma*, CF 9:71 where William admits ignorance of what this outer darkness is.

38. This paragraph paraphrases Origen, *On Roms*, PG 14:875C. The triad, carnal-animal-spiritual, is found in Origen and drawn ultimately from St Paul, I Thess 5:23.

39. The discussion of Rm 2:6-7 to here is verbatim from Origen, *On Roms*, PG 14:879–880.

40. From 'This glory of incorruption . . . ' down to this point condenses several columns of Origen, *On Roms;* PG 14:883–886.

41. William condenses a couple sentences of Origen, *On Roms*, for this sentence; see PL 14:884.

42. William's imagery of sin as a physical wound is from Origen, *On Roms*, PG 14:885.

43. These last two sentences paraphrase a section in Origen, *On Roms*, PG 14:886.

BOOK TWO

Continuation of ROMANS, CHAPTER TWO

Rm 2:11-12

VERSES ELEVEN AND TWELVE. **For there is no respect of persons with God** Whenever a rational soul thinks or reasons, even when blinded by cupidity, whatever truth is manifest to it in its reasoning should be attributed not to it but to the very light of truth by which the soul, at least slightly illuminated, senses some truth by its reasoning. No soul which can reason at all is so perverse that God does not speak in its conscience. For the hand of our Creator wrote in our hearts, 'What you do not wish done to you, do not do to another',* and, 'Whatever you wish men to do to you, do similarly to them'.* No one was allowed to be ignorant of this, even before the law was given, so that there might be something by which even those who had not received the written law could be judged. But that which men were forced to see in their conscience was written down and set before their eyes, lest they complain that they lacked something. Only Jews received the written law; both Jews and Gentiles received the natural law.

Cf. Tob 4:16
Mt 7:12

The works prescribed by the written law are twofold; part of them concern sacraments and part of them morals. Circumcision, the Sabbath, and so forth, for example, pertain to sacraments. The commands, 'You shall not kill', 'You shall not commit adultery', and so on, concern morals. If observances are not understood as well as observed, they are sheer slavery. If they are both understood and observed, they are beneficial, but in their own time, and this is how they were observed by Moses and the prophets. Such servitude would still be useful in keeping man subject to a tutor and fear. Nothing so frightens a soul in its piety as a sacrament that is not understood, but when it is understood, it generates joy, and it is celebrated freely, provided the time is suitable. If not, it is merely read about with spiritual sweetness and discussed.

Every sacrament when it is understood is referred either to the contemplation of truth or to good morals. The contemplation of truth is founded on the love of God alone, but good morals are founded on love of God and love of neighbor, on which depend the whole law and the prophets.*[1] As far as pertains to morals, the written law and the natural law are about the same and are equally common to the Jews and Gentiles, except that one has it written both on tablets and in their minds, and the other has it only in their minds. The same natural force is present in both, and by it a rational animal judges something to be legitimate and does it. Therefore, as our text says, 'there is no respect of persons', but he 'who sinned under the law', that is, he who was bound to observe the written law, will be judged according to the law which forbids sins and assigns to each sin its penalty. He who sinned without the written law will be judged without the law, that is, not through the written law which he did not receive. The law which he did receive will suffice for his judgment.

Mt 22:40

Rm 2:13

VERSE THIRTEEN. **For not the hearers of the law**, whether written or natural, **but the doers shall be**

Cf. Rm 11:6   **justified before God** The Apostle's statement that only the doer of the law shall be justified before God requires a correct understanding, lest it seem contrary to what he said elsewhere, 'If by works, then not by grace', and 'grace is not grace'.* Heaven forbid that justice should come to one who keeps the law and from the works of the law; rather, justice comes that he may keep the law. He is justified by grace in the act of keeping the law. He is not first a doer of the law so that he is made just for having kept the law, but as a man is created in order that he may be a man, so the doer of the law is justified in order that he may be just, or that he may appear to be what he is in keeping the law, namely just. We should remember that the Apostle here speaks to Jews who have been converted to the Lord and who fulfil the law in a spiritual way. The Gentile convert carries out the prescriptions of the law naturally, and by doing that he is justified, because the spirit of grace restores in him the natural law that was written naturally in his heart by God, but deleted by vice. For one who has turned to the Lord, to have the law of God written in his heart and not on tablets is to embrace the justice of the law with the intimate affection of his

Cf. Gal 5:6   heart. Here faith works by charity.* The text continues:

Rm 2:14-16   VERSES FOURTEEN THROUGH SIXTEEN. **For when the Gentiles, who do not have the law, do by nature those things that are required by the law, although they do not have the law, they are a law to themselves. They show that the work of the law is written in their hearts, with their conscience bearing witness to them, and with their thoughts accusing, or even defending them on the day when according to my gospel God shall judge the secrets of men through Jesus Christ.** In speaking of 'their thoughts accusing', the latin translator seems to follow the greek custom of using the genitive case for the ablative, since Greek does not have the ablative.[2]

The Apostle speaks of our thoughts, because by thoughts works are judged and a person

is judged innocent or guilty. Also, he speaks
of thoughts, not of those which were, but of
those which exist now, because even though all our
thoughts and acts may perish from the memory,
they do not perish from the conscience. All of them
will be brought to light before God the Judge. That
will be a fearful judgment where nothing will be
introduced from outside, but everything will be
produced from the conscience: the accuser, the witness, the judge, and the case.

Rm 2:17

VERSE SEVENTEEN. **But if you are called a Jew, and rest in the law** Here the Apostle addresses himself to a vigorous and necessary disputation about the law, directed not only against the Jews but also against the enemies of grace and those contentious persons mentioned above.* Here the reader will be greatly helped if he keeps in mind the four degrees of the law, or of progress in the law.[3] The first stage of man is when he lives according to the flesh, in the deepest darkness of ignorance, with his reason making no resistance. The second stage of man occurs when knowledge of sin is acquired through the law. Unless the divine spirit helps, the man wishing to live according to the law is conquered and knowingly sins. Knowledge of sin rouses every kind of concupiscence in man, so that he commits sin, and when a great amount of prevarication has been added, the words of Scripture are fulfilled, 'The law entered in, that sin might abound.'* The third stage of man, and one of good hope, occurs if God looks kindly on a man and helps him fulfill what he commands, and the man begins [to be moved by the spirit of God] with greater strength of charity when the lusts of the flesh are aroused. Although there is still something in him which fights against him and his weakness is not totally healed, still the just man lives by faith, and lives justly, as long as he does not yield evilly to concupiscence. And thus delight in justice conquers. The final stage: if anyone succeeds with pious perseverance, peace will remain which will be fulfilled after this life in the repose of the spirit, and

Above at Rm 2: 8–9.

Rm 5:20

[PL omits]

then in the resurrection of the flesh. In regard to these four stages, the first one is before the law, the second under the law, the third under grace, and the fourth in full and perfect peace. Grace, however, was not formerly absent from those to whom it should have been given, although it was veiled and hidden according to the requirements of the time. The whole body of this Epistle uses these four distinctions, speaking sometimes of the man of God individually, and sometimes of the people of God in general.

'If you are called a Jew,' he says. This skilful doctor of souls, seeing that of two sick men, one of them, that is, his own race, is much more dangerously sick, is infirm with the infirm. He rebukes the Gentiles severely and does not spare them; he notes that the same crimes exist among the Jews and lightly censures them so that by the obedience of the Gentiles he may stimulate his own people to patience until in the manner of a doctor he has lessened the cause of the disease, that is, pride. Thus, he follows the practice of doctors who can treat more securely the cause of the illness when that cause has been mitigated. In like manner, in order to relieve the malady he has not until now singled them out for rebuke, but dealt with them along with others. But now after the common warning has been given, he watches for a freer approach to his sick man, and strides forward with the strong bonds of reason to bind the madman, so that having the Gentiles easily in hand, he may adapt even the hardness of the Jews to grace. Both of them according to the distinctions given above are found to be under the law, either written or natural.

Rm 2:17-20   VERSES SEVENTEEN THROUGH TWENTY. But if you are called a Jew and rest in the law, and make your boast of God, and know his will, and approve the more profitable things, being instructed by the law, you are confident that you are a guide of the blind, a light to those in darkness, an instructor of the foolish, a teacher of infants, having the form of knowledge and of truth in the law Know that all these statements which are brought forward as though in praise of the false Jew are spoken in irony. Whatever is said here is like a plaster which makes pride swell so that its vanity can be reduced and its worthlessness deflated. What is so worthless as to boast of what one does not have, and to preach what one does not perform? That people was apathetic in regard to the second item concerning the people of God on the above list, namely the law. The people gloried in having accepted it, but did not fulfil it even in a carnal sense and, presuming on itself, that people reluctantly approached grace. If it had truly rested in the law and boasted of God, it would not have done what it proclaimed should not be done.

'If you are called a Jew,' Paul says, but you are not, for the Church is the true Judaea and the Lord God has clothed himself with the beauty of her confession.* You seem to draw your name from the Fathers from whom you are disgraceful descendants. They had circumcision of the flesh as a sign of faith, but circumcision of the heart on account of that faith. You used to have kings from the tribe of Judah, and therefore you were called Jews. But when you denied Christ the King from the tribe of Judah, you lost both the kingdom and the name.

Ps 92:1

'You rest in the law,' condemning and mocking the various errors of the Gentiles; or resting in a carnal understanding of the law, you decide that nothing more should be sought. 'And you make your boast of God,' as though you were God's own people and as though God were known only in Judaea.* 'And you know his will, because he has not done the same for every nation, and his judgments he has not made manifest to them.'* And of many profitable things, 'you approve the more profitable'. 'Being instructed by the law, you are confident' in a presumptuous way that without the guidance of the Holy Spirit 'you are a guide of the blind', so that both of you fall into the ditch.* You trust in yourself as 'a light of those who are in darkness' as though they were to be enlightened by you, an instructor of the Gentiles as if they were foolish in regard to the law, 'a teacher of

Ps 75:2

Ps 147:9

Cf. Mt 15:14

infants' as though they would learn from the law to speak the nonsense in your fables. Finally, you trust that you have 'the form of knowledge and of truth in the law,' that is, a perfect and true knowledge of the law to which no one dare add anything.

Rm 2:21

VERSE TWENTY-ONE. **You therefore who teach another, do you not teach yourself? You who preach that men should not steal, do you steal?** The Jews stole property among themselves and, what is worse, they wished to steal a correct interpretation from the law, grace from the Church, and Christ's coming from the world. And so they committed adultery, in a carnal sense first, and then in a spiritual sense, by pursuing their own concupiscences. They paid suit to the idols of the Gentiles, and still more so to the idols of their own hearts. In both they were sacrilegious, not putting sacred things in sacred places. They dishonored the God of the law by their transgression of the very law in which they thought they should boast. They dishonored him because they made his name to be blasphemed among the Gentiles. 'Christian' is a name derived from Christ, and when it is blasphemed, the blasphemy falls back on the author of the name. This statement is taken

Ezek 36:20-23

from the prophet Ezekiel.* Those Jews who are rebuked here already share the christian name, but because they stupidly boasted of their former status and set themselves before the Gentiles, the Apostle prudently humbles them from their former status. He proves that what they thought made them more remarkable and glorious—the law and circumcision— is useless and unnecessary. These were more to their confusion than to their glory. He has already spoken about the law; now about circumcision.

Rm 2:25

VERSE TWENTY-FIVE. **Circumcision profits indeed, if you keep the law,** the law of circumcision of course. Circumcision is the cutting away of evil from oneself, and the law of circumcision is to be earnest in good works, so that the words of Scripture

Ps 36:27

are fulfilled, 'Turn away from evil and do good.'*

True circumcision is circumcision of the heart, that is, a will free from all concupiscence; this is not accomplished by the letter which teaches and threatens, but by the spirit which helps and heals.

Circumcision profits, if you keep the law; but if you are a transgressor of the law, observing only the circumcision of the flesh, **your circumcision is made uncircumcision,** that is, it is reckoned as infidelity. The text continues:

Rm 2:26-27

VERSES TWENTY-SIX AND TWENTY-SEVEN. **If then the uncircumcised keep the justices of the law, shall not this uncircumcision be counted for circumcision? And shall not that which by nature is uncircumcision, if it fulfil the law, judge you, who by the letter and circumcision are a transgressor of the law?** The Apostle compares those who keep the justices of the law with the Jews who through the letter and carnal circumcision transgress the law. Let them not, he says, keep the law, that is, the law which prescribes works or sacraments, but rather the justices of the law, that is, its moral discipline. By keeping it the uncircumcised are so much preferred to the circumcised who break the law that they will judge them.

The author did well to say 'If they fulfil the law'. One who lives according to the letter observes the law, but one who lives according to the spirit fulfils it. But perfection is in him who says, 'I did not come to destroy the law, but to fulfil it'.*

Mt 5:17

Rm 2:28-29

VERSES TWENTY-EIGHT AND TWENTY-NINE. **He is not a Jew who is outwardly so; nor is that circumcision which is outwardly in the flesh; but he is a Jew who is one inwardly; and circumcision of the heart is in the spirit, not in the letter. His praise is not from men, but from God.** The sense of the Apostle's discourse must be watched carefully, lest, while he is addressing now this group of persons, now that group, the reader lose his way and become confused, and miss the end to which the Apostle intends to bring him. This end is grace, or the recommenda-

Above at Rm 2:17 tion of grace. As we said a little earlier,* Paul cherishes both the Jews and the Gentiles with fatherly love. He embraces the Jews both in flesh and in spirit, and the Gentiles for the sake of the grace of the gospel and the honor of his own ministry. He threatens the contentious of both groups with anger and its consequences, and promises glory and honor to those of both groups who act well. He humiliates and lifts up and then makes equal, first this group and then that, always striving to temper and govern everything so that neither group has more glory or more envy.

And then concerning the Gentiles he adds, 'Whoever sinned without the law shall perish without the law',* and immediately in regard to the circumcised he says, 'Whoever sinned under the law shall be judged by the law'. Again, raising up the Gentiles he says, 'When the Gentiles who do not have the law,'* etc., and then turning to the Jews, he says, 'If you are called a Jew,'* and so on. Then lest he seem too excessive in rebuking the Jews, he adds, 'Circumcision is profitable, if you keep the law'.* But immediately setting a limit to the boasting of the Jews against the Gentiles, he says, 'If you are a transgressor of the law, your circumcision is made uncircumcision'. Then raising up the Gentiles a little, he says, 'If the uncircumcised keep the justices of the law,' etc., and then lifting their spirits even more, he says, 'That which is by nature uncircumcision, if it fulfils the law, will judge you, who by the letter and circumcision are a transgressor of the law'.* Then because there were certainly many promises in the law and the prophets which seemed to apply to the circumcised, he says the following in order to open the way for the Gentiles to hope for those promises also. 'For he is not a Jew, who is outwardly so, nor is that circumcision which is outwardly in the flesh; but he is a Jew, who is one inwardly,' etc. Then there follows what we now have in our hands.

Rm 2:12

Rm 2:14

Rm 2:17

Rm 2:25

Rm 2:26-27

CHAPTER THREE

Rm 3:1-2

VERSES ONE AND TWO. **Then what advantage does a Jew have?** Let us proceed by laying down the groundwork so that afterward we may move more easily to our conclusion regarding grace. **Much more in every way.** For the Jew there were many preparations and instructions for the faith of Christ; for the Gentile there were none of these except their natural intelligence. 'Do we excel them? No, not so,'* because if you do not believe, a greater preparation for the faith is for you nothing except a greater damnation. But if you believe and the other man believes, your faith does not at all surpass his faith in merit. But as far as merit is concerned, it has been demonstrated with certitude that before grace all were subject to sin. The law only gave knowledge of sin not its remission. 'But now, that is, in the time of grace, justice is made manifest',* not the justice of the law or of merits but of God through the blood of Christ. This is grace. Therefore, a little later, as if to conclude, he adds, 'We account a man to be justified by faith without the works of the law'.*

Rm 3:9

Rm 3:21

Rm 3:28

At this point let us back up a little. He says 'There is no respect of persons with God'.* What does God respect then? Patience in good works.* Where does this come from? Either from grace or from the law. If from the law, it would not be beyond the law. But it is found beyond the law, because the Gentiles who do not have the law do by nature those things that belong to the law,* that is, they bring forth fruit in patience.*

Rm 2:11
Rm 2:7

Rm 2:14
Lk 8:15

Rm 2:17

Then follows 'But if you are called a Jew,' etc.* It is as though the Apostle says, 'You who are called a Jew, where does the justification of the law come from, from the law or from elsewhere? It is not from the law, because you who boast in the law dishonor God through transgressions of the law. Therefore it comes from elsewhere. It comes from the Spirit, in whom the true and hidden Jew is justified, and whose praise is not from men but from God.'

'Then what advantage does a Jew have, or what

good is circumcision? Much in every way,' because they received more preparations for the justification of faith, either spiritually or carnally. But the Gentiles received more faith; as the Lord says, 'I have not found such great faith in Israel.'* Why was there less faith for the Jew? This is the abyss of God's wisdom. If good works proceed from grace and if justification comes from the Spirit, then both Jew and Gentile have the capability and the opportunity for these things. But since the Jew before grace received more preparations, which were also temporal consolations for him, he received more in every way. In the time of grace, however, Jew does not excel Gentile, because the Gentile received more faith in the present time and, as regards the past, grace found both equally subject to sin. Therefore grace was equally necessary for both. Let us now return to our reading of the text.

Mt 8:10

Rm 3:2-3

VERSES TWO AND THREE. **First, indeed, because the words of God were committed to them,** that is, in the law and the prophets, showing them mysteries, instructing them in morals, and preparing them to receive the coming of Christ. Among them were some few who believed, but the multitude which did not believe **did not make the faith of God without effect,** that is, did not wholly separate that people from the faith of Christ. Since God's promises to them are good, they cannot be falsified, for the following reason:

Rm 3:4

VERSE FOUR. **God is true, but every man a liar,** including that mendacious man, whoever he is, who does not believe or admit that God's gifts and calls are without repentance. He says, 'What if some of them have not believed then? Shall their unbelief make the faith of God without effect?'* Faith is here to be taken as that which God has toward those to whom he has entrusted his words, or else that which they have toward God who merited that God's words be entrusted to them. **God forbid!** He says God forbid that the evil of some particular one should

Rm 3:3

destroy the good of the whole. God forbid that the truth of God who promises should be brought to nothing by the sin of an unbelieving man, because **every man is a liar, but God is true, as is written, 'That you may be justified in your words, and may overcome when you are judged'**. Every man is a liar, but not those men to whom the word of God was addressed, whom Scripture pronounced to be not men but gods.* And the Lord in the gospel confirms this.* God is true and justified in his words. The meaning of these words is to be sought in the earlier verses of the psalm. It says, 'Against you alone have I sinned,'* because I am king and thus subject to no man's judgment. Against you alone have I sinned because I was not afraid to sin before you, you who are everywhere present. Have mercy on me according to your great mercy, so that you may be justified, that is, appear just in your words by which you promised that you would build me a house, that my seed would remain after me, and that my kingdom would stand firm forever.* You will show yourself just and truthful when you fulfil these things for me, judging me according to true mercy, which you love, and restoring to me the spirit of prophecy, in which you have made manifest to me the uncertain and hidden things of your wisdom. You will overcome the judgments of men who rashly and superficially criticize both you in your indulgence and me in my penitence and the good things of your promises which are granted to me.

Ps 81:6
Jn 10:35

Ps 50:6

2 Sam 7

The Apostle uses this lengthy discourse to prove the truthfulness of God, 'that you may be justified in your words, and may overcome when you are judged'. In this should be noted a comparison in the example which has been introduced. Just as the rash judgment of men deprived David after his sin of all forgiveness and of the grace of the promises, so it deprived the whole Jewish race after the Lord's passion. But mercy, judged unjustly, conquered when from its own unjust death it most mercifully brought about justice unto life even for its own killers. When the false blasphemy against God was heard and the general calumny of damnation against his own kind, the Apostle, as if impatient, exclaimed, 'God forbid! Every man is a liar, but God is true!' On the occasion of this blasphemy as if with his spirit placed on the blasphemers he says, 'Thus, they speak with this sentiment':

Rm 3:5 VERSE FIVE. **If our iniquity commends the justice of God, what shall we say? Is God unjust who executes wrath?** To show that he is speaking with the voice of the blasphemers, he says, **God forbid! I speak according to man.** True it is that he speaks according to man, but not a man who is very wise in human matters. That God's justice is commended by our iniquity is in no way the result of our sins but is an actual consequence of reason, by which contraries are proved by contraries. As a worthy and proper consequence justice is the hostile adversary of injustice, even as light is of darkness and life of death, and it is just that God in whom there is supreme justice should execute wrath on men in whom there is injustice. And perhaps it was therefore that the Apostle does not say that unjust men commend the justice of God, but our injustice, so that he could show that it was not God who was opposed to men, but justice to injustice.

Otherwise, how shall God judge this world? He who will judge the world justly cannot be unjust. This is another argument for the justice of God. Then the Apostle exaggerates the calumny in order to reject it, for he says,

Rm 3:7 VERSE SEVEN. **They say, 'If the truth of God has abounded through my lie to his glory, why am I also still judged a sinner?'** But the Apostle explains that we are not the ones saying this or that which is thought to follow from it.

Rm 3:8 VERSE EIGHT. **Some say that we say, 'Let us do evil that good may come,'** when rather we preach that good be done, lest evils come. Consciously sinning, they say this and therefore their condemnation is just.

Rm 3:9-11

VERSES NINE THROUGH ELEVEN. **What then? Do we excel them? No, not so.** Having rejected the calumny, the Apostle returns to the thread of his argument and asks, 'What do we possess more than they do?' Since it is obvious that before grace both parties were under sin and, when grace came, it made both equal as much as it could, there is no longer a cause for contention or boasting by either party.

For we have charged both Jews and Greeks, that they are under sin. This he confirms by Scripture as is his custom, and in this he gives the Doctors of the Church an example that they should strengthen and fortify what they say with the testimonies of Scripture.

There is not any just man. There is none who understands, there is none seeking God. No one is just because no one understands, and no one understands because no one seeks after God. If anyone would seek, he would understand; if he understood, he would be just by loving the one whom he understood.

Rm 3:12

VERSE TWELVE. **All have turned away.** Birds deserve to be caught, a certain wise man said; the heavens are given to them, so what do they seek on earth where there are traps? We too have abandoned the heavens toward which nature has directed us even by the stature of the body, and we all lie prostrate among earthly things; we are useless and we corrupt each other by example. **There is no one who does good.** It is one thing to do good and another to act well. To act well happens casually and as if fleetingly; to do good is the result of effort and inner disposition. Just as conversely concerning evil, take pride for instance: it is one thing to be proud, and another to act proudly. Some men suffer pride in themselves, but others act proudly and encourage pride. Of them the prophet says, 'He who acts proudly shall not dwell in the midst of my house'.*

Ps 100:7

There is not so much as one. Count them one by one. You will not find one who is perfectly good until you arrive at the supremely good, who says, 'No one is good except God alone'.*

Lk 18:19

VERSE THIRTEEN. Their throat is an open sepulchre when they talk, because they are 'dead from the heart' as the prophet says.* The rotting corpse inside them emits a stench through their unclean words. **The venom of asps is under their lips** since they talk wickedly, and more wickedly keep silent, since their incurable wickedness cannot accomplish what it wants and wastes away in their hearts.

Rm 3:13

Ps 30:13

VERSE FOURTEEN. Their mouth is full of cursing and bitterness, because they curse aloud when they dare, and when they dare not, their heart is full of bitterness.

Rm 3:14

VERSE FIFTEEN. Their feet are quick to shed blood. They are quick to every sin in their actions, because they are not restrained or ruled by the judgment of reason.

Rm 3:15

VERSE SIXTEEN. Destruction and misery are in their ways, because the hard necessity of bodily labor and affliction, and the misery of a suffering conscience are in all their acts.

Rm 3:16

VERSES SEVENTEEN AND EIGHTEEN. And the way of peace they have not recognized, because **the fear of God is not before their eyes,** which is the beginning of wisdom and of entering upon that peace, of which it is said, 'There is much peace for those who love your law'.*

Rm 3:17-18

Ps 118:165

These evils which the Apostle has gathered together here seem to be introduced especially for the Jews, since at the beginning of the psalm about the Gentiles it is said, 'The fool has said in his heart, "There is no God".'* But the pride of the Jews was especially to be smashed by recalling to them their transgressions of the law in which they gloried. For, glorying in Abraham and the rest of the Fathers, they boasted that it

Ps 13:1

was almost natural for them to possess justice. Therefore the Apostle adds:

Rm 3:19-20

VERSES NINETEEN AND TWENTY. **We know that whatever the law says, it says to those who are under the law, that every mouth may be stopped** and opened only in praise of God. The Gentiles were quickly brought to humility through consciousness of their past error, and the Jews were humbled through transgression of the law, about which they seemed to boast. The greater the knowledge of the law and the more personal the acceptance of it, the less excuse there is, and the [less excuse there is the] more evident is transgression and the more certain is condemnation, because even if the works of the law are performed, by the works of the law, no one will be justified by observing it carnally **before God,** who sees the inner heart & will, where he sees that one who fears the law would prefer to do something else if it were lawful.

[PL omits]

That all the world may be made subject to God, and may understand what it owes to him and what it receives from him. From the law it has the knowledge of sin, but from grace the manifestation of justice and equally justification itself.

For through the law is the knowledge of sin; not that sin would not be known, but that it was thought to have been committed with impunity. Even if grace cannot help overcome a known sin the law works wrath just the same.

Rm 3:21-22

VERSES TWENTY-ONE AND TWENTY-TWO. **But now,** that is, under grace, **the justice of God is made manifest.** Although it justifies without the help of the law, **it receives witness from the law and the prophets,** so that when the law announces, faith fulfils, and perfection is achieved. Faith should not lack the witness of the law, and the justice of the law could be fulfilled only in faith. Therefore the justice of God is made manifest without the law, but receives the witness of the law and the prophets.

It has been observed here by those who know the greek tongue or the writing of the Greeks that because

of the many different kinds of laws, the mosaic law
in their writing is noted by the placement of the
definite article.[4] When the word 'law' occurs twice
in this verse, the first time without the article and the
second time with it, it is given to understand that it is
the mosaic law which testifies to the justice of God,
but that no law, whether given in paradise, conferred
by nature, or promulgated in writing, helps to fulfil
the justice of God.

Note also that he says that sin is known and justice
is manifested, because everything that is manifested
is light; sin is more known than manifested, because it
belongs to darkness.

What is this justice? **The justice of God,** answers
the Apostle, when faith obtains what the law commands. It is the justice of God, not of men, not of
works, not of one's own will. Not that it can be done
without our will, but that our will, shown through
the law to be weak yet healed by the grace which
comes from faith, fulfils the law. The law has this
useful aspect, that since it cannot heal, it sends those
to be healed to grace with ample testimony and experience of their weakness; [it sends them] to grace *[PL omits]*
and the life-giving Spirit, where all sins are destroyed
and the charity to act well is breathed into man.
This is **the justice of God through the faith of Jesus
Christ, passing into all and over all who believe in
him.** It passes into all, as regards the universality of
believers, and over all, since it surpasses all the merits
of those who receive it. **There is no distinction**
between Jew or just man, as to who is in less need,
nor between Gentile or penitent sinner, as to who
should receive less.

Rm 3:23   VERSE TWENTY-THREE. **For all have sinned,
and need the glory of God** God does not need to be
glorified by anyone, but everyone in every way needs
God to be glorified in him. Each man's glory consists
Cf. Rm 3:24   in being justified freely by God's grace,* and whoever
has grace also has glory.

Rm 3:24–25   VERSES TWENTY-FOUR AND TWENTY-FIVE.

Through the redemption which is in Christ Jesus our Lord Those had to be bought back who had sold themselves. Man sells himself in consenting to sin, which is the death of the soul, when he receives the pleasure of sin and in return in some way gives up the hope of life and eternal life. Then came the Man who alone was born just, and who did not accept the pleasure of sin, but did not refuse sin's punishment; and he gave this justice to man who was sold and who had nothing in the substance of his nature whereby he could buy himself back, so that by Christ's punishment man might destroy the bond of his debt. And this is the justice of God that, clinging in faith to him who died for us, we might have from him what we cannot have from ourselves. And because this is conferred on us gratuitously, it is a grace. That all things might respond to grace, God predestined Christ before the ages, but in this time he presented him openly as the **Propitiator in his own blood,** when he revealed his justice in the sight of the nations.* By this justice God appears just by not leaving sin unpunished, and he justifies the unjust man in a just way, remitting his sins atoned for by the voluntary shedding of the blood of the Propitiator. When the sinner clings to Christ by faith, he comes away in his justice to the glory of him who justifies, justified in the atoning blood of the Propitiator, in his healing charity, in his justifying justice. In order to manifest his justice, therefore, God for a long while put up with sinners, even time and again, but in the time of grace he prepared and brought about justice for the unjust. Thus God showed his justice in regard to times past by mercifully bearing with sinners, and in regard to the present by granting them the indulgence of grace and by justifying them freely. He did this once for all men, and he does it continuously for each man individually. He bears with and continues to bear with the sinner; he inspires and prepares his conversion. Sometimes he even introduces force; he heals the will, helps the weakness, and when he has done everything, he ascribes to the recipient the total merit for what has been done. This is grace, this is that justice

Ps 97:2

of God about which the prophet says, 'Deliver me in your justice.'*

Ps 30:2

The whole of the human race lay subject to punishment, and if the punishment of damnation which was due to all were rendered, without a doubt it would not have been done unjustly. Who therefore is so completely out of his mind that he does not give unspeakable thanks to him who mercifully liberated whom he willed, and who in no way could rightly be blamed for injustice if he completely condemned everyone? Since this is a most just conclusion, it is most evidently out of the question that anyone should glory in himself, or in the law, or in anything except in the Lord.

Rm 3:27

VERSE TWENTY-SEVEN. Then where is your boasting? It is excluded. By what law? Of works? No, but by the law of faith. If the Apostle meant that boasting was praiseworthy, then he intended the boasting which is in the Lord and he said it was 'excluded', not driven back so as to be removed, but pressed out so as to stand in relief. Thus, some silversmiths are called 'excluders'. Therefore also there is found in the psalm, 'that they may be excluded who are tried with silver,'*[5] meaning that those who are tried by the word of the Lord should stand out prominently.

Ps 67:31

But if the Apostle wished to refer to a wrong type of boasting arising from the pride of those who seem to themselves to live justly and so boast as if they had not received this, then he says it is excluded, that is, rejected and cast away, not by the law of works, but by the law of faith. By the law of faith each one recognizes that if he lives well it is by God's grace, and that he will not attain the perfection of the love of justice from any other source. This consideration makes him pious, because piety is true wisdom. I mean by 'piety' what the Greeks call THOCEBIAN.[6] It is recommended in the Book of Job[7] which says, 'Behold, piety is wisdom'. THOCEBIA is the worship of God, and it chiefly consists in the soul's not being ungrateful toward God.

This type of pride is not vulgar like pride over eloquence or riches, but is that exulting about those things which are the proper goods of good men, such as justice, as when the Jew presumes to appropriate to himself justice by reason of the works of the law, or when a proud man does this in regard to the merits of his works. Although it is certain that justice comes to no one except from faith, care must be taken lest this be thought a reward deserved by faith or be spoken of as such by those who are puffed up as though wise in regard to justice. For although faith obtains justification according to the measure of faith imparted to each by God, nothing of human merit precedes the grace of God, but by merit grace merits to be increased so that it even merits to be perfected. For in regard to faith, 'What have you that you have not received'?* And elsewhere the Apostle says, 'I obtained mercy that I might be faithful'.* He did not say, 'because I am faithful', but 'that I might be faithful'. Faith, indeed, is not a thing of merits or of one's own will. It is a free gift of God and with it all good things begin. Good works are, indeed, performed by men, but faith is worked in man and without it good works are performed by no man. 'Everything which is not of faith is sin.'* Even the merit that comes from prayer should not boast of itself, even if the prayer asks only for God and the things of God. When help is given to him who prays, faith is praying which was given to him who was not praying, and if it were not given he could not pray. In all these things, O Jew, O proud man, 'Your boasting is excluded. By what law? By the law of works? No, but by the law of faith.'

1 Cor 4:7
1 Cor 7:25

Rm 14:23

We should know in what way the law of works and the law of faith differ, since both of them equally say, 'You shall not covet'* and under this prohibition are contained all the sins committed through concupiscence. Also we should know that both of them have their own sacraments of works, although they are different. In the law of works there is the justice of the God who commands; but in the law of faith, the mercy of the one who comes to help. What the

Rm 7:7

law of works commands with a threat the law of faith obtains by belief. By the law of works God says, 'Do what I command'; by the law of faith it is said to God, 'Grant what you command.'* Therefore, the law commands so that it can admonish what faith should do, that is, so that the person to whom a command is given, if he is now unable to do it, may know what to ask for, and if he can do it immediately, and obediently does it, he may know by whose gift he is able to do it. This is that wisdom which is called piety, by which the Father of lights is worshipped by whom every best gift and every perfect gift is given.* He is worshipped by the sacrifice of praise and of thanksgiving so that the worshipper glories in God and not in himself. The good son of the faith knows from whom to hope for what he does not yet have, and from whom he holds what he already has.

Cf. Aug. Confessions 10.29.40 and 10.37.60

Cf. Jm 1:17

The law of works is 'a holy law, and a holy, just, and good commandment',* but by means of its goodness sin works death, since the law prohibits and yet causes all manner of concupiscence. It commands but does not help; it punishes but does not liberate.

Rm 7:12

The law of faith has certain practices in the sacraments of the Church, which are easier to perform than the sacraments of the law of works, of better use, of greater power and fewer in number. It is as if the justice of faith has been revealed, and the sons of God have been called to liberty, and the yoke of slavery has been removed, which befitted a hard and carnal people.[8] Yet these will also cease in their own time, for just as the first coming of Christ put an end to those, so the second coming of Christ will put an end to these when the kingdom of revealed truth shall shine forth. The text continues:

Rm 3:28

VERSE TWENTY-EIGHT. **For we account a man to be justified by faith without the works of the law.** What then? Does faith not work through love?* Of course it does. But because there were some Jews who boasted of the works of the law which they performed not out of love but out of fear, and because

Cf. Gal 5:6

they wished to seem just and to be preferred to the Gentiles who did no works of the law, the Apostle boldly exclaimed that a man can be justified by faith without the works of the law. Those who did what they did out of fear were not more just than those whose faith worked through love in the heart, even without appearing outwardly in work. Do not for a minute think that the Apostle said that a man can be justified without works, so that if a believer were to have time for works, he would not need to perform them. He said this rather, that no one should think that he came to the justification which is through faith by the merits of previous works. He says, therefore, that a man can be justified without works, meaning previous works, but that he is justified by faith and grace, which cannot lie idle in him if he has time to do works. But if he does not have time, the justice of faith remains with him. On the contrary, he insists that the faith which is unfruitful when it has time to act is useless, so that he says, 'If I have all faith so that I can move mountains, and have not charity, I am nothing'.* A charity which is faithful is always operative and this is without a doubt what is meant by 'to live well, for charity is the fulfillment of the law'.* 'Very well,' says the Jew, 'let it be that a man is justified only by faith, but this applies only to the Jew, because faith belongs only to him who has the law.' To this Paul answers:

1 Cor 13:2

Rm 13:10

Rm 3:29

VERSE TWENTY-NINE. **Is God the God only of the Jews** who accept the law of works, **and not also of the Gentiles,** to whom has been given only the law of faith? **Yes, of the Gentiles also,** because he who created both will save both.

Rm 3:30

VERSE THIRTY. **For it is one God, who justifies circumcision by faith, and uncircumcision through faith.** The expressions 'by faith' and 'through faith' seem to be variations in wording only, not in meaning, because elsewhere he says that uncircumcision is justified by faith and circumcision through faith. However, some persons who are literalists have thought that the phrase 'circumcision is justified by faith' should mean that the beginning of faith is in circumcision. They wish to construe 'uncircumcision is justified through faith' in second place. Whether this agrees well enough with what is written let us leave to the reader's judgment. For the time being let this conclusion stand: man is justified by faith without the works of the law.

Rm 3:31 VERSE THIRTY-ONE. **Do we then destroy the law through faith? God forbid; but we establish the law.** Through the law comes knowledge of sin, through faith comes the obtaining of grace against sin, through grace the healing of the soul from the blemish of sin, through the soul's healing comes freedom of will, through freedom of will comes love of justice, through love of justice comes the fulfillment of the law. And in this way the law is not destroyed through faith but established, because faith obtains the grace by which the law is fulfilled.

CHAPTER FOUR

Rm 4:1 VERSE ONE. **What then shall we say that Abraham found according to the flesh?** The Apostle, commending the justice which is from faith against those who boasted in the justice which is from works, presents Abraham as an example. There is no doubt that he was pleasing to God. This statement of Scripture seeks to draw our attention to that. We believe and the Apostle says that Abraham has glory before God.

Rm 4:2 VERSE TWO. **But if Abraham was justified by works, he has glory, but not before God.** But he has glory before God. Therefore he was not justified by works. By what then? The text continues:

Rm 4:3 VERSE THREE. **For what does Scripture say?** That is, from what source does Scripture say that Abraham was justified? In that which follows:

Abraham believed God, and it was reputed to him as justice. Therefore, Abraham was justified by faith.

Rm 4:4 **VERSE FOUR. But for him who works,** that is, who presumes on his works and through their merit attributes to himself the grace of God which was given to him, **there is a reward because it is not reckoned to him according to grace, but according to merit.** But woe to any justice of man if it is judged without mercy.

Rm 4:5 **VERSE FIVE. But for him who does not work, yet believes in him who justifies the ungodly, his faith is reputed to justice.** The act of believing is a work of grace. Christ works this in us, but certainly not without us. For he says, ' "The works that I do he also
Jn 14:12 shall do,"* because I act in order that he may act, and so a just man is made from a sinner.' Then faithful charity acts, and without a doubt this is to live well.

PL: ut It is important that one trust God or* believe in God. He trusts God who trusts him when he speaks or promises; or he trusts God who entrusts himself to him. Therefore the prophet says about a certain
Ps 77:8 people, 'Their spirit was not entrusted to God'.* To believe in God is to approach God by trust and love and to become a member of his body or to offer oneself in obedience to his good pleasure, whatever it is, just as Abraham did, for whom, because he believed perfectly, his faith was reputed as justice. He trusted God who promised him posterity. He believed in God when, leaving his land and his family, he obediently
Gen 12 went into a land which he did not know,* or when he
Gen 22 offered the son in whom he had received promises,* or when he rejoiced to see the day of the Lord, and
Jn 8:56 he saw it and was glad.*

According to the purpose of his grace God so decreed and arranged that, with the cessation of the law, faith should justify.

Rm 4:6 **VERSE SIX. So also David speaks of the blessedness of the man** who has been accepted, that is, made acceptable, and **to whom God reputes justice without** works. 'Blessed are they whose iniquities are forgiven.' Because sins are found in all men, it remains that the only blessed ones are those whose iniquities have been forgiven. And this is grace where there are no merits of your own and the remission of your sins is given to you freely. Therefore, the Apostle does not say, 'who have no iniquities', but 'whose iniquities are forgiven', or 'whose sins are covered', or 'whose sin is not imputed, although it occurs'. But the sins are not covered in order that they may exist and live, but lest they be seen, noticed, or observed.

Notice the different order: first, he says that iniquities are remitted, then sins are covered, and finally that sin is not imputed. The beginning of conversion is to leave aside evils, and this merits the remission of former evils. Then individual evils are covered by individual or even additional goods, and when the matter has come to perfection, by the grace of God and zeal for a good life the very affection for sin is radically removed from the depths of the heart by an affection for virtue. Sin is no longer imputed to have been committed before God; it has thus been amputated from the soul now renewed by God's justification. Iniquity, called in Greek ANOMIA,[9] and sin seem to differ in this, that iniquity is that which is done against the law, but sin is committed either against nature or against the rebukes of conscience.

From what has been said we find that our father Abraham found his justice coming from faith and not from works, but his blessedness came from justice, except that there is hesitation on this last point because of what is said: 'To him who works, the reward is not reckoned according to grace, but according to debt; but for him who believes in him who justifies the ungodly, his faith is reputed to justice.'* This passage seems to show that in faith lies the grace of him who justifies, but in works seems to resound the justice of him who punishes. But to one who weighs well the gravity of the words which assert that to the worker a reward is imputed according to debt, it will be strange if he can persuade himself that any work can demand God's reward as a debt, since

Rm 4:4-5

whatever good we are capable of, which we do or which we think, is a gift of God, and nothing can be offered to him which is not a gift or a present from the Father of lights. See, therefore, whether the word 'debt' should not be understood of an evil deed. You will often find the word 'debt' applied to sin in the sacred books, as in 'Forgive us our debts,'* and in regard to the slave called to a reckoning, 'Pay your debts'.* Consider, therefore, whether the sense of this passage 'the reward of works which is rendered according to debt' is not likewise applied by the Apostle to those who work as Cain worked the earth,* or to those to whom it is said, 'Depart from me, you workers of iniquity'.*

Mt 6:12

Mt 18:28

Gen 4:2

Lk 13:27

Therefore, since it is evident that blessedness comes from grace through faith, he continues:

Rm 4:9

VERSE NINE. **This blessedness then, does it remain in circumcision only, or in uncircumcision also?** Already he had said earlier that Abraham trusted God, and that it was reckoned as justice to him, and that he had shown what beatitude this kind of faith had. But now he proposes a question, and from its answer teaches that even from a temporal reckoning—and this is wholly victorious for grace and against the Jews—the blessedness of justification was given to Abraham through faith, not while he was circumcised, but while he was still uncircumcised. Scripture says, 'Abraham trusted God, and it was reputed to him as justice'.* But if Abraham while still uncircumcised was justified by faith, so can everyone who trusts God be justified through faith, although still uncircumcised. The blessedness spoken of in the psalm belongs to him also, since his faith also is reputed to justice. The blessedness, in fact, belongs more to the unjust than to the just, since faith is reputed as justice to those who, before they had this faith, had no justice. Therefore, the Apostle says:[10]

Gen 15:6, Rm 4:3

Rm 4:10-12

VERSES TEN THROUGH TWELVE. **How then was it reputed? In circumcision, or in uncircum-**

cision? He responds to himself: **Not in circumcision, but in uncircumcision.** If Abraham had been found in the time of circumcision, uncircumcision would seem to have been excluded from faith and grace, but now it is shown that his faith was reputed as justice while he was still uncircumcised. Therefore, it is declared that Abraham, still uncircumcised, was justified by faith, and without a doubt is rightly the leader and father of all those who believe while still uncircumcised. But because after the profession of faith which he made while still uncircumcised Abraham received circumcision, the Apostle explains the reason for his acceptance of circumcision.[11] He says, 'So that it might be a seal of his faith, which he had while uncircumcised, so that by it he might become the father of those born in circumcision, provided they belong to that faith which justified Abraham while he was uncircumcised. In this way he is made the father of both races, of the uncircumcised through faith, and of the circumcised through faith and through the flesh.'*[12] Thus the posterity of Abraham takes its beginning in a double mystery. The faith is Abraham's, and so is the seed. Whoever are like him in faith have a claim to the promised inheritance.

Cf. Rm 4:11-12

Before we pass on from here we should investigate more carefully how Abraham's faith is reputed as justice, and whether anyone who trusts God is also immediately just and his faith reputed to him as justice, since justice does not seem to embrace the fullness of one virtue only, but of all virtues. A man is convicted of injustice through proof that any element of justice is lacking to him. But it was the opinion of the ancient philosophers concerning the virtues that if a person had one of them he had them all. But the same opinion also exists in the christian religion about those virtues proper to christian piety. Whoever has faith has hope, love, and works, according to the degree of his faith. Whoever has hope has it according to the degree of his faith, love and works. The same for him who loves and who has works. This is God's full, flawless, and perfectly proportioned justice.

Therefore, when Abraham's perfection was put to the test, a perfect work of faith was enjoined on him, so that through a father's affection the believer's faith might be proved; and it was found perfect. He does not understand the perfection of Abraham's work who does not take note of the greatness of the temptation. He was ordered to immolate the son whom he had generated in old age from a sterile wife. This was his only son, in whom he had received the promises; he could not hope for another. The Lord said, 'Take your son Isaac whom you love and offer him to me as a holocaust.'* 'What did father Abraham do? He did not weep, hesitate or make excuses, but openly showed which he loved more, God or his son; and since he believed perfectly and loved perfectly, he also undertook a perfect work. Therefore, he merited to receive his son back, and his faith was reputed as justice to him. He had heard words carefully chosen to rip and tear a father's guts, but armed with the breastplate of faith,* he passed through the temptation untroubled and did not disturb the tenderness of his fatherly affection but increased it. Rightly then, faith was reputed as justice to him, as has been frequently repeated.

Gen 22:2

1 Th 5:8

Whoever has Abraham's faith and offers God the laughter of his heart,* that is, his carnal pleasures and the desires of his soul, on the altar of a holy profession, will hear from the Lord these words, 'By my own self have I sworn, because you have done this thing and have not spared your soul for my sake, I will surely bless you,'* and his faith will be reputed to him as justice.

Cf. Gen 21:3-6

Gen 22:16-17

The Jews, therefore, are forced to confess that Abraham was justified through faith, and we also are forced to understand that all the ancients who were justified were justified by this same faith. What we believe, in part concerns the past and in part the future, but they believed in all this as pertaining to the future only, with the Holy Spirit revealing himself to them that they might be saved.

In regard to Abraham's circumcision and our baptism, we should know that each of them was a seal of faith in its own time, signifying circumcision of the heart or cleanness of conscience, because the circumcised man begot an uncircumcised son, just as the baptized man begets an unbaptized son; each of them passes on a defect of origin which he himself has. Just as at that time everyone who wished to be saved had to be circumcised, so now he must be baptized. Each of these sacraments will pass away, but what these signs or seals signify will remain forever.

The Apostle set down both words 'sign' and 'seal', and there seems to be some difference between them. A sign is that which, when seen or thought, calls to mind some other thing of which it is the sign. Jonah in the belly of the whale for three days and three nights was a sign of the Lord Jesus Christ who was to be in the heart of the earth for three days and three nights.* And carnal circumcision is a sign of spiritual circumcision. But a seal is what is impressed as a protection on something which is to be guarded for a time; and no one else should add a seal, except the person who impressed the first one.[13] This is the justice of faith, through which it is shown that Abraham will be the father of many nations. We believe that a resealing will take place with the entry of the fullness of the Gentiles, and when all who then make up Israel are saved and the holy posterity of Abraham appears as one. An alternate understanding is that the mysteries which were foreshadowed in the law and the prophets or the patriarchs were such as had to be indicated by signs and covered by seals. In those mysteries which were to be indicated by signs to the believers among the Gentiles, father Abraham is said to have received a sign; in those which were to be concealed and kept for circumcised believers, Abraham is said to have received a seal. A resealing will take place when, as said before, the fullness of the Gentiles have entered in and all Israel is saved.*[14]

Abraham, therefore, is the father of the circumcised and the uncircumcised, and it was while he was uncircumcised and not when circumcised that faith was reputed as justice to him, and he received the sign of circumcision, the seal of the justice of faith which he had when he was uncircumcised, that is, which he had before he was circumcised, so that he might be the father of all those who believe through uncircumcision, that is, in uncircumcision. The result is that just as to him faith is reputed, so also it **is reputed to them as justice, and that he is the father of circumcision, and not for those only who are of the circumcision, but for those also who follow the steps of the faith which is in the uncircumcision of our father Abraham.** For the promise is not through the law, for if it were it would be only for them who served the law.

Rm 4:13

VERSE THIRTEEN. **For not through the law was the promise to Abraham or to his seed, that it would be heir of the world,** so that its inheritance would be extended through the whole world so that in his seed all nations would be blessed.* Not through the law, **but through the justice of faith,** because observance of the law scarcely escapes punishment, but the merit of faith looks to the hope of the promise. Moreover, a precept is imposed on slaves, but faith is demanded from friends.

Cf. Gen 22:18

Rm 4:14-15
PL: Rm 4:14-21

VERSES FOURTEEN AND FIFTEEN. **For if they alone who are of the law be heirs, faith is made void,** that is, the faith of Abraham by which he merited to be justified, and the faith which was produced by no one's merits, and **the promise is made of no effect,** so that there are no longer heirs. If that were so, Abraham should first have fulfilled the law, but he would have worked at that in vain, because **the law works wrath.** Where there is wrath there is no inheritance. But wrath is attached to the law where there is transgression. **For where there is no law neither is there transgression.** Transgression is a double sin. What is simply sin without the law becomes sin and transgression of a commandment with the law. When there is the transgression of one who defies a law, what can result except anger on the part of the one who orders? Therefore, there is no inheritance from the law, because the law works wrath. The inheritance is from the promise, because God himself does what he promises. The man who thinks that he fulfils the precepts of the law by his own free will without the spirit of grace wishes to establish his own justice and not to receive the justice of God. God did not promise this to Abraham. Not from the power of our will but from the grace of his own predestination God promised what he promised to Abraham. He promised what he himself would do, not what men would do. Even when men do some good which pertains to the worship of God, he makes them do what he commanded; they do not make him do what he promised. Otherwise, the fulfilment of God's promises would be in men's power, not in God's, and what was promised by the Lord would be rendered to Abraham by man. This was not the way Abraham believed, but he believed, giving glory to God, because he is able to do what he promised.* Scripture tells what God does, not what he predicts or foreknows. [Now he could predict or foreknow the actions of others.] He promised his own action, not other people's when he promised sons to Abraham in the faith of the Gentiles, and they could not be sons unless they had faith. Therefore, he gave the faith itself. But according to some people, when Scripture says, 'He who believes shall be saved,'* one of these acts is demanded, and the other is offered. What is demanded from man is in man's power; what is offered is in God's power. But why should not both of them be in God's power, both what he commands and what he offers? Indeed, what he commands is made the object of a request, when the disciples who believe in him ask him to increase their faith.*

Cf. Rm 4:20-21

[PL omits]

Mk 16:16

Lk 17:5

Rm 4:16 VERSE SIXTEEN. **Therefore everything is of faith, that according to grace the promise might be firm for all the offspring, not only for him who is of the law,** that is, those who came from the Old Testament to the New, **but also for him who is of the faith of Abraham,** meaning the imitator of Abraham's faith, claiming nothing for itself from the promised law, the guileless son of him who, in regard to faith, is the father of us all, both Jews and Gentiles.

Rm 4:17   VERSE SEVENTEEN. As it is written, 'I have placed you as the father of many nations before God, whom you trusted, who gives life to the dead, and calls those things that are not, as those that are'. He calls them, because he made those things which are going to exist. He predestined both nature and grace in us. God causes us to be men, and to be faithful, and he creates our justice, if we are just. And whomever he chooses for this he holds before himself not in his nature, but in his foreknowledge, and this is what is meant by 'before God'. Before God has already been done what will exist according to his disposition. 'And he calls those things that are not, as those that are.' He does not call them to be, but calls them as those things that are. Those who were promised were not yet in existence, lest anyone should glory about merits. And those persons to whom promises were given, were themselves promised, so that the whole Body of Christ should say, 'By the grace of God I am

1 Cor 15:10   what I am'.*

This is grace, which Noah, Moses and other saints are said to have found like a great treasure. Scripture

Gen 6:8   says, 'He found grace in the sight of the Lord'.* But notice that the Apostle says, 'Therefore it is of faith,

Rm 4:16   that according to grace the promise might be firm',* as if wishing to show that if the promise had been from the law it would not have been firm. And

[PL omits]   rightly so, because what is in the law is [beyond us, but what is of grace is within us, that is, what is of the law is] written on tablets or parchment, but what is of grace is written by the finger of God, the Holy Spirit, in our minds. The faithful soul unsealing the faith given it by God offers it faithfully to the Holy Spirit like wax tablets prepared so that he can write what he pleases, and what is written by the Spirit through the love of the Spirit interior affection should hold firm forever. And this is faith which is reputed as justice and which is made capable of grace.

This happens to the offspring of Abraham, not only those who are from the law, that is, those who came to grace from the observances of the law, but those who are of faith, that is, those who solely by imitation of Abraham's faith are counted as his sons. In this he is made the father of all believers, both Gentiles and Jews.

Who gives life to the dead, either those who are dead in soul by the death of sin, or those who worshipped idols, and were made like them, according to the prophet.*

Cf. Ps 113:8

'He calls those things that are not, as those that are.' The Apostle must mean those who have no share with him who says, 'I am who am'.*[15]

Ex 3:14

Rm 4:18-19 VERSES EIGHTEEN AND NINETEEN. **Against hope he believed in hope.** Abraham was an obstacle to his own hope, because his advanced age and the age and sterility of his wife denied him hope of begetting children. Against all this he believed in hope, because he trusted God who gave him hope, and he knew that it was easy for God to fulfil what he had promised. It is well said that he believed in hope, because he progressed from faith to hope. Faith in its progress is hope, and in its perfection is charity.[16]

And he was not weak in faith, although many things seemed capable of weakening his faith, as has been said.* Believing, Abraham gave glory to God, knowing most fully that he would not deceive in promising nor fail in fulfilling what he had promised. **Neither did he consider his own dead body, since he was almost a hundred years old, nor the dead womb of Sarah.** It was not incontinence that loosened the seed of Abraham, nor did womanly lust act on his holy wife; in them it was more by religion than by nature that their dead members revived. But when they heard a hope of offspring and posterity so great that God promised that its glory would equal the heavens and the stars then they no longer looked to their own good or to the grace of continence, but counted all things as loss that they might gain Christ from Abraham's seed.* So it was said to him, 'Your

Above at Rm 4: 10-12

Cf. Phil 3:8

seed shall be as the stars of heaven and as the sands of the sea.'* By the stars of heaven here are to be understood the spiritual sons of Abraham who are conspicuous for the light of virtues;* by the sands of the sea is to be understood the infinite multitude of a carnal and sterile generation.

VERSES TWENTY AND TWENTY-TWO THROUGH TWENTY-FIVE. In the promise of God he did not stagger by distrust, but was strengthened in faith, giving glory to God. And therefore it was reputed to him as justice. Now it was not written only for him that it was reputed to him as justice, but also for us to whom it shall be reputed if we believe in him who raised up our Lord Jesus Christ from the dead, who was delivered up for our sins, and rose again for our justification.

We should inquire carefully why the Apostle, in this place naming God in whom we believe and in whom Abraham believed, does not say 'if we believe in God the Most High', or 'in God who made heaven and earth', but only 'who raised up the Lord Jesus from the dead'. The answer is that it is much more magnificently to God's praise that he raised the Lord Jesus Christ from the dead than that he created heaven and earth. The latter consists in making what did not exist, the former in repairing what had perished. The latter was the institution of something new, the former was the restoration of what was destroyed. The mystery of this matter had already occurred previously in Abraham's faith, for when he was ordered to sacrifice his son, as Scripture says, he believed 'that God is able to raise up even from the dead'.* Rejoicing on account of this he offered his only son, because in him he was not thinking of the destruction of his posterity, but of the reparation of the world and the renewal of all creation, which would take place through the resurrection of the Lord. In this way, therefore, a comparison seems to be well made between Abraham's faith and the faith of those who believe in God who raised up the Lord Jesus Christ. What Abraham believed would be, we believe has been.

'He was delivered up for our sins and rose again for our justification.' The death of Christ both signifies and demands the mortification of the old man in us and the resurrection of justice. For that reason a man should hate his own sin implacably, for because of it he knows that his Lord was handed over. Let no one therefore think that his faith in Christ will be reputed to him as justice, unless he puts off the old man with his acts, and puts on the new man,* making himself conform to, and share in, his death and resurrection. Otherwise, there is no concord between justice and injustice.*

Cf. Eph 4:22-24

Cf. 2 Cor 6:15

NOTES

1. The previous paragraph and this one to here are from Augustine, *Exposition on Epistle to Galatians;* PL 35:2117. Also see Florus, PL 119:284. William condenses the passage from Augustine.
2. The Vulgate has *cogitationibus accusantibus.* The Pauline text in MS 49 has *cogitationum accusantium* as William has here. Origen in Rufinus' translation has both ablative (PG 14:877) and genitive (PG 14:1138). Origen lacks any grammatical discussion on this point. However, this sort of discussion is commonplace in medieval exegesis. Cf. Lombard on Rm 2:15; PL 191:1346BC.
3. These four degrees are taken from Augustine, *Propositions on Romans;* PL 35:2065ff. The remainder of this paragraph draws on Augustine's development of these four steps or degrees. William's text for the remainder of this paragraph is a direct quotation from a gloss on fol. 7ʳ of MS 49 attributed to Augustine.
4. William's source here is Origen, *On Roms,* PG 14:944. Note that William speaks of those who know the greek tongue or the writing of the Greeks as authorities for this observation. He does not say this on his own. This can be construed as an indication of his ignorance of Greek.
5. For a similar treatment of 'exclude', see Augustine, *On Psalm 67,* section 39; PL 36:836.
6. The Greek word meant here is θεοσέβειαν. This word and William's discussion are taken from Augustine, *On Spirit and Letter 11.18;* PL 44:211. In MS 49, fol. 128ʳ this word appears in small roman capitals with a line over it, the customary method of writing a foreign word in a medieval text. It does not appear in the PL.
7. The statement 'Behold, piety is wisdom' is found in Augustine, *On Spirit and Letter 11.18;* PL 44:211. The Vulgate has a different reading of Job 28:28. William relies here, and elsewhere, on Augustine.
8. This and most of the previous sentence are taken from Augustine, *Against Faustus 19.13;* PL 42:355.
9. This Greek word appears on fol. 130ʳ of MS 49 as ANORMIAN in small roman capitals, corrected probably during the fourteenth or fifteenth century to ANOMIA, also in small roman capitals. William's source here is Origen, *On Roms,* PG 14:966.
10. This paragraph is based on Origen, *On Roms,* PG 14:966.
11. This paragraph is based on Origen, *On Roms,* PG 14:967.
12. This paraphrase of Rm 4:11-12 is drawn from Origen, *On Roms,* PG 14:967.

13. The definition of 'seal' is from Origen, *On Roms*, PG 14:585.

14. This paragraph is from Origen, *On Roms*, PG 14:968-9.

15. The previous four paragraphs are condensed from Origen, *On Roms*, PG 14:975-978.

16. This sentence is a paraphrase of one in Origen, *On Roms*, PG 14:981.

BOOK THREE

CHAPTER FIVE

Above on Rm 2:17

WE HAVE ALREADY devoted two books to various aspects of the states mentioned above;* that is, those things which concern the first and the second states of the man of God or the people of God, and as we commence with the third state we salute the grace of God and his wonderful light and we adore him in that light from which he has begun to rise over us. The progression of these different steps does not follow the order of the text exactly; rather, they are indicated in different ways and places throughout the text, just as they usually occur at different times in the heart of the man who is making progress. There each one finds these different stages according to the successes or failures of his interior life. Sometimes a man must be tempted and shown to himself, and left to himself by God. Then he is found to be so totally lawless and senseless that he does not know his right hand from his left, as the saying goes. This pertains to the first stage of man. Sometimes an eye is given to a blind man so that he sees what should be seen. But it is not profitable, and it does not please the wretched man when his sense reports nothing to his mind of what it sees as is proper to natural vision. This pertains to the second stage of man. Sometimes a certain vision presents itself to the eyes of reason not so much by nature as by grace, so that the seer does not so much attract the object seen as the thing seen attracts the seer to it and conforms and adapts him to itself. When this happens without resistance it is a token or pledge of approaching health. When this occurs, yet not without strife and contradiction, it is a warning that weakness still continues. This pertains to the third stage of the man of God.

    The people of God were first left to themselves under the natural law so that they could understand by themselves what they were. Then the written law was added for some of them, lest there be some way in which man could excuse himself before God. Finally grace was sent to all men so that man could understand what he was in himself, what he was in relation to God, and what God was to him, and thus he could praise God but accuse himself.

    It is to this point that the apostolic discourse seems to have come, both in regard to the man of God and to the people of God, and from here the discourse enters the realm of grace, although up to this point the Apostle often draws the eyes of the reader to the need of grace and depicts the state of man or of men who were prior to the law or who are under the law. 'Justified therefore by faith, let us have peace with God through our Lord Jesus Christ.'* Until now the discourse has concerned the notion of faith[1] which is reputed as justice and the difference between circumcision and uncircumcision. Now let us see how those who are justified by faith and not by works are formed by the Apostle for grace. Since it is clear, he says, that the law of Moses harms not the Gentile, nor the law of faith the Jew, let us all, Jews and Gentiles, have peace toward God. First of all, let whoever understands and rejoices that he is justified through faith take care lest he be ungrateful for grace. That is, let him not have a proud faith and say to

Rm 5:1

himself, 'If it is from faith how is it free?' as though he himself gives faith and receives back justification. Let the faithful man not say this, because it will be said to him, 'What have you that you have not received?'* *(1 Cor 4:7)*

CHAPTER FIVE

Rm 5:1 — VERSE ONE. **Being justified by faith** They are just because they are made just. Made just by whom? By him who gave the faith which made us just.

Let us have peace toward God. The Lord said, 'In the world you shall have distress; but have peace in me'.* *(Jn 16:33)* As waves cannot be lacking in the ocean, so they cannot be lacking in the world, nor can some commotions in ourselves. Some neglect peace toward God in order to have peace with the world, although all peace is to be considered secondary so we may have peace with God. 'Love truth and peace,'* *(Zech 8:19)* says the prophet. First truth and then peace, that is, peace which is in harmony with truth. This peace which pertains to truth 'is patient, is kind, does not envy, does not deal perversely, is not puffed up, is not ambitious, does not seek its own, is not provoked to anger, thinks no evil, does not rejoice in iniquity, but rejoices with the truth.'* *(1 Cor 13:4-6)* This is peace toward God. The reward of this peace is peace in God; that is, to will all things in a good way and to have all that one wills. This is the definition² of true blessedness, whose first fruits the sons of God receive in this world and whose fullness they receive in the next. This pertains to the fourth stage of the man of God or the people of God. This is peace toward God through our Lord Jesus Christ, who is our peace, and who makes two things one, either the wall of circumcision and of uncircumcision, or the earthly and the heavenly, or man and God.* *(Cf. Eph 2:14-16)*

Rm 5:2-3 — VERSES TWO AND THREE. **And by him we have access through faith,** because we cling to him, **into this grace in which we stand and boast in the** hope of the glory of the sons of God. The teaching of Christ showed this way of approach to God, his example made it, his passion constructed it, grace draws and truth lifts it up, and all this through faith. We stand in grace when we labor with constancy on its behalf; we stand in it when we hope for and love what we believe. O to stand in the hope of the glory of the sons of God; how sweet it is to labor at that! The Lord said to Moses, 'Stand here with me',* and I will teach you. But the people were playing and adoring the calf's head. And David said, 'In the morning I will stand before you and I will see.'* He who stands in front both sees and loves to be seen. Therefore, those who prove to be faithful ministers are said to stand before the faces of kings. Some minor king of this world will say to you, 'Stand and obey me, and I will adopt you as a son in the glory of my kingdom.' What insults, what hard labor, what delays would you not tolerate? 'Stand with me', God says to you, and I will adopt you as a son; all that is mine is yours; you will be my kingdom, and I will be your good. As hostage you have my Son dying for you while you were still wicked.* When you are justified you hold as a pledge my Spirit.'

Deut 5:31

Ps 5:5

Cf. Rm 5:6

Grant, O Lord, grant, O Father of Lights, what you command. Grant what you promise to your servants; namely, the hope of the glory of your sons. **And not only that** but grant also that **we may glory on your behalf, in tribulations** [which, even if they seem to weigh us down by their presence, urge us toward you.] May these tribulations produce in us the inner disposition of patience to the accomplishment of our trial and the increase of holy hope.

[PL omits]

Rm 5:5-6

VERSES FIVE AND SIX. **And hope confounds not,** because wherever hope is faithful to you, immediately the object of hope is present also, **because the charity of God is poured forth in our hearts by the Holy Spirit,** whom you give us. When he comes into us by your gift, he teaches us all truth, making known to us that in you, O Father, is the source of highest divinity; in you, O Son, the eternal birth of

eternal consubstantiality; in you, O Holy Spirit, the
holy union of the Father and the Son; and in the
Three the one simple equality of holy OMOUCION.³
And what, O Lord, is this glory of your sons, what is
the hope of their journey, what is the solace of their
exile, no matter how prolonged, except that you wish
us to have communion among ourselves and with
you through that which is common to you, holy
Father, and holy Son. You gather us into one through
that gift which you both possess in common.

In this we are reconciled to your divinity,⁴ in this
we are hidden in the secret of your face,* in this we *Ps 30:21*
are cheered by the delights of your right hand until
the end.* For what would whatever we are as men *Cf. Ps 15:11*
have profited us unless we had progressed unto you
by loving you, O God? Surely just as we learn through
truth, so we love through charity, with the result that
in learning we perceive more fully and enjoy more
sweetly what we have learned.⁵ This is your prayer,
O Lord, which you prayed for us to the Father,
'I will that just as you and I are one so they may be
one in us.'* You wish this and vehemently wish that *Cf. Jn 17:21,24*
you may love us in yourself through the Holy Spirit,
your love, and you wish to love yourself through us
and in us. That precious substance by which we love
you is not in us from ourselves,* but from your Holy *Cf. 2 Cor 3:5*
Spirit whom you give us. Give him to us, therefore,
and dwelling in us, O God, love yourself through
us by moving us and arousing us to your love, by
enlightening us and stirring us up. And since we have
been estranged from the possession of true goods by
our sins, may your charity cover up the multitude of
our sins.*⁶ When you do this, O pleasant and sweet *Cf. 1 Pet 4:8*
one, those of your servants who have become your
sons find it pleasant and sweet to meditate on or
to speak of you, and in their speech and meditation
their heart is made to burn for you, and they speak
of you much more fully, seeing you with their sense
of enlightened love, but most profusely when you
deign to speak to the heart of the one loving you.
You speak to your lover, and it is like adding oil to
the flame,⁷ so that he who loves loves still more, and

Jb 4:12	he who burns burns more intensely. You speak to him interiorly in his conscience by the enlightenment of your Holy Spirit, and he understands 'the breath of your whisper', as it is said in Job.* And
PL: we passim	why did Christ, when as yet you* were weak, according to time die for the impious? Why, indeed, O Lord?
Rm 5:7-11	VERSES SEVEN THROUGH ELEVEN. Scarcely anyone will die for a just man; yet perhaps for a good man someone would dare to die. But God commends his charity toward you; because when as yet you were sinners, according to time Christ died for you. Therefore, being justified now by his blood, you shall be saved all the more from wrath through him. For if when you were enemies you were reconciled to God by the death of his Son, now that you are reconciled, you shall be saved by his life all the more. What, is there no other exit from sin for me except through the death of Christ your Son? None. For great love must be set against great hate, the love of the Son against the hatred of the enemy; love of you even to contempt of self against the sin of self-love, by which you loved yourself even to the contempt of God. By these realities and the sacraments of these realities, by these mysteries and the affections of these mysteries, the love by which we go to God and cling to him was to be purified. Without this love completely cleansed and purified there is no return to God, no clinging to God. But the man who has been cleansed and who sees and enjoys, what does he say? 'Not only so; but also we glory in God, through our Lord Jesus Christ, no longer in sacraments but in the very reality of all the sacraments, not in mysteries but in the light of revealed truth.' Because, even if that man knew Jesus according to
Cf. 2 Cor 5:16	the flesh, now he no longer knows him thus.* He has passed through the flesh into God, **through our Lord Jesus Christ, by whom we now** in the meantime **receive reconciliation.** There with him we shall have blessed union.

God continually calls this to remembrance in the

heart and conscience of the son of grace commending his charity toward us. With due respect to the other sacraments of our salvation and faith, God-made-man had this purpose in being born and in suffering and in doing whatever else he did on earth, that he should commend his charity toward us and so provoke our charity toward him, for love responds most strongly to love. But he wished to be loved by those whom he undertook to save, whom he could not save unless they loved him, those whose measure of salvation is in the measure of their love. This is why it was for the impious, the weak, and the sinner that he died. The Apostle prudently uses these three terms,* designating by them all classes of sinners. He calls impious those who fail in the worship of God; weak, those who fail through weakness or ignorance; sinners, those whom neither weakness nor ignorance excuses, but whom willing malice drives to sin.

Rm 5:6,8

For why did Christ, when as yet we were weak, according to time die for the impious? 'According to time' means either the three days' time in which he rested in the tomb, or according to what he received from time, that is, according to the flesh.

But God commends his charity towards us, etc. Imagine a doctor who had undertaken to cure a sick man, whom he could not cure except by the death of his only son. Would that sick man not be hateful and detestable to the doctor? 'But God spared not even his own Son, but delivered him up for us all.'* The Son also 'loved us and delivered himself for us'.* The more bitter was the necessity of death for the sake of saving, the sweeter the joy gleamed forth in the one saved through the life of him who rose in his resurrection.

Rm 8:32
Eph 5:2

Consider how the author connects the individual items to each other. Sinners are justified, enemies are reconciled, and reconciled through death they are saved through life.* The wrath of God, who judges all things with tranquillity, is nothing but just punishment. We were enemies of God only in the sense that sins are hostile to justice, and when sins were remitted the hostilities were ended. If the just punishment of

See Rm 5:8-10

God receives the name of wrath, what more correct understanding of the reconciliation of God can be had than when such wrath ceases? He is not moved by affection when he who is always the same loves us, but his love for us is goodness. Our love for him is the Holy Spirit, whom he gives us, through whom the charity of God is poured forth in our hearts. He commended his charity toward us by loving first. We were loved first in order that we might be made worthy to love and to be loved even more. God did not begin to love us at the moment when we were reconciled through the death of his Son, but before the foundation of the world he loved us so that [before we were anything at all] we might be his sons together with his Only-begotten Son.* Thus, we had to be shown how much he loved us, so that we would not despair, and of what quality we were, lest we become haughty. The preceding sentence, in which the author says, 'When as yet we were weak, according to time Christ died for the impious', goes with the two following sentences, in one of which he calls us sinners, and in the other enemies of God. As if assigning one to the other he refers 'sinners' to 'weak', and 'enemies of God' to 'impious'.

[PL omits]

Eph 1:4

Therefore, as by one man sin entered into this world and, by sin, death; so death passed into all men, in which all have sinned. The Apostle here disputes at greater length about two men, the first Adam, through whose sin and death we, his posterity, are bound by hereditary evils, and the second Adam, who is not only a man but also God. By his paying for us what he did not owe we are freed from debts, both our fathers' and our own. Because on account of the former man the devil held all men who had been begotten in concupiscence through his deteriorated flesh, it is right that on account of the latter man the devil should relinquish all those who were spiritually regenerated through his spotless grace.[8]

This passage of Scripture is interpreted in different ways by different persons; the reason for it seems to be a certain obscurity not so much in the meaning as the letter, which perhaps comes from the carelessness of the translator. This seems to be an easy way out without complete loss of meaning. We have received reconciliation through the one Lord Jesus Christ, just as sin entered into the world through one man. It seems right that just as the latter came through one man, so should the former come through one man. In the following lines the Apostle makes these two equal in many aspects and counterparts, although one of them far excels the other. But there are some who want the verse which appears much later—'Therefore just as by the offence of one' *—to correspond to this in such a way that all the intervening matter is given as a supplement to the meaning. Although these people avoid the obscurity and perplexity of the intervening reasoning, they incur greater complexity in the meaning. But there are others who say that after the Apostle has taught the difference between faith and the law and has revealed the secrets of the mystery that when we were enemies we were reconciled to God by the death of his Son, he then suitably expounds the causes of the enmity and of the reconciliation. And therefore he introduces the reason of the other secret saying:

Rm 5:18 (margin)

Rm 5:12 (margin)

VERSE TWELVE. **Therefore as by one man**, etc. When the author says, 'Just as by one man sin entered into this world, and by sin death, and so it passed into all men,' it remained for him to say, 'So by one man justice entered into this world, and through justice life, and thus it passed into all men, in whom all have been brought to life'. But Paul did not omit this from lack of eloquence, but because he saw some useful point to be gained. When this prudent dispenser of the word comes to those portions of his argument which seem to say something outstanding about God's goodness, he usually says them somewhat obscurely and briefly, or altogether covers them over in silence on account of the more tepid, lest he make them more lazy by a slackening of hope. Therefore when he had here said, 'Just as by one man sin entered into this world', he was silent about what should be inferred, leaving it to the prudent to understand it clearly, and prudently veiling it from the imprudent. At the same time he showed that even if through one man justice and life passed into all men, still this would not happen immediately for the idle, but for those who are able with much labor and sweat to search out what is obscure, to knock at what is closed, and to desire what is hidden.

Through one man. It is one thing to imitate Adam in sin, another to be born from Adam with sin originally. For Adam, in addition to his example for imitation, also made all those who would come from his lineage equal to himself. On the other hand, whoever clings to the Lord is one spirit by the secret communication and inspiration of spiritual grace, in addition to his example for imitation.

'Through one man.' Not through the deceitful serpent, and not through the woman who was seduced into transgression, of whom it is written, 'From a woman came the beginning of sin'.* Rather it was through one man, because woman conceives through the seed of generation which she receives from man. From a man came the beginning of generation. The only man who appeared in the world without sin was unwilling to be born in this way, although he was born of a woman.

Those who declare that not even one syllable in Paul's writings is void of mysteries note that he did not say that sin entered all men, but that it entered into the world. Again, he did not say that death entered but passed through, not the world, but all men. Now, by the 'world' may be understood earthly men and those who remain in their earthly habits, while 'men' may designate those who begin to recognize that they are made in God's image. Into those who are called 'the world', that is, the earthly, sin is said to have entered, and the Apostle nowhere speaks of its exit, but into those who are called 'men' he says that sin passed—that is, it was there but it was expelled by conversion and penitence and passed through and did not stay in them any longer.[9]

And through sin, death. The chaste duty toward

Si 25:33

a spouse carries no guilt, the origin of sin brings with it its due punishment. The husband does not escape death because he is a husband, nor is he subject to death for any reason except sin. The Lord was also subject to death, but not because of sin. He undertook our punishment in order to cancel our guilt.* He was the only infant who could be innocent, because he was not born from Adam's sin, that is, from concupiscence. Concupiscence appeared in Adam immediately after the sin of disobedience, as both a sin and the punishment of sin, when the eyes of those first men were opened in mutual concupiscence, and through this concupiscence both original sin and what is called the law of sin in our members pass through all men.

PL: punishment

And sin is death. The Apostle no doubt means that death of which the prophet speaks, 'The soul that sins shall die'.* Corporeal death is rightly called the shadow of that death, because wherever that death occurs corporeal death is bound to follow, as a shadow follows a body. The Saviour alone appeared without sin, and death pursued even him because he was made sin for the sake of our sins.* Voluntarily he underwent death, for he said, 'I have the power to lay down my life, and to take it up again.'* The grace of God, through the baptism of him who came 'in the likeness of sinful flesh',* has emptied sinful flesh. It is emptied not in the sense that concupiscence born in living flesh and mingled with it is suddenly removed and no longer exists, but in the sense that it is no longer an obstacle to a mortal being, although it was in him when he was born. If it survives baptism, man has it as something to fight and overcome with the help of the Lord, provided he has not received his grace in vain and does not wish to be reprobate. Except by an ineffable miracle of the omnipotent Creator, it does not happen in baptism that the law of sin, which is present in man's members fighting against the law of the mind, is completely and entirely extinguished and ceases to exist, but what happens is that whatever evil is done, spoken, or thought by man while he, with his mind in subjuga-

Ezek 18:4

Cf. 2 Cor 5:21

Jn 10:18

Rm 8:3

tion, is a slave to concupiscence is totally abolished and is as if it had not been done. When the bond of guilt by which the devil held the soul has been dissolved, and the obstacle by which he kept man away from his Creator has been destroyed, the law of sin remains in the battle in which we castigate our body and bring it into subjection. Temporal death remains in the meantime even in those who have been redeemed by the death of Christ, as an exercise of faith and a battle in the present struggle in which even the martyrs did combat. Even it will be taken away in the renewal of the body promised by the resurrection.[10] Both sin and death passed into all men, for if sin had not passed into all men, every man would not have been born with the law of sin existing in his members. If death had not passed into all men, all men would not die the death of the body.

In whom all have sinned. Either in that sin, of which he says sin entered into this world, in which all have sinned, or else, 'in whom' that is, 'in that man'. For, indeed, men die in him, because it is just that the punishment also be transmitted to them along with the crime. If Levi, who was born in the fourth generation after Abraham, is said to have been in the loins of Abraham,* all the more were all men in the loins of Adam when he sinned, and they sinned in him and were expelled from paradise with him; and through him death passed into all those who were in his loins.[11]

Heb 7:10

Rm 5:13

VERSE THIRTEEN. **For until the law sin was in the world.** Whatever entered the world through the first man, not only original sin but whatever other sin could be contracted from a corrupt beginning, remained in the world until the time of the law, because the law could not take away sin, for it entered the world so that sin might more abound.* Either the natural law is meant, by which each one who has the use of reason begins to add his own sins to original sin, or else the written law which was given the people through Moses.

Rm 5:20

But sin was not imputed, because there was no law.

It was by the rebuke of the law that sin was pointed out, although it was not treated by the Lord God as though it did not exist. Sin is said to be in the world up to the time of the law and including the law, so that the law is not outside the realm of sin which is said to have existed until then. The law existed until John,* and sin until the time of Christ's coming. Only the grace of the Saviour frees [men] from it: 'But sin was not imputed, when the law did not exist.' Those who acquiesce to this reasoning are silent here and say nothing, but there are those who think we should inquire here about which law is meant. Man's rational nature was never without natural law, which not only directed its attention to the sins of original concupiscence, but sometimes noted them more sharply. Therefore, Cain said against himself, 'My sin is greater than that I may deserve pardon'.* And Noah said against his son, 'Cursed be Canaan as a servant.'* From the time the earth was cursed in the work of the first man, both sin and the law imputing it were always in the world. Original sin was neither evident to everyone, nor hidden from everyone. It was not hidden from [the foreigner] Job, nor from Abraham and his household. Abraham received circumcision for that reason, for circumcision did for him what baptism does for us by faith in his seed, who is Christ. Therefore, David groaning said, 'Behold I was conceived in iniquities; and in sins did my mother conceive me'.*

There have been those who believed the course of the expression should be interrupted here and who thought that the whole sense of this passage should be carefully examined so that they could discover the Apostle's meaning on these matters not so much from their own understanding of it as from his words. And after a while these authors, finding that the Apostle had said, 'For without the law, sin was dead; and I lived some time without the law',* discovered that he said this of the natural law. They held his meaning to be that until the natural law, which begins when man reaches the age of reason and starts to discriminate between good and evil, sin was intrinsically dead in

Marginalia:
Lk 16:16, Mt 11:13
Gen 4:13
Cf. Gen 9:25
[PL omits]
Ps 50:7
Rm 7:8-9

me, because there was no law forbidding what was not to be done, or reason which showed what had to be done. They hold that this passage can only be understood of the Apostle himself, since he plainly speaks of himself. According to this opinion it does not seem altogether absurd if this passage says that up to the time when the natural law was understood, sin springing from a corrupted origin was in the world, but furthermore that it was dead because it was not imputed, being excused by natural weakness or ignorance. The holders of this opinion explain the phrase 'in the world',* instead of 'in men', by saying that only those who are capable of reason and who have the natural law should be called men. But [they say] that age which is not yet capable of the natural law should be called 'the world' rather than 'men', for they are part of the world but do not, like men, yet merit to put on the image of the Creator. But because this opinion about the law is also applied to the mosaic law by others, let it be left to the reader's judgment which opinion should be preferred. What follows is sufficiently applicable to either.

Rm 5:13

Rm 5:14

VERSE FOURTEEN. **But death reigned from Adam to Moses,** that is, from the first man until the divinely promulgated law, for not even it could remove the kingdom of death. The kingdom of death means a state in which the guilt of sin so dominates men that it keeps them from arriving at eternal life, which is true life, and even drags them to a second death which is eternal in its punishment. The kingdom of death is only destroyed in man by the grace of the Saviour. Even before Christ came in the flesh this grace operated among the saints of antiquity who looked to his helping grace and not to the letter of the law, which could only command and not help. For that was held concealed in the Old Testament which is now revealed in the New Testament, according to the just ordering of times. Therefore, death reigned from Adam to Moses over all those who were not helped by the grace of Christ so that death's reign might be destroyed in them. Now see in whom death reigned.

Even over those also who have not sinned after the likeness of the transgression of Adam. This is the better interpretation of these words. When the Apostle had said that death reigned even over those who had not sinned, as though we were disturbed by death's reigning even over those who had not sinned, he added 'after the likeness of the transgression of Adam', because there was in their numbers a likeness of Adam's transgression. The text can also be understood in this way: 'Death reigned from Adam to Moses and even over those who had not sinned in the likeness of Adam's transgression', because, although already born, they did not yet have the use of reason which Adam had when he sinned. They had not received the command which he transgressed, but were bound only by original sin, through which the kingdom of death dragged them to condemnation. The kingdom of death is non-existent only in those who are reborn by Christ's grace and belong to his kingdom, for although temporal death, itself propagated by original sin, kills their body, it does not drag their soul to punishment. Here the Apostle wants the kingdom of death to be so understood that the soul which is renewed through grace does not perish in gehenna, that is, is not separated or alienated from the life of God.

What the author adds about Adam, **who is a figure of him who is to come,** is understood in more than one way also. The phrase means either that Adam is a contrasting figure to Christ because just as in Adam all die, so in Christ all are made alive; and as by the disobedience of Adam many were made sinners so by Christ's obedience many are made righteous;* Or else, the Apostle called Adam 'the figure of him who is to come' because he would inflict the form of death on his posterity. However, the better understanding of the phrase is that he is a contrasting figure, for the Apostle stresses this. Then he makes this additional statement lest the two contraries be thought completely equal.

Cf. Rm 5:19

Rm 5:15

VERSE FIFTEEN. But the gift is not equal to the offence. For if by the offence of one many died, much more will the grace of God and the gift, by the grace of one man, Jesus Christ, abound for many. The words 'much more' do not mean 'many more men' are justified than condemned, but that grace will abound much more.[12] Adam by his one sin generated guilty men; but Christ by his grace dissolved and deleted all the sins that men added by their own will to the original sin in which they were born. The

Rm 5:17-21

Apostle says this more clearly later in the text.* But note carefully what he says, 'by the offence of one many died'. Why should he say 'by the offence of one' and not rather 'by their own offences', if in this passage he meant imitation and not propagation. But notice what follows.

Rm 5:16

VERSE SIXTEEN. And the gift is not the result of the one sin. For judgment indeed was by one unto condemnation; but grace is of many offences unto justification. The Apostle says, 'by one unto condemnation'. One what, unless one sin? He explains this by adding, 'grace is of many offences unto justification'. Why is judgment by one unto condemnation; why is grace of many offences to justification? Is it not true that, if there is no original sin, then not only does grace lead men from many sins to justification, but also judgment leads men from many sins to condemnation? Does grace not forgive many offences, and judgment condemn many offences? Let us understand the Apostle, and let us see that judgment is said to be from one offence unto condemnation, because it would suffice for condemnation even if there were nothing in men except original sin. Although there is graver condemnation for those who also add their own sins to original sin—and so much graver as the sins are graver—nevertheless, that one sin alone which is contracted from man's origin not only separates from the kingdom of God where even heretics agree deceased children without the grace of Christ cannot enter, but also makes them strangers to salvation and eternal life, which cannot exist outside the kingdom of God where only the fellowship of Christ grants admission.

Thus we have drawn from Adam, in whom we all have sinned, not all our sins but only original sin. But in Christ, in whom we are all justified, we attain the remission not only of original sin, but also of the others which we ourselves have added.

Therefore, 'the gift is not like the result of the one sin'. For, indeed, judgment is from one offence, that is, the original, and if it is not forgiven it can lead to condemnation, but grace leads to justification from many sins which are forgiven, that is, not only original, but even all others.

Rm 5:17

VERSE SEVENTEEN. **For if by one man's offence death reigned through one, all the more shall they who receive an abundance of grace and justice reign in life through one, Jesus Christ.** Why did death reign on account of one man's offence through one man unless they [all] were held in the bond of death in that one man in whom all sinned, even if they did not add their own sins? Otherwise death did not reign through one man and on account of his sin, but on account of the sins of the many and through each one sinning. Why do they receive an abundance of grace and justice except because that sin in which all sinned is not alone remitted to them, but also the grace of remission is given for those sins which they added, and to all of them such justice is given that, although Adam consented to him who was persuading him to sin, these do not yield even to one who compels them to sin. And what does the phrase mean 'they shall reign much more in life', when the kingdom of death drags many more into eternal punishment, unless we understand that in both parts of the verse those are spoken of who pass from Adam [to Christ], that is, from death to life, because they shall reign in eternal life without end, more than death reigned in them temporally and with an end?

[PL omits]

Rm 5:18

VERSE EIGHTEEN. **Therefore, as by the offence of one it is unto all men to condemnation; so also by** the justification of one it is unto all men to justification of life. If we think of imitation, then this "offence of one" will be only that of the devil. But since the passage is manifestly about Adam and not the devil, we have to understand not the imitation of that sin, but its propagation. The Apostle's words about Christ, 'by the justification of one', express this more clearly than if he had said 'by the justice of one'. He speaks of the justification by which Christ justifies the wicked, and he does not propose this as something to be imitated, because only Christ can do it. The Apostle could rightly have said, 'Be imitators of me, just as I am of Christ',* but he could never say, 'Be justified by me as I am justified by Christ'. There can be, there are, and there have been many just men who are to be imitated, but there is none who is just and who justifies, but Christ. So it is said, 'To him who believes in him who justifies the ungodly, his faith is counted'.* Anyone rash enough to say 'I justify you', should also say 'Believe in me', but none of the holy ones could rightly say this except the Holy of Holies, who said, 'Believe in God; believe also in me'.* Because he justifies the wicked, faith in him is counted as justice. For if mere imitation made men sinners through Adam, why should not the mere imitation of Christ make men just? But if Christ is the one in whom all are justified because not only the imitation of him, but also grace regenerating them through the Spirit makes them just, then also Adam is the one in whom all have sinned, because not only the mere imitation of him makes them sinners, but also the penalty generating through the flesh. This is the reason why the word 'all' is used twice. Those who are generated through Adam are not all the same as all those regenerated through Christ, but the phrase is still right because just as there is no carnal generation of anyone except through Adam, so there is no spiritual generation except through Christ. If some could be generated in the flesh and not through Adam, then some could be generated in the spirit and not through Christ. And then the word 'all' would not make sense in both places in the sentence. The

1 Cor 11:1

Rm 4:5

Jn 14:1

same persons whom he calls 'all' in one place, he
calls 'many' in another, for in some situations 'all'
can be a few. Carnal generation has many subjects
and so does spiritual, but not as many as the carnal.
Just as carnal generation has all men, so spiritual
generation has all just men, because even as no man
escapes carnal generation, so no just man exists
without spiritual generation, and in both categories
there are many persons.

Rm 5:19-20 VERSES NINETEEN AND TWENTY. **For as by the disobedience of one man many were made sinners, so also by the obedience of one man many shall be made just. Now the law entered that sin might abound.** This text does not pertain to that sin which is contracted from Adam, about which it was said above that 'death reigned through one'. Let us understand by 'law' here either the natural law which appears when one attains the use of reason, or the written law, given through Moses. Even the latter could not give life and liberate from the law of sin and death which is contracted from Adam, but rather it bestowed additional transgression. 'Where
Rm 4:15 there is no law, neither is there transgression.'*
When the law given in Paradise was transgressed man was born from Adam with the law of sin and death, of which it is said, 'I see another law in my members
Rm 7:23 fighting against the law of my mind,' etc.* This law is easily conquered unless it is later fortified with bad habits, but it is not conquered without the grace of God. When the other law is transgressed, which consists in the use of reason by a rational mind in those men who are already using reason, then all the sinners on the earth become transgressors, but the sin becomes much greater when the law given through Moses has been transgressed.

'Now the law entered so that sin might abound', either when men neglect what God commands, or when they presume on their own strength and do not ask the help of grace and so add pride to their weakness. But when by a divine call they understand to whom they should groan, and when they call on him in whom they believe, saying rightly, 'Have mercy on me, O God, according to your great mercy',* and also, 'I said, "O Lord, have mercy on me, heal my soul for I have sinned against you",'* and when a man reaches out toward him and groans in this way, then will come to pass what follows, **Where sin abounded grace abounded more,** and 'Many sins are forgiven her because she has loved much'.* Then 'the charity of God is poured forth in his heart'* and by it the fullness of the law is accomplished, not through the power of the will which is in us, but through the Holy Spirit who was* given to us, so that as sin has reigned to death, **so also grace might reign by justice to everlasting life through Jesus Christ our Lord.** When the Apostle says 'as sin has reigned to death', he did not add 'through one man', or 'the first man', or 'through Adam', because he had already said, 'The law entered that sin might abound'. This abundance of sin does not pertain to descent from the first man but to the transgressions of human life. This abundance is added to that one sin by which infants are bound, and comes in adult age from a fullness of iniquity. But because the grace of the Saviour can loosen even that which does not pertain to original sin, therefore, when the Apostle said, 'So grace might reign by justice to everlasting life,' he added the words, 'through Jesus Christ our Lord'.[13] Next he puts a question to himself.

Ps 50:1
Ps 40:5

Lk 7:47
Cf. Rm 5:5

PL: is

CHAPTER SIX

Rm 6:1

VERSE ONE. **What shall we say then? Shall we continue in sin that grace may abound? God forbid.** The Apostle saw that the perverse might perversely understand what he had said, '[The law entered in that sin might abound.] Where sin abounded, grace abounded more,' as though he said sin was a profitable thing on account of the abundance of grace it produced. To remove this impression he replied, 'God forbid.' And he added:

[PL omits]

Rm 6:2

VERSE TWO. **How shall we who are dead to sin**

live in it? That is, since grace has done this for us, that we die to sin, what are we doing except being ungrateful to grace if we live in sin? He who praises the benefit of medicine does not teach the diseases and wounds from which medicine cures the patient. Rather, the more medicine is praised, the more disgraceful and horrible are reckoned the wounds and diseases from which the medicine frees a patient. So the praise and commendation of grace is the censure and condemnation of offences. Man had to be shown the foulness of his sluggishness, which caused the holy and good commandment to be of no avail against his wickedness, and by which his wickedness was increased rather than decreased. 'The law entered in that sin might abound'* so that, overcome and confounded in this way, he could see that he needed God not only as a healer but as a helper by whom his steps might be directed lest every iniquity should have dominion over him,* and so that he could be cured by fleeing to the power of divine mercy. Thus 'where sin abounded, grace abounded more',* not by the merit of the sinner but by the help of him who came to rescue him. Then the Apostle shows that the same medicine has been mystically demonstrated in the passion and resurrection of Christ, saying:

Rm 5:20

Cf. Ps 118:113

Rm 5:20

Rm 6:3-4

VERSES THREE AND FOUR. **Do you not know that all we who are baptized in Christ Jesus are baptized in his death? For we are buried together with him by baptism into death, that as Christ is risen from the dead by the glory of the Father, so we also may walk in newness of life.** The Apostle illustrates in the mystery of the Lord's death and resurrection the figure of the setting of our old life and the rising of the new, the destruction of iniquity and the renewal of justice. From where does such a great benefit come to men except through the faith of Jesus Christ? This holy thought preserves the sons of men who hope in the protection of God's wings, so that they are inebriated with the plenty of his house and drink of the torrent of his pleasure; for with him is the fountain of life and in his light shall we see light.*

Cf. Ps 35:8-10

For Christ was immolated once in himself, and yet in the sacrament he is immolated not only in every celebration of Easter but every day among the people. Neither is he lying who, when asked, says that he is immolated. For if the sacraments did not have a certain likeness to the things of which they are sacraments, they would not be sacraments at all. For the most part they take their names from this likeness to those things. So, therefore, in a certain way the sacrament of the Body of Christ is the Body of Christ, and the sacrament of the Blood of Christ is the Blood of Christ, and also the sacrament of faith is faith. To believe is nothing else than to have faith. That is why the response is made that the infant believes, although he does not yet have an awareness of faith; the response is made that the infant has faith because he has the sacrament of faith, and that he turns to God because he has the sacrament of conversion. The response itself belongs to the celebration of the sacrament, as the Apostle said of baptism itself.

'We are buried together with Christ by baptism into death.' He did not say, 'We have undergone a symbolic burial', but said plainly 'We are buried'. He called the sacrament of such a great thing by nothing less than the name of the thing itself.

Thus even if the faith which exists in the will of the believer does not yet make the infant one of the faithful, the sacrament of that faith does. For just as the response is given that the infant believes, so also the infant is called one of the faithful, not by assenting to the matter with his mind, but by receiving the sacrament of the reality. When man begins to have the use of reason, he does not seek the sacrament a second time, but understands, and is conformed to its truth by the consent of his will. As long as he cannot do this, the sacrament acts to protect him against hostile powers, and it is so effective that if he leaves this life before growing up, he is by means of this sacrament and the recommendation of the Church's charity freed by christian help from that condemnation which came into the world through one man. Whoever does not believe this and thinks it impossible is an unbeliever even if he has received the sacrament of faith; and the child is far better than he, because even if he does not yet have faith in his intellect, still he does not place the obstacle of antagonistic thinking in its way.[14]

There was no sin in our Lord, and yet in a certain way he died to sin when he died to the flesh in which there was the likeness of sin. Although he had never lived according to the old line of sin, he sealed our life with his new resurrection, reviving us from the old death by which we were dead in sin. The great sacrament of baptism which is celebrated in us consists in this: that those who attain to this grace die to sin, just as he is said to have been dead to sin because he was dead to the flesh, which is the likeness of sin, and they live, no matter what their age, by being born again from the washing, just as he lives by rising again from the tomb. Just as no one, from the newborn infant to the decrepit old man, is forbidden baptism, so there is no one who cannot die to sin in baptism. But children die to original sin only, and adults to all the other sins which they have added by their evil lives to that sin which they contracted in birth. So the Apostle closes this passage as he began it. He brings in the death of Christ in such a way that he says even He died to sin. What sin, except the flesh, in which there was not sin but the likeness of sin, and which was called sin for that reason?

The Apostle then speaks to those baptized into the death of Christ, not only the adults but also the chilren. 'Consider that you also are dead to sin, that is, like Christ, but alive to God in Christ Jesus.'* Whatever was done on the cross of Christ, at his burial, in his resurrection on the third day, in his ascension into heaven and his sitting at the right hand of the Father, was done so that the life of the Christian, as lived here, is shaped and molded to these events, not only as they are spoken of mystically, but even as they were lived. For it is on account of the cross that the Apostle says, 'Those who are Jesus Christ's have crucified their flesh with its vices and concupiscences.'* [On account of the burial, 'We are buried with Christ

Rm 6:11

Gal 5:24
[PL omits]

through baptism unto death.'] On account of the resurrection he says, 'So that as Christ is risen from the dead by the glory of the Father, so we also may walk in newness of life.'* On account of the ascension and the sitting at the right hand of the Father he says, 'If you are risen with Christ, seek the things that are above, where Christ is sitting at the right hand of God. Mind the things that are above, not the things that are upon the earth. For you are dead and your life is hid with Christ in God.'* That statement pertaining to the death of the soul is applied to the mystery of our interior man, not only in the psalm but also on the cross: 'My God, my God, why have you forsaken me?'* The following words of the Apostle agree with this statement. 'Knowing that our old man is crucified that the body of sin may be voided so that we may serve sin no longer.'* By the crucifixion of the inner man are understood the pains of penitence and a certain salutary suffering of continence, and by this death the death of impiety is put to death, but in this God does not abandon us. By such a cross the body of sin is emptied and voided, so that we do not yield our members as instruments of iniquity unto sin,* because even if the inner man is renewed day by day he is still old before he is renewed. Within is enacted what the Apostle says, 'Strip yourself of the old man with his deeds'.* And he continues his exposition saying, 'Putting away lying speak the truth'.* Where is it that lying is put away except inwardly, in order that 'he who speaks truth in his heart' may dwell on the holy mountain of God.*

Now the form of the past Adam and that of the future Adam have been described. The form is not altogether uniform. It is similar in genus and contrary in species. In genus similar in that just as it was diffused from one Adam to many men so it was infused from the one Christ into many men. In species contrary, because from Adam's transgression many were made sinners, and from Christ's obedience many are made just.*

Now that the forms of the first and second Adam

have been compared both in similar and dissimilar aspects, because we have diffusely drawn out the text, it seems that the order and sense of the words should be drawn together and discussed more precisely. The Apostle compares the death which comes from Adam with the life that comes through Christ, and says, 'The gift is not like the offence'.* Afterwards he says that the law entered in that sin might abound, but where sin abounded grace abounded more.* By these words he resolved what seemed to be a contradiction, and says, 'How shall we who are dead to sin live any longer in it?'* Then wishing to show what it in fact means to be dead to sin, he says, 'Do you not know that all we who are baptized in Christ Jesus' etc.* By this he teaches that if anyone is first dead to sins he must necessarily be buried with Christ in baptism; but if anyone is not first dead to sin he cannot be buried with Christ, for no one is ever buried alive. If he is not buried with Christ, he is not legitimately baptized.

 Then he goes on, 'What shall we say, then? Shall we remain in sin, that grace may abound?'* First, notice how balanced his expression is. He says, 'Shall we remain in sin?' To remain is not to desist from what is begun. Whoever does this in regard to sin has certainly not received even the beginning of conversion. Since penitence for sin is properly the work of grace, where there is obstinate impenitence nothing abounds except judgment and condemnation.

 'For if we are dead to sin, how shall we continue to live in it?'* Inspect more carefully the mystical order. First we must die to sin in order to be buried with Christ. Burial is for the dead. But buried to sin, we should in no wise still live in it. Indeed, our Lord Jesus Christ, buried in a new sepulchre and wound in a clean winding sheet, points to the newness of life and cleanness of conscience in the one buried with him. 'Do you not know that all we who are baptized in Christ Jesus are baptized in his death?'* The baptismal font, which is used for no other purpose, signifies this, as does the white clothing. We should also recognize that no baptized person with the use of reason should be ignorant of the faith or of the mystery of his own baptism. The Apostle seems to speak with a certain agitation when he says, 'Do you not know' etc. Therefore, whoever is baptized in Christ Jesus is baptized in his death; he has died with him by the renunciation of sin; he is buried with him by the profession of his holy intent.

The question might be raised that here we are said to be baptized in Christ alone, whereas he who baptizes says, 'Baptizing them in the name of the Father and of the Son and of the Holy Spirit'.* But in this passage it was not baptism that was being discussed but the death of Christ, in the likeness of which the Apostle was saying that we would die to sin and be buried with Christ. It did not seem germane that the Father or the Holy Spirit should be mentioned when it was a question of the memory of that death. The Apostle here is following his practice by which, when he takes something from Scripture, he takes only what is required by the matter at hand.

Mt 28:19

'So that as Christ is risen from the dead by the glory of the Father, so we also may walk in newness of life.'* Christ arose from the dead and the Father was glorified. If we rise with him and walk in newness of life, men will see our good works and glorify our Father who is in heaven.* We must walk and not quit, so that the last day shall find us still making progress.

Rm 6:4

Cf. Mt 5:16

Rm 6:5

VERSE FIVE. **For if we have been planted together in the likeness of his death, we shall also be in the likeness of his resurrection.** All this pertains to the question whether he gave permission to sin when he said, 'Where sin abounded, grace abounded more'.* Therefore he says that we were baptized in the death of Christ, and we died, were buried and planted together with him, adding also the hope of resurrection.[15] For the death of Christ is in the Church like the tree of life planted in the midst of paradise.* Whoever dies with him is planted with him so that, mortifying his members on earth, he sends his root downward, as the prophet says,* and thus bears fruit upward, the fruit of flesh in bloom again and the

Rm 5:20

Cf. Gen 2:9

Cf. Is 37:31

fruit of a spirit renewed in the glory of the resurrection and in the fertile buds of the holy virtues.

Rm 6:6   **VERSE SIX. Knowing this, that our old man is crucified with him so that the body of sin may be destroyed, to the end that we may serve sin no longer** What dying, being buried and rising again with him means is that our old man—that is, the life we formerly led in sin—should come to an end and perish by faith in the cross of Christ, and that those members of ours which served sin should be destroyed so that they no longer serve anyone but God. In that way our root is planted in the root of the tree of life, that is, our love is conformed to the love of Christ, so that it produces the branches of justice and the fruits of life from the juice of his root.

'That the body of sin may be destroyed.' This body of sin means either the totality of sin, whose members are fornication, uncleanness, avarice, etc.;[16] or else it means our body itself as infected from its very origin by the poison of the ancient serpent. It is destroyed when a man dies to sin and begins to live to God, for then it no longer belongs to the man himself, or to sin, but to him who redeemed it with a great price so that it should serve him. Whoever is dead to sin is justified as long as he does not serve sin but the Lord his God, for to serve him is just. But what is the fruit, what the pay, what the reward?

Rm 6:8   **VERSE EIGHT. Now if we be dead with Christ we believe that we shall also live together with him.** With what sort of life, a temporal one or an eternal one?

Rm 6:9   **VERSE NINE. Knowing that Christ rising again from the dead dies now no more; death shall no more have dominion over him.** If he were to die again, we would have to die again with him. The words added by the Apostle, 'We believe that we shall live together with him', show that, although the resurrection is a certitude, we shall not obtain it except through the mediation of faith. 'Knowing that Christ rising again from the dead dies now no more; death shall no more have dominion over him.' Whoever dies together with Christ, if he expects the glory of the resurrection, must know that he owes three days of burial, the belief of his heart and the confession of his mouth so that he may be saved,* also the mortification of his members, and finally resurrection to a new life. In other words he must renounce the world, renounce vices, and then achieve perfection in the light of wisdom.

Cf. Rm 10:9-10

Rm 6:10

VERSE TEN. For in that he died to sin he died once; but in that he lives he lives unto God. He who took the likeness of sinful flesh for our sakes and was made sin died once by turning over to sin and the law of the flesh what belonged to them; but in that he lives he belongs to God, because he is conformed to God's incorruptibility.

Rm 6:11

VERSE ELEVEN. So do you also reckon that you are dead to sin, but alive to God. The Greek text has ΚΟΓΙΤΑΤΗ;[17] that is, not 'reckon' but 'consider thoroughly', which seems to agree better with the meaning and certitude of faith. We should always think and keep before our eyes what we have sworn and declared in baptism; death to sin and life to God. The words added by the Apostle, 'In Christ Jesus our Lord', give the manner of paying our vow. It is the same as saying, 'Living to God in wisdom, in peace, in justice and sanctification; all of which things are Christ.' To live in them is to live in Christ Jesus our Lord.[18]

Cf. I Cor 1:30

Rm 6:12

VERSE TWELVE. Therefore let not sin reign in your mortal body. If sin reigns it is king. Indeed sin is a king and has its own army fighting for it and obeying its laws, which are written in the flesh and the members of the body, over which sin has obtained the right of governing. Its army is what the Apostle calls 'the works of the flesh, fornication, uncleanness' etc.* Because they pertain to the kingdom of sin, whoever does these works 'shall not obtain the

Cf. Gal 5:19-21

Gal 5:21 kingdom of God'.* Included in that army are heresies, which spring from an inflated sense of the flesh. Also the prudence of the flesh constitutes this kingdom, which the Apostle pronounces to be both death and
Cf. Rm 8:6-7 an enemy of God.* This wicked army is always ready for battle, besieging the stronghold of the virtues as long as the flesh lusts against the spirit. Unless it were in our power to exclude the power of sin from our body, the Apostle would not have given the precept, 'Let not sin reign in your mortal body'. But he who gave the precept did not leave us without counsel, saying elsewhere, 'Mortify your members which are
Col 3:5 on earth',* and 'Always bearing about in our body
2 Cor 4:10 the mortification of Jesus'.* For sin hates the memory of Christ's cross, and flees from the desire to imitate him. When the standard of the cross appears, that whole spiritual army of malice immediately disappears; sin does not hold its ground. What the Apostle commands is not impossible. For he did not say, 'Let it not exist', but 'Let sin not reign in your body'. Sin is present in you when you feel pleasure; it reigns when you consent. Not to feel pleasure sometimes is altogether impossible, but never to consent is not impossible, with the help of grace. You are partly heir to God and partly heir to the world. Your own part, your flesh, rebels against you in the sickness of its concupiscence. That sickness is a tyrant. Let not the mind which clings to God collapse; let it not surrender itself. It has great help. It will conquer if it perseveres in fighting. When concupiscence is restrained often, it will diminish and begin to die.

'In your mortal body,' he says. He did not add the word 'mortal' for no purpose, but meant to suggest either that the body is mortal in the sense that it is capable of mortification, or that it is mortal as a reminder of what is written, 'In all your works remember
Si 7:40 your end and you shall never sin'.*

The seat of the kingdom of sin is the body; the
Cf. Rm 7:23 law of the kingdom is the law of its members;* its army is described above; its power is concupiscence; its realm is the obedience shown to desires; the prop and stay of the kingdom is shown in this statement,

And do not yield your members as instruments of
iniquity unto sin. To do this is to fight on behalf of
the kingdom of sin, and it is most wicked to yield to
sin the members created by God and dedicated
to him.

Rm 6:13   VERSE THIRTEEN. **But present yourselves to
God as those who are alive from the dead and your
members as instruments of justice to God.** Notice in
detail Paul's wisdom. When he says that instruments
are not to be given to sin or iniquity, he does not say
'us' but rather 'our members', but when he persuades
us to give ourselves to God, he does not wish us to
give God our members before ourselves, and by that
he means the soul or the heart's resolution. First we
should give ourselves and cling to God, and only then
will we make our members instruments of justice.
Again, if we mortify the sinful concupiscence in our
mortal body, we are made like men coming back
alive from the dead, dead to sin and alive to God. Our
members are instruments of justice fighting for him,
and for them to serve him is most just. The Apostle
carries through the previous metaphor well, calling
our members instruments of iniquity in the kingdom
of sin, and again instruments of justice in the kingdom of God. He continues:

Rm 6:14   VERSE FOURTEEN. **For sin shall not have
dominion over you.** See here too the Apostle's
wonderful caution. When he speaks of us he says, 'Sin
shall not have dominion over you', but when he
speaks of the Saviour, he says, 'Death shall not have
dominion over him'. There was room for death in
him, but no room for sin. To us it should not be said,
'Death shall not have dominion over you', because
we cannot avoid it, but rather, 'Sin shall not have
Rm 6:9   dominion over you',* because we can, without a
doubt, avoid that.

For you are not under the law, but under grace.[19]
The law was given so that grace might be sought.
Grace was given so that the law might be fulfilled. It
was not the fault of the law that it was not fulfilled,

but the fault of the prudence of the flesh. This fault was to be demonstrated by the law and to be healed by grace. Those under the law and not under grace were under the dominion of sin, and from it a man is not freed through the law but through grace. Not that the law is bad, but it makes those under it guilty by commanding and not helping. Grace helps in order that each one may be a doer of the law; without grace anyone placed under the law will be only a hearer of the law.* *Cf. Jas 1:22*

Rm 6:15 VERSE FIFTEEN. **What then? Shall we sin because we are not under the law, but under grace?** The meaning seems to be the same as that above, where he says, 'What shall we say then? Shall we continue in sin that grace might abound?'* The only difference seems to be that in the earlier text the Apostle seems to be telling those who have not yet left sin not to remain in it; in the later text the question seems to be put by those who have already left sin. In the former case the purpose is that grace, not yet in existence, should abound; in the latter he speaks with grace already present, 'because we are not under the law, but under grace'. [God forbid!] [20] *Rm 6:1* / *[PL prints with v. 16]*

Rm 6:16 VERSE SIXTEEN. **Do you not know that to whom you yield yourselves as obedient servants, you are servants of him whom you obey, whether it be of sin unto death or of obedience unto justice?** The phrase 'either of sin or of obedience unto justice' seems imperfect, since he should rather have said, 'either of sin or of justice through obedience'. But since the meaning is clear, it is useless to get involved with the wording. This is what the Apostle teaches: that on whichever side a person inclines his obedience, either to justice or to sin, he makes himself a slave to that side.[21] We should carefully avoid either a sudden fall into sin or a rash leap into it, because what is done once makes for greater pleasure, pleasure demands repetition, repetition creates a habit of the will, habit injects a necessity to servitude. It is within our competence to accept the yoke of servitude if we so desire, but once it has been accepted, we are unable to cast it off when we desire.

VERSE SEVENTEEN. But thanks be to God that you were the servants of sin, but have obeyed from the heart that form of doctrine into which you have been delivered. The Apostle is speaking here of those perfect ones from whom he gave thanks to his God also at the beginning of this epistle,* because their faith was spoken of in the whole world. He gives thanks not because they were servants of sin, but because having become servants of justice they cast away the necessity imposed by habit and the unworthy slavery to sin. It is rare and it is difficult for one to change one's inner disposition, and as worldly wisdom says, it is impossible to separate members that are united without the loss of blood.

'You obeyed according to that form of doctrine into which you have been delivered.' Look at the changed dispositions for which thanksgiving is truly appropriate. It seems to some people that the Apostle does not reckon 'doctrine' and 'form of doctrine' to be the same, but holds that 'form of doctrine' is something less than 'doctrine' itself, so that 'form of doctrine' is what we see here 'through a mirror and in a dark manner',* but 'doctrine' is what we shall see 'face to face'.[22] But others hold that the 'form of doctrine is the perfect and well-formed doctrine of justice. Others expound the matter in another way. They propose three forms for the doctrine of faith: the rational, the spiritual and the intellectual. The rational form of doctrine concerns mysteries and morals, and it is suitable to those men to whom the Lord says that the kingdom of heaven is to be announced in parables. The spiritual form of doctrine consists in zeal for reading and meditation and the teaching of the ancients, and befits those to whom the Lord says, 'To you it is given to know the mystery of the kingdom of God.'* The intellectual form of doctrine consists in the inner disposition of an enlightened love, which is proper to the clean of heart who merit seeing God. The rational form of

---

Rm 6:17

Cf. Rm 1:8

1 Cor 13:12

Lk 8:10

PL: *ultimately*	doctrine requires willing obedience and active perfection; the spiritual form of doctrine requires a sober mind and humble contemplation; the intellectual form of doctrine calls for peaceful and familiar experience. This last type of understanding, coming down from above, is not formed by reason but rather conforms reason to itself, not so that reason can grasp it, but that illuminated by it, reason can in some way* consent to it. Accordingly, it is of the first form of doctrine that the Apostle is here speaking, for it was to it that these persons gave themselves who gave themselves obediently.
Rm 6:18	VERSE EIGHTEEN. **Being then freed from sin we have been made servants of justice.** When the will is added either to sin or to justice, there is a necessity to servitude. He continues:
Rm 6:19	VERSE NINETEEN. **I am speaking in human terms because of your infirmity.** The prudent steward of the word, seeing them make progress in the first form of doctrine, judges that human things should be committed to human beings, although he would have preferred to give them divine things if he had noticed they were progressing in a somewhat superhuman way. He says, 'I am speaking in human terms' which you can bear. When you yielded your members to wickedness for the commission of great sins, was it fear that led you to sin or was it the sweetness of sin? You will answer that it was the sweetness of sin. Sweetness leads you to sin then, but does fear drive you to justice? This is inhuman. Or rather it is human in that the two things resemble each other. Just as up till now the desire and pleasure of sin has been in you, so now let there be the delight and love of justice. This does not yet seem to be perfect justice, but it is in some way mature justice. More servitude is owed to justice than men usually give to sin. Bodily penalties, even if involuntarily suffered, still restrain men from sinful deeds, but justice should be so much loved that even bodily punishments should not restrain men from its deeds. Just as he is most wicked

whom not even bodily punishments deter from the unclean works of sordid pleasure, so he is most just who is not restrained by fear of bodily pains from the holy works of luminous charity. But I tell you something human, O man: love justice as you have loved evil. In evil you pursued pleasure; for justice's sake put up with persecution. When you come to the harsh, the terrible, the savage, the threatening, trample on it, break it and pass on. O to love, to progress, to die to self, to reach God! 'He who loves his life loses it; and he who lost his life for my sake will discover it in eternal life.'* So should we love the lover of justice; so should we love the lover of invisible beauty.

Jn 12:25, cf. Mt 10:39

Rm 6:20

VERSE TWENTY. **When you were servants of sin you were free men from justice.** I ask you, what kind of freedom is there for a miserable slave except when he takes pleasure in sin? He freely serves as a free man who willingly does the will of his master, and in this way the slave of sin is free in the act of sinning. He will not be free to act justly unless, freed from sin, he begins to be the slave of justice. True freedom is to rejoice over right actions; at the same time it is loving slavery to embrace a command obediently. But for a man who has been bound and sold, from where will this liberty to act rightly originate unless he redeems him of whom it is said, 'If the Son shall make you free, you shall be truly free'.* Men are free from justice only through their free will; they are free from sin only through the grace of the Saviour. For this reason the wonderful teacher also set forth these words:

Jn 8:36

Rm 6:20-21

VERSES TWENTY AND TWENTY-ONE. **When you were the servants of sin you were free from justice. What fruit therefore did you have in those things of which you are now ashamed?** There is a certain useful momentary confusion: the disturbance of a soul looking at its sins, and in looking being horrified, and in its horror blushing, and in its blushing correcting itself. Whoever does not have this type of confusion will have everlasting confusion. Therefore, the Apostle continues.

Rm 6:21-22   VERSES TWENTY-ONE AND TWENTY-TWO. **For the end of them is death. But having now been freed from sin and become servants to God, you have your fruit unto sanctification, and its end is life everlasting.** Note here the careful choice of words. He called them 'free from justice', and not 'freed', lest they should attribute this to themselves; but then he most carefully chose to call them 'freed', referring this to that saying of the Lord, 'If the Son shall make you free, you shall be truly free'. But this will, which is free in evil things because it delights in them, is therefore not free in good things because it is not freed. Man cannot will anything good unless he is helped by him who cannot will evil. We call free to perform works of piety those whom the Apostle referred to when he said, 'But now freed from sin and having become servants to God, you have your fruit unto sanctification, and its end is life everlasting'. This fruit of sanctification, which is no doubt charity and its works, we can in no way possess of ourselves, but we have it through the Holy Spirit who is given to us. About this fruit the Master—that is, God—spoke when he said to the branches abiding in

Jn 15:5   him, 'Without me you can do nothing'.* Therefore the Apostle calls even eternal life, which is certainly the reward of good works, the grace of God when he says:

Rm 6:23   VERSE TWENTY-THREE. **For the wages of sin**
[PL omits]   **is death [, he says.]. But the grace of God is life everlasting in Christ Jesus our Lord.** Wages are paid for military service; they are not given. Therefore the word 'wages' is well chosen here where eternal death is given as a debt, so to speak, to the devil's soldiers. Where he could have said and said rightly that eternal life is the wages of justice, the Apostle preferred to say, 'But the grace of God is life everlasting', so that we would understand that God leads us to eternal life not by our merits but by his grace.[23] For eternal

life is the wages of justice, but to you, O man, it is a grace, just as justice itself is a grace. Therefore, lest this be sought in any other way except through the Mediator, the Apostle adds the words, 'In Christ Jesus our Lord'.

NOTES

1. The expression 'notion of faith' is *ratio fidei* in Latin. For William's development and use of the concept see *Enigma*, CF 9:22-24.
2. For this definition of blessedness see Augustine, *Letter 130;* PL 33:498. Also see William's discussion in Book 5 at Rm 8:26 for a definition borrowed from Augustine.
3. Migne (PL 180:591) gives this word as *consubstantialitatis*, ignoring the reading on fol. 136ᵛ of MS 49. Or, perhaps, the Migne text, which is the Tissier text, is witness to another manuscript of the *Expo on Roms* of William. This is a possibility which has not been explored. William uses small roman capitals for this word. He uses *homoousion* in *Enigma*, CF 9:57, 58, 59, 63.
4. 'except that ... to your divinity' is Augustine, *Sermon* 71.12.18; PL 38:454.
5. 'Surely ... we have learned' is Augustine, *Sermon* 71.12.18; PL 38:454.
6. 'And since ... of our sins' is Augustine, *Sermon* 71.12.18; PL 38:454.
7. Horace, *Satire* 2.3.21. See also William's *On the Nature and Dignity of Love*, PL 184:396, for the same expression.
8. This paragraph is from Augustine, *Trinity 13.16.21;* PL 42: 1030-31. Florus refers to it, PL 119:290.
9. From 'that he did not say ... ' down to this point is almost a direct quotation from Origen, *On Roms*, PG 14:1012-13.
10. 'Temporal death ... by the resurrection' is Augustine, *Letter* 157.3,19; PL 33:683.
11. This sentence is from Origen, *On Roms*, PG 14:1009-1010. William adds a few words in the middle of Origen's sentence: '. . . when he sinned, and they sinned in him ... ' This seems to affirm William's western, augustinian view of original sin and inherited guilt.
12. Verse 14: 'This is the better ... ' to 'abound much more'. See Augustine, *Letter* 157.3.19-20; PL 33:683-4.
13. The entire discussion of verses 19-21 is from Augustine, *Letter* 157.3.15-17; PL 33:681-2.
14. 'For Christ was immolated ... ' down to here is a long passage taken from Augustine, *Letter 98.9-10;* PL 33:363-364.
15. This paragraph so far is from Origen, *On Roms*, PL 14:1043.
16. This paragraph down to here is from Origen, *On Roms*, PG 14:1043.
17. On fol. 148ʳ of MS 49 the text is ΚΟΓΙΤΑΤΗ in small roman

capitals with a gamma as the third letter. This word has a gloss above the line: *id est non existimate sed cogitate.* Another hand, in a Greek script uncharacteristic of the twelfth century, has excised ΚΟΓΙΤΑΤΗ and added above the line λογίζεσθε. This is probably a fourteenth or fifteenth century addition. William's source here is Origen, *On Roms,* PG 14:1054 where Rufinus' Latin reads: *Existimate vos mortuos esse peccato, quod melius quidem in Graeco habetur Cogitate vos mortuos esse peccato.*

    18.   These two sentences are from Origen, *On Roms,* PG 14:1056.

    19.   The discussion of verse 13 and that of verse 14 down to this point are Origen, *On Roms,* PG 14:1058.

    20.   The discussion of verse 15 is Origen, *On Roms,* PG 14:1059.

    21.   This paragraph down to here is Origen, *On Roms,* PG 14:1059.

    22.   This sentence is a paraphrase of a section in Origen, *On Roms,* PG 14:1061.

    23.   'where he could . . . itself is a grace'. See Augustine, *Letter* 194.4.20-21; PL 33:881.

BOOK FOUR

CHAPTER SEVEN

In his already somewhat lengthy discussion in the preceding sections about the justice of law and the justice of faith for Jews and Gentiles, the Apostle taught that both are ultimately justified by faith and have peace with God. Then by comparing the old Adam and the new he demonstrated to them the primacy of the grace in which God had reconciled them, and he incited them, positioned in [grace], to ANATERTON,[1] that is, sinlessness, as they call it, and to the works of faith especially from the mystery of the baptism they had received, and he urged them to pass from the slavery of the letter to the freedom of the spirit. These things pertain to the third stage of the individual man or the people of God.* Now imitating him whom he served in the gospel of his Son,* of whose mercy the earth is full,† and who has made the heart of each person and who understands all their works,* our author—who is rude in speech but not in the knowledge* by which he can address each man's conscience—more deliberately takes up the form of moral doctrine. He demonstrates

See above on Rm 2:17

*Cf. Rm 1:9
†Ps 32:5

Ps 32:15
Cf. 2 Cor 11:6

in a reasonable way the effect of any kind of law on them, the effect of grace, the effect of faith, of the letter, and of that which is called freedom of will. But also he describes the contention between the law of the mind and the law of the members, and shows that there is no liberation from this body of death except by the grace of God through our Lord Jesus Christ. First, by means of a parable based on the law he puts an end to the law, so that every mouth may be stopped, and so that with the destruction of the glory of the Jews concerning the law an equal case might be made both for the Jews and for the Gentiles, and that there might be the grace of a similar doctrine for them both. He says therefore:

CHAPTER SEVEN

Rm 7:1-3   VERSES ONE THROUGH THREE. **Do you not know, brethren, for I speak to those who know the law, that the law has dominion over a man as long as he lives? For the woman who has a husband, while her husband lives is bound to the law. But if her husband is dead she is loosed from the law of her husband. Therefore, while her husband lives she shall be called an adulteress if she is with another man; but if her husband is dead she is delivered from the law of her husband, so that she is not an adulteress if she is with another man.** This passage is understood in different ways by different people. Some interpret the woman subject to her husband as mankind subject to the law; for just as a woman is judged an adulteress if she is joined to another man while her husband lives, though when her husband dies she is loosed from his law and can marry whomever she wishes, so when the law was alive, i.e., was in good standing, mankind subject to it could not withdraw its neck from the yoke of the law. But when the law was dead and fell from its good standing, then mankind was free to apply itself to another law. This interpretation as applied to the mosaic law and the people of the circumcision is very easy to understand, and there is nothing questionable about it. When the prophet appeared of whom Moses said, 'God will raise up for you a prophet from your brethren; listen to him as to me',* then the ancient and ageing law came to its end, and a new song began to be sung, and a new commandment was preached, and all things were made new. Immediately a choice was made among the Jews and the Church was formed, the new bride of the Lamb, and, without spot or wrinkle,* she clung to the new Bridegroom without any hint of adultery, since her former husband was dead and abandoned.

But others discussing this parable more subtlely in order to include both Jews and Gentiles in it have noted three elements in the parable and three elements in the reality which is referred to by the parable, and these elements are aptly joined together to explain the parable. The three elements in the parable are the wife, the husband, and the law, since the wife us subject to her husband through the bond of the law. So much for the parable. In the reality portrayed by the parable there are also three elements: mankind, sin, and the law, because man is under the law as long as he lives in sin, just as the wife is under her husband's law as long as the husband lives. Although we find three things in the parable—the wife, the husband, and the law—and three things in the reality portrayed by the parable—the soul, sin, and the law of sin—only one thing is different, that in the parable the husband dies in order that the woman may be loosed from the law of the husband, but in the reality of the parable it is the soul itself which dies to sin in order to marry Christ. When it dies to sin, it also dies to the law of sin. Sin in this case is to be understood as that which is added by means of the law, and it is called 'sin beyond measure',* because, although it is already known to be sin, it is increased by added transgression. 'For where there is no law there is no transgression.'* This is what is meant by 'sinner beyond measure' and 'sin by the commandment'.* These were the passions, not passions then but rather delights, which were increased by the law and worked in man's members to bring forth fruit unto death, and beneath which the soul was held captive as beneath a domineering husband, before the time when grace came through faith. The person who serves the law of God with his mind dies to these passions, although the passions themselves are not yet dead as long as man serves the law of sin in his flesh. Something of the passions still remains in one who is under the regime of grace. It cannot conquer him but instructs him, it cannot capture him but disquiets him, until everything fortified by evil habits has been mortified.

The true spouse of Christ understands the distinction between the letter and the spirit, which are called law and grace by another terminology. And now that she is no longer serving God in the oldness of the letter but in the newness of the spirit, she is not under the law but under grace.* So when the letter is joined to the spirit and the law is joined to grace, these two things are not simply called 'letter' and 'law', since under that aspect they kill by multiplying sin. For the law is called 'the power of sin'* because it increases the harmful pleasure of sin by its severe prohibition, but even so the law is still not evil; but 'sin, that it might appear sin, worked death by that which is good'.* Thus many things which are not evil things are harmful to people. This spouse of Christ then is dead to the law, that is, to sin, which is made more plentiful through the prohibition of the law, since the law orders but does not help when it is unaccompanied by grace. Dead to such a law then, in order to belong to another who is risen from the dead, she makes distinctions with no injury to the law, lest she commit a sacrilege against its author. The same law 'which was given by Moses' becomes 'grace and truth through Jesus Christ',* when the spirit is added to the letter with the result that the justice of the law begins to be fulfilled. If it is not fulfilled, it makes men guilty of transgression. There is not one law which is holy and good and just,* and a different law through which sin works death* and to which we have to die in order to belong to another who rose from the dead, but it is one and the same law. Therefore, the text continues:

Cf. Rm 7:6, 6:14

1 Cor 15:56

Rm 7:13

Jn 1:17

Cf. Rm 7:12
Cf. Rm 7:13

Rm 7:4

VERSE FOUR. **Therefore, my brethren, you also have become dead to the law by the body of Christ.** That is, you have died to the shadow by means of the reality; you have died to the letter through the spirit, and to the law through grace, so that you are no longer the wife or spouse of the dead man, but of him who is risen from the dead, so that you no longer bear fruits in dead works for a dead man, but you bring forth living fruit to God. The law foreshadowed such a thing when it commanded a wife to transfer from her deceased first husband by whom she had no children to the bed of the brother of the deceased who was obliged to raise up seed for his brother who was unable to do so.* The brother in this case seems to be the more fertile spiritual understanding of the letter. The text continues:

Cf. Deut 25:5

Rm 7:5

VERSE FIVE. **For when we were in the flesh, the passions of sins which existed through the law worked in our members to bring forth fruit unto death.** When we were in the flesh, that is, when we were wholly immersed in the concupiscences of the flesh and placed all our hope in them, the passions of sins which were increased, not taken away, by the law worked in our members to bring forth fruit unto death, for the law made the sinner, who presumed in himself, a transgressor, because he did not have God for a helper. Your concupiscence conquered you, O man, because it found you in a bad place, that is, in the flesh. Leave the flesh. Living in the flesh, do not desire to be in the flesh, but exist in the spirit. What does it mean, 'exist in the spirit'? Put your hope in God. If you put your hope in that spirit by which man exists, your spirit will fall back upon the earth, because you did not give it to him upon whom it depends, for it does not possess itself unless it is possessed. Do not put your hope in yourself, but in him who made you. He is your life, and whatever fruit you bear for him, you bear for your own life. It continues:

Rm 7:6

VERSE SIX. **But now we are loosed from the law of death in which we were detained, so that we should** serve in newness of spirit and not in the oldness of the letter. The law of death is the letter which kills, and those who die to sin are freed from it. The law is the letter only to those who read it, and this is characteristic of the Old Testament; but it is not the letter to those who fulfil it through charity, which is characteristic of the New Testament. The law is no help to those who read it, but is rather a witness to those who sin; those who are renewed through the spirit are freed from its condemnation, because 'the letter kills, but the spirit gives life'.* Man serves through fear in the oldness of the letter, but through love in the newness of the spirit where slaves were made sons. We know it is the Lord's doing that we who are slaves are not that former kind of slave, for we are sons of grace. But the kind of slave who 'knows not what his lord does'* does not know this, because he glories in himself and not in the lord.

2 Cor 3:6

Jn 15:15

Rm 7:7

VERSE SEVEN. What shall we say then? Is the law sin? God forbid. But I do not know sin but by the law; for I would not have known concupiscence had the law not said, 'You shall not covet.' If the law is not sin but only that which makes sin known, it is still blamed in these words. When the human soul was, as it were, secure in its ignorance, the law by showing it sin made it guilty. 'But I do not know sin but by the law,' he said. He did not say, 'I did not do it but by the law', but 'I did not know it but by the law'. Yet the law was usefully given for the sake of pointing out sin. Since sin could not be overcome except by the grace of God, anxiety over guilt made the sinner turn to God to receive grace. Therefore, guilt was not implanted in man through the law, but was recognized through the law; the law did not remove it, but showed by whom it could be removed. The result was that, because the soul which had not yet received grace could not resist concupiscence, concupiscence increased, because it has greater vigor with the addition of transgression when it acts against the law than it would have if no law forbade it. Therefore, the Apostle chose concupiscence as a kind of all-inclusive concept, as if the precept of the law which forbade all sin was, 'You shall not covet'.² Whoever fulfils the commandment commits no sin. No sin is committed except by concupiscence. Sin sometimes happens to a man which he neither performs nor commits, because there is no desire in that sin; but it is imposed through weakness or ignorance. Yet if it were not a sin the prophet would not pray, 'Do not remeber my ignorances'.* Therefore, it is a good law which prescribes, 'You shall not covet', but when the Spirit does not help by breathing into us a good desire in place of an evil desire, i.e., pouring charity into our hearts, then the law, although good, increases our evil desire by prohibiting it. Somehow or other what is desired is made more attractive when it is forbidden. This is what the Apostle says later, that sin deceives by means of the commandment and through it kills.* Therefore, the text continues:

Ps 24:7

Rm 7:11

Rm 7:8-9   VERSES EIGHT AND NINE. **But sin, seizing the opportunity, worked in me all manner of concupiscence through the commandment.** Concupiscence existed even before sin but not in all its strength. The river was restrained by the law but not dried up. Concupiscence led you even when there were no obstacles, but when the obstacles were breached, it overwhelmed you. It was in its lesser stage when it moved your lust, but it was in full force when it transgressed the law. Do you wish to know how great it is? Then see what it broke: the precept of God saying, 'You shall not covet'.* Man did not say this; God said, 'You shall not covet'. **Without the law sin was dead,** that is, it was in hiding, it did not appear, it was as though buried in the darkness of its own ignorance. **And I lived sometime without the law,** that is, I was not terrified by any death springing from sin, because it did not appear when the law did not exist. I was alive, that is, it seemed to me that I was living. **But when the commandment came sin revived.** It stood out, it became obvious; it did not so much live, as live again. It had lived once already in paradise when it was

Ex 20:17

obviously committed against the precept which had been given. When sin is contracted by the new-born it lies hidden as though it were dead until the evil which is opposed to justice makes itself felt by means of a prohibition. When one thing is commanded and approved and yet another thing pleases and dominates, then sin somehow revives in the knowledge of the man who is born, the same sin which lived once before in the knowledge of the first man who was made. It lived again, that is, made itself felt; it began to wage war again and to make its appearance.

Rm 7:10

VERSE TEN. **And I died.** That is, I became a transgressor, or I knew I was dead, or the sure penalty of death hung over me as the result of my transgression. Of all these things I was ignorant when I followed my own desires without knowledge, because there was no prohibition of them.

And the commandment that promised life, if it were obeyed, I found to offer death, when it was disobeyed. Not only is there sin as before, but now the sin is committed by one who knowingly transgresses. The commandment not to covet is well designed for life, for the only true life consists in not coveting. O happy life, and happier than the pleasures of desire. Happy the soul which takes pleasure in delights of this kind where it is not defiled by dishonor and where it is purified by the serenity of truth; that is, when the law of God gives pleasure, and such pleasure that all lascivious delights are overcome. But this does not happen immediately when a man comes to grace, but concupiscence gradually slackens in a man making progress to the degree that he progresses toward justice.

Rm 7:11

VERSE ELEVEN. **For sin, finding opportunity in the commandment, deceived me, and by it killed me.** For sin, using the law illegitimately, was committed more pleasurably, with a zest increased by prohibition, and in this way it deceived me. A pleasure is deceitful when more numerous and more bitter penalties are attached to it. Because what is forbidden is committed with more sweetness by men who are not yet spiritual, sin deceives with a false sweetness. Because the guilt of transgression is attached to it, it kills.

Rm 7:12 **VERSE TWELVE. Therefore the law indeed is holy, and the commandment holy, and just, and good.** For the law commands what should be commanded and prohibits what should be prohibited. The fault is in the one who uses it badly, not in the commandment which is good, for the law is good if one uses it lawfully. The law is used badly by one who does not submit himself to God with loving humility in order that the law may be fulfilled by grace. A little before, the Apostle had defended the law from the charge of being a sin; now he gives it due
Rm 7:7 praise. Then he said, 'Is the law sin? No!'* Truth is defended by one word because the defender has great authority. Here he says, 'The law indeed is holy, and the commandment holy, and just, and good.' Therefore, accept the commandment. Know that it is your weapon, not meant to kill you, but to kill your enemy, provided you are humble like little David. If you are a great and proud Goliath, you will be killed by your
1 Sam 17 own arms. Goliath gloried in his shield and lance,*
Cf. Ex 14-15 Pharaoh in his chariots and horses,* but you glory in the name of the Lord. The law is always good, whether it is an obstacle to those devoid of grace or a help to those full of grace, just as the sun is always good, whether it harms afflicted eyes or soothes healthy ones. What health is to eyes for seeing the sun, grace is to minds for fulfilling the law. Just as healthy eyes do not perish by their delight in the sun but are enlightened by it, and unhealthy eyes are beaten back by the harsh intensity of the rays into denser darkness, so the soul which has been saved by the charity of the spirit is not said to be dead to justice, but that soul which is liable to guilt and transgression, which are caused by the letter of the law as long as grace is absent.

Rm 7:13 **VERSE THIRTEEN. Then did that which is good become death for me? Certainly not.**[3] But sin, so that it might appear as sin, worked death in me by that which is good. The law is not death, but sin is death. Already the Apostle had said, 'Without the law sin was dead',* and we explained the word 'dead' as 'hidden'.* Sin is hidden; it does not appear. Now see how truly that was said. He says, 'sin, that it may appear sin'. He did not say, 'that it might exist', because it already was in existence even when sin did not appear. What does the phrase mean, 'that it might appear sin'? The answer is, 'I did not know concupiscence until the law said,"You shall not covet".'* He did not say, 'I did not have concupiscence', but 'I did not know concupiscence'. So too in this place he does not say 'in order that sin may exist', but 'that it may appear sin, it worked death in me by that which is good'. What death? **In order that sin, through the commandment, might become sinful beyond measure.** Why beyond measure? Because now it is transgression. 'Where there is no law there is no transgression.'* 'And the commandment which promised life (for what is so pertinent to life as not to covet?) I found offered death. For sin, finding opportunity in the commandment, deceived me, and by it killed me.'* The law frightened concupiscence but did not extinguish it; it caused fear of punishment but not love of justice. What then? Why do we doubt that the law was given for this purpose: that man should discover himself? As long as God did not forbid him evil, man lay hidden from himself. He did not discover that his strength was feeble until he received the law of prohibition.

Rm 7:14-15   VERSES FOURTEEN AND FIFTEEN. **For we know that the law is spiritual; but I am carnal, sold under sin. For that which I do I do not understand. For I do not that which I will, but what I hate I do.** It is clear enough from these words that the law cannot be fulfilled except by spiritual men, and they become such only by the grace of God. The more a person resembles a spiritual law, that is, the more he rises to a spiritual affection, so also the more he fulfills it and delights in the grace which forgives sin and infuses the spirit of charity, with the result that justice is not troublesome but even sweet and joyous. When all the circumstances of this text are carefully considered, it is correctly understood that the Apostle said these things and those which follow, both in his own person and in that of others living faithfully under grace but not yet taken up into that peace in which death is absorbed in victory, according to what the Apostle says, 'If the Spirit of him who raised up Jesus from the dead dwells in you, he shall give life to your mortal bodies, because of his Spirit dwelling in you'.* When our mortal bodies are raised to life again, not only will there be no consent to sin, but no carnal concupiscence will remain to which consent can be given. The only man who was able, while still in mortal flesh, not to have this carnal concupiscence, which resists the spirit, was that man who alone came to men without it.

Rm 8:11

The body will be spiritual in heaven, and whoever is there will be completely a spiritual man, that is, according to both his constituent parts, since even the body will be spiritual. Nor is it absurd that even the body will be spiritual in that life, if in this life it can happen in those who still savor carnal things that even the spirit is carnal. This is the fourth stage of the man of God,* which is begun here in the sanctification of the Spirit and is perfected in that blessed state of eternal happiness. And so the Apostle says here, and with him every spiritual man, 'But I am carnal', as if he did not yet have a spiritual body, just as he could have said, 'I am mortal', because he still lived in a mortal body. The same should be understood of the other things said here. When they are attributed to spiritual men they seem incongruous, but we will discuss them better in the proper places.

See above on Rm 2:17.

'We know that the law is spiritual,' he says. Indeed the law is spiritual, because, as we have already said,* 'it is the very law which was given through Moses, but grace and truth came through Jesus Christ'.* When the spirit was joined to the letter and charity to the commandment, then true liberty was joined to the slave of sin, and a servitude which was free because it

See above on Rm 7:3

Jn 1:17

was voluntary was joined to the freedman of justice.

The law is spiritual but I am carnal, says the Apostle. I am still in the flesh. Dying daily, I shed the flesh, but I have not yet perished as long as I have not perfectly obtained the absence of concupiscence. I shall obtain it perfectly when I wholly shed the flesh, when my spirit puts on a spiritual body, and I shall no longer be carnal in any part of me, since both parts of me will be spiritual.

I am sold under sin. Who sold you, Paul? He replies, 'O man, I am the man'. Man sold himself to be a slave under sin. I sold myself when I consented to the seducer. I could sell myself, but I cannot redeem myself. I sold myself when I gave consent to sin and received death. But again I give faith and receive justice from him who also gave faith, the faith of his blood, which the devil shed unjustly. In this blood I was justified by him, who alone is just and is not justified, because he alone was born just. For this reason the Apostle says, 'We also who have the firstfruits of the Spirit groan within ourselves, waiting for the adoption of sons, the redemption of our body'.* I know that I am redeemed with a great price, but my body is not yet exempt from its own corruption, and therefore being still corruptible and mortal, it has not yet received the hope of its redemption. Therefore, all of us, no matter what first fruits of the Spirit we have received, still groan daily within ourselves, knowing that we are redeemed, but not yet exempt from the servile condition of the flesh.

Rm 8:23

This is why we call daily to our Redeemer with anxious prayers, 'Redeem me, O Lord, and have mercy on me'.* You redeem us, O Lord, when you fulfil in us the work of your redemption. You had given man delight and joy in you, which that wretch gave up in order to possess delight and joy in himself, but, given over to death and corruption, he obtained neither of these, in you or in himself. But you gave yourself into slavery in order to buy back liberty for him. You gave yourself up to shame in order to buy

Ps 25:11

back glory for him. Your blood is the price of all these goods. It is the fountain of David lying open for the washing of the menstruous woman.* Have patience with us, Lord Jesus. You made so much of us that when you would redeem us you willed that you yourself should be the price. But we, addicted to vile things, again withdrew ourselves for sordid pleasures, being the vilest slaves of the flesh. Afterwards we bring the stink of our filthiness to you to be washed in the fountain of your precious blood, which is not tainted however much it washes. Indeed the more it washes the more salubrious it becomes, just as he loves more to whom more is forgiven.* Spare us, O Lord, and would that men would spare themselves and not bring here their excessive filth, that is, that they would not come here excessively filthy. Yet your price is enough to redeem them all; your fountain is enough to wash them all. Those who are guilty of their price, namely your blood, those who have sinned against your grace, and who return and weep before you, you know how to forgive in a most kindly way. Yet you turn the guilty over to punishment by the law, so that just as it was an eye for an eye and a tooth for a tooth, so blood is demanded for blood. These sinners sweat out the depraved pleasures of sin by the bloody sweat of penitence, and they wash them away by the bloody tears of the heart. But since he does not have these things except with the help of your grace, miserable man who is sold under sin releases himself to your grace when he accepts his price from you. When he returns to grace he immediately discovers a struggle and he suffers the darkness of ignorance, which is dangerous for those entering a struggle.

'For that which I do I do not understand. For I do not that which I will, but what I hate I do.' Not that the Apostle did not understand sin, since sin became apparent through the commandment, but 'I am ignorant', that is, 'I do not know' or 'I do not approve', as when the Lord says, 'I never knew you'.* Or else the Apostle means, 'I think it good when I act to fulfil my lust to the uttermost', or 'I do not doubt that it is evil, but I act through blind lust', or 'I do not pay sufficient attention to the struggle within me of willing and not willing'. We certainly should not understand the Apostle's words to mean that he willed to be chaste but was unchaste, or merciful but was cruel, or pious but was impious, when he said, 'I do not that which I will'. He says, 'I will not to covet, and yet I covet'. Yet the law says, 'You shall not covet'. Man heard the law, recognized vice, declared war upon it, and found himself captive. Not all men except the Apostle; all men including the Apostle because he is a man. He has set before your eyes his own battle so that you would not fear yours. If the blessed Apostle had not said this, perhaps you would despair of yourself when you saw concupiscence stirring in your members without your consent, and would say, 'If I belonged to God I would not be so moved'. See the Apostle struggling and do not despair. He says, 'I do not do that which I will, because I do not wish to covet and yet I covet'. This is a general disease and an unavoidable infection stemming from Adam. For in paradise he committed the disobedient act that had to be punished, and he discovered in himself a shameful stirring. Their eyes were opened to what they had never sensed, what they had never feared in their bodily activity. Their eyes were opened not to see but to be aware; therefore, they took care to cover themselves. From this comes original sin which no one escapes;[4] because of this the flesh lusts against the spirit, and no one does not feel this. This is the sin which almost naturally dwells in the body of each man who is born from that sin; it is the sin which causes all other sins. Reason hates concupiscence; the son of grace does not will it. But the flesh delights in concupiscence and wills to fulfil that in which the son of Adam takes delight. Therefore the Apostle does not do what he wills; namely, not to covet, because the man in him does what the Apostle hates; that is, he covets.

Rm 7:16　　VERSE SIXTEEN. **If then I do that which I do not will, I consent to the law because it is good.**

Transgressions of the law would not be bad unless the law itself were good. If it were not good, it would not be bad to transgress it. Because it is bad to transgress it, therefore, the law is good. What is as good as, 'You shall not covet'? So the Apostle says, 'My weakness does not fulfil the law, but my will praises it. I reject what I do, and in this rejection I consent to the law even if I am opposed to the law in what I do. My will, which is the will of the law, is not to covet. Although I do not act in this way, nevertheless I would approve of such restraint both in myself and in the law if I could act this way; I consent to the law because it is good.'

Rm 7:17

[PL omits]

Cf. 1 Jn 3:9

VERSES SEVENTEEN AND EIGHTEEN. **Now then it is no longer I who do it but sin that dwells in me.** [For I will what the law wills, not to covet, but I covet and it is no longer I who do it but sin that dwells in em.] Where in you? The text continues, **For I know that good does not dwell in me, that is to say, in my flesh.** This is the seed of Adam in our body, and contrary to it is that seed of God in our spirit of which John says in his Epistle, 'If anyone is born of God he does not sin, but his seed which is in him preserves him'.* Sin dwells in the body, but by not consenting to it he lives by faith who invokes God in his fight against sin. For to will that sin not exist is present in man, but is dormant, that is, powerless without the help of grace, since the act of will is itself the work of grace. Therefore, the Apostle adds, **I am not able to accomplish that which is good.** He does well in not consenting; he does well to hate his own concupiscence; but he cannot accomplish what is good. He shall accomplish it when the concupiscence in his members is annihilated. Now the defect of the flesh in a good undertaking is not good, but when the defect has ceased to exist the flesh will remain, but will no longer be tainted or depraved. This same learned man shows how this relates to our nature when he says, 'I know that good does not dwell in me,' which he then expounds saying, 'that is, in my flesh'. He calls his flesh himself;

therefore, it is not an enemy. Even when its defect is resisted the flesh is loved, because it is taken care of. *Eph 5:29* 'For no one ever hated his own flesh.'*

For to will is within my power; but I am not able to accomplish that which is good. Volition is present to both the flesh and the mind, but neither one can accomplish anything as long as the concupiscence of the flesh cannot bring the will of the mind to consent to evil, and the will of the mind cannot drive concupiscence out of existence. Thus, the text continues:

Rm 7:19-20 VERSES NINETEEN AND TWENTY. **For the good which I will I do not; but the evil which I do not will, that I do. Now if I do that which I do not will, it is no more I who do it, but sin that dwells in me.** When I will correctly, I will what the law wills. I find therefore that the law is good to me when I will to act well, because by its command it directs me toward the good; but I do not find myself able to accomplish the good. To will is close to me, it is near me, but sin dwells in my body as a household enemy. Everyone who makes progress with a right intention, as he progresses, draws away from all sin, and puts it ever farther away as he draws nearer to justice and perfection, because concupiscence, which is sin dwelling in our flesh, continuously lessens in those who make progress, although it still remains in their members. It is one thing to withdraw from all sin, and that is the business of the present; it is quite another thing to have withdrawn, and that belongs to perfection. The guilt of original concupiscence is forgiven in baptism, but the weakness remains until the life to come. In that life there is perfect peace for those who are fighting well, and everyone who is making good progress struggles hard until he is healed to arrive at it. This is that hidden sin and that dormant evil which is spoken of above, 'It is no more I who do it, but sin that dwells in me.' Again evil lies in wait for me, like a snake watching for my heel. This sin, of which the Apostle said, 'It is no more I who do it, but sin that dwells in me,' is at work in us but we do not take part in it when our will in no way consents to it. It holds the members and prevents them from obeying the desires of the will. For what does sin produce in us when we are unwilling except unlawful desires? If the will does not give its consent, the members are stirred but nothing comes of it. Sin produces desires; if we obey them, we cooperate, but if we do not obey them, we do not produce them, but the sin which dwells in us produces them. If we had no unlawful desires, neither we nor sin would bring about anything evil in us. We are said to take part in an inclination toward an illicit desire, even though by resisting it we do not cooperate with it, since it is not a question of an outside force, but of our own weakness. We shall be healed of this feebleness when we become immortal in body and soul. The guilt of this weakness was taken away in baptism, as was said above, together with all the sins which we committed in obeying it, and it would be no further obstacle to us if we would give no further obedience to its desires.

Rm 7:21   VERSE TWENTY-ONE. **I discover a law when I will to do good,** that is, I find that the law is something good. But when I will to do good, I find a struggle in myself, for, as he adds, **evil is close to me.**

Rm 7:22-23   VERSES TWENTY-TWO AND TWENTY-THREE. **For I am delighted with the law of God, according to the inward man; but I see another law in my members fighting against the law of my mind and holding me captive in the law of sin that is my members.** Did no weakness remain because all evil was wiped out in baptism? If none remained, we would live here without sin. But by reason of that part which is freed we are free and we serve God; by reason of that part in which we are still slaves we serve the law of sin. 'I am delighted with the law of God according to the inward man,' he says. Notice, where we are free, we delight in the law of God, for liberty delights us. As long as you do what is right out of fear, God does not delight you. As long as he does not delight you, you still act as a slave; let him delight you and you are free. Do not fear punishment but love justice. You cannot yet love justice? Then at least fear punishment so that you can come to love justice. The Apostle already felt himself free in his superior part, and therefore he said, 'I am delighted with the law of God according to the inward man'. The law delights me; what the law commands delights me; justice itself delights me.

'But I see another law in my members, fighting against the law of my mind, and holding me captive in the law of sin, that is my members.' This is the weakness that remains. He feels himself captive in that part of himself where justice is not complete. Now insofar as he is pleased with the law of God he is not a captive but a friend of the law, and therefore free, because a friend. What about the remainder? 'If the Son shall make you free, you shall be free indeed.'* *Jn 8:36* This is the law which fights against the law of the mind, which the first human beings merited to have in their mortal members after they transgressed the precept. Even down to the present day this law is regulated by marriage among the sons of Adam, and it is confined and restrained by continence, so that just as punishment comes from sin, so merit comes from punishment. This is the law that leads me captive, but captive only in part, only in my flesh. My mind fights back, and takes delight in the law of God, and does not consent to sin as it titillates, suggests, and cajoles, since the mind has other inner delights of its own in no way to be compared with the delights of the flesh. Therefore, there is something dead in me [and something living.] The mind does not consent, *[PL omits]* but death presses its claim. Just as there is a living element in me, so there is also a dead element in me.

Rm 7:24   VERSE TWENTY-FOUR. **Unhappy man that I am, who shall deliver me from the body of this death?** What is he asking? If it is the dissolution of the body, that is not far off. Does such a heartfelt groan come from the Apostle for that reason? Far from it! Not everyone who finishes this life is freed from the body of this death, but only the one who is worthy to receive that other life. The Apostle does not ask to be freed from the substance of the body, which is good, but from the fleshly vices, and from them not even a dying man is freed except through the Saviour's grace. For death separates from the body, but the vices contracted through the body hold fast, and just punishment is due them, as that rich man found out even in hell.* The Apostle asks not only that, by an act of divine kindness, he not be punished for his past sins, but also that he be strong and valiant against sin in the future. He is delighted with the law of God, but sees another law in his members. He sees that it is; he does not recall that it was. He is impelled by the present; he does not recollect the past. He sees something not merely fighting him, but even leading him captive into the law of sin, which is, not was, in his members. He could have used the phrase 'this mortal body'. What does he mean by 'the body of this death'? Before sin the bodies of the first human beings were animal, yet spiritual, but they were not the kind that had to die. They became such on the day when they touched the tree contrary to the prohibition. Thus, indeed, those men had animal bodies, which would not die unless they sinned, but which were to receive an angelic form and a heavenly quality. As soon as they transgressed the precept, death was conceived in their members like some fatal disease, and it altered that condition by which they dominated their bodies so that they could not say, 'I see another law in my members fighting against the law of my mind'. Even if the body was animal and not yet spiritual, it was not yet mortal like that from which and with which we are born. Why is it that once we are born—or better, once we are conceived—we begin what is nothing less than a kind of sickness, by which after diseases and many bodily deaths, afflictions, and captivities of soul, we finally, in addition to all this, have to die? It is not so necessary for a person afflicted with dropsy, consumption or elephantiasis to die as it is for him who has begun to possess this mortal body. In this body all men are by nature children of wrath,* because it was the punishment of sin alone which effected this condition. The concupiscence with

Cf Lk 16:19-31

Cf. Eph 2:3

which we are born cannot be brought to an end as long as we live. It can be diminished daily but it cannot be ended. For this reason our body is called the body of death.

Rm 7:24-25

VERSES TWENTY-FOUR AND TWENTY-FIVE. **Who shall deliver me from the body of this death? The grace of God.** It is grace, because it is given freely; it is grace, because it anticipates all our good merits. It will free us from the body of death, when this corruptible thing puts on incorruption. Through whom? **Through our Lord Jesus Christ.** For 'as in Adam all die, so in Christ all shall be made alive'.* Paul, who was sure that the crown of justice had been set aside for him, must be forgiven when he said, 'I know whom I have believed, and I am certain that he is able to guard until that day that which has been committed to him'.* It is difficult for the laborer not be seek the end of his labor. It was good for him still to remain in the flesh on account of the brothers, but to be with Christ would be much better.* O Lord, whose grace frees us, the prophet who says 'You are my hope' is right in saying too that you are his patience.* The body of death, the slavery of the soul under the law of sin, the world seated in wickedness,* and all the evils of this life press us toward you, the supreme good in which there is no evil. You indeed promise yourself to us, but you do not tell us when we shall have you. You make the evil which forces us away from here; you prolong hope to torment us in our misery. If in all these things we say, 'Unhappy man that I am, who shall deliver me from the body of this death?', your grace answers, 'I will'. If we ask when, we are rebuked for impatience. If we presume anything further, we are overwhelmed by ignorance of your judgments. Therefore those who dwell within the bounds of your grace are troubled at your signs, and the outgoing of this morning and evening delights them very much,* when, because they shall belong to your grace, they fear no further failure. Beyond that, they shall no longer desire progress, since they shall have that perfection by which you will be all in all to

1 Cor 15:22

2 Tim 1:12

Cf. Phil 1:23-24

Ps 70:5
Cf. 1 Jn 5:19

Cf. Ps 64:9

them. O Lord, you will give them peace; in the meantime give them patience.

Therefore, I myself serve the law of God with the mind, but with the flesh the law of sin. The structure of the meaning of the preceding passage is as follows: Because grace liberates, I myself serve the law of God with the mind, and the law of sin with the flesh. But if I serve the law of God with the mind, and if I also serve the law of sin in my flesh unwillingly, already I am in Christ. If I am in Christ, there is no condemnation for those who are in Christ Jesus'.* We who have fled to Christ have escaped whatever pertains to damnation, because we have found a liberator.

Rm 8:1

CHAPTER EIGHT

Rm 8:2-3

VERSES TWO AND THREE. **For the law of the spirit of life in Christ Jesus has delivered me from the law of sin and of death.** In the law of the spirit is fulfilled that justice which could not be fulfilled in the law of the letter, for **since the law was weak God sent his Son.** Therefore, the Apostle says, 'With my mind I serve the law of God'. Up to this point the man of God did not clearly perceive himself or understand what was happening; now he begins to discern himself and to understand who is working in him. Therefore, he says, 'It is not one person in my flesh and another person in my mind, but I am both in my flesh and in my mind. These are not two contrary natures, but one man in both of them, just as there is one God by whom man was made. I serve the law of God with my mind by not consenting, and with my flesh I serve the law of sin by coveting. Yet in the latter I take pleasure and in the former I am not subdued.' O old man, a new type of life is proclaimed for you. You are walking on air with the joy of newness, but you are weighed down with the burden of oldness. There begins for you a war against yourself. To the extent that you displease yourself, you are joined to God; and to the extent that you are joined to God you will be prepared to conquer yourself, because he who conquers all things is with you. But we grow weary of daily struggle, and we would not always will to conquer; we would sometimes will to find peace. Whatever worth there is in our desires, in our will and in our prayer when we say 'Lead us not into temptation but deliver us from evil,'* to that extent we desire that not even evil desires should exist in our flesh; but as long as we live here, we cannot accomplish this. Human nature in itself deserved as much: its sickness comes from sin; once this is healed, it is no more. This discord works for peace. The flesh works for its desires; work for your own also. The desires of the flesh are not suppressed or extinguished by you; do not let yours be extinguished lest you perish in the combat. Serve the law of God with your mind not giving consent to evil concupiscences; serve the law of sin with the concupiscences of the flesh, but not with your own service. As long as you are in that state you are in Christ Jesus, and there is no condemnation for those who are in Christ Jesus. Although they are in the flesh, and the flesh serves the law of sin, yet they do not walk according to the flesh, for with their mind they serve the law of God. 'Now'—meaning in this state—'there is no condemnation for those who are in Christ Jesus.' Or else, the word 'now' means that during this time of combat, as long as we are still fighting, we have already escaped the peril of condemnation. Peace will come and then there will be no concupiscence to fight against.

'The law of the spirit of life in Christ Jesus has delivered me from the law of sin and of death.' The Apostle seems to have proposed three laws here, and it is necessary for the reader to keep them separate. The first is the law of the spirit of life; the second is the law of sin and death; and the third is the law which cannot justify. The law of the spirit of life is the law of faith, the law of mercy, of which it is said, 'By your law have mercy on me'.* It is the grace of God, granting forgiveness of sins and capable of adopting. The second law is concupiscence, and it is rightly called a law since it is legitimate that the man who refused to obey the Lord his God should have his

Mt 6:13

Ps 118:29

Gen 2:17

flesh disobey him. It is the law of sin and the law of death, for sin is death according to what is said: 'Whatsoever day you shall eat of it, you shall die the death'.* The third law is that of the letter which is powerless to fulfil what the law of the spirit of life fulfilled; namely, the liberation from the law of sin and death. It is the law of deeds, which can threaten but not help, command but not aid. One of the laws reveals sin, and the other takes it away. Taking away sin was impossible to the law of the letter since it was weakened through the flesh. With the flesh in victorious rebellion, man listened to the law and was more excited in his own concupiscence. What he could not do through the law of the letter was fulfilled through the law of grace.

Rm 8:3-4

VERSES THREE AND FOUR. **God sending his own Son in the likeness of sinful flesh has condemned sin of sin in the flesh, that the justification of the law might be fulfilled in us who walk not according to the flesh, but according to the spirit.** O Lord, open the Scriptures, which speak of you, to those who seek in them you alone, and especially [open] this text which you have spoken to us through your Apostle, which reveals traces of your hand and has the style of your Spirit. Especially in it loose for us the seal which no one in heaven or on earth or under the earth was found worthy to loose except you, who hold the key of David.* Open for us then what that is **which the law could not do, because it was weakened through the flesh.** This could not be revealed to the world unless your Only-begotten Son came and appeared in the world in the likeness of sinful flesh. What can this mean except what follows: the destruction or condemnation of sin, and the fulfillment in us of the law's justification?

Cf. Rev 5:3-5

Therefore, he says to the Hebrews, 'For if sprinkling the blood of goats and calves and the ashes of a heifer sanctifies the defiled to the cleansing of the flesh, how much more shall the blood of Christ, who by the Holy Spirit offered himself unspotted to God, cleanse our conscience from dead works, to serve the living God?'* What in one place is called the 'condemnation of sin' is called the 'cleansing of dead works' in another, and the service of a clean conscience toward God is the same as the perfect fulfillment of justice. In the law of the letter man sinned, and a goat paid the penalty; in this case not the spirit but the flesh seemed to be cleansed or sanctified, because the law, conscious of its own weakness, required nothing more for its cleansing than that external rite of cleansing. The law seemed to possess powers only over the flesh; as far as cleansing the conscience, it was weakened by the flesh. After the commission of a sin which did not require stoning or death, something was threatened on behalf of the people, but nothing was done about the conscience being cleansed by the Lord God; this could only be done in the fulfillment of the justice of the law.

Heb 9:13-14

We should ask therefore, 'What is the justice of the law'? That which is called the justice of the law is so called because it was given for the fulfillment of the law. What is that but satisfaction for the past and precaution for the future? But there can be no satisfaction from a nature spoiled by sin which has grown to be one with that nature, and no precaution for the future from what would be outside of grace. Notice, this is the infirmity of the law through the flesh. Therefore, the Only-begotten came from the Father, full of grace and truth,* so full of grace that it not only abounded in him, but overflowed from him into us, and from his fullness we have all received grace for grace. First of all, he gave us faith, and then hope as though the reward of faith; but hope does not disappoint, because soon the charity of God is also poured forth in our hearts through the Holy Spirit.* When he is given to us, we must hope as much as we believe, and we must love as much as we hope and believe. This is the fulfillment of the law and of justification. When the Only-begotten of God came into the world, he met the prince of this world, and he permitted himself to be killed by him for the sake of justice, although he had nothing on him.* He gave the justice of his innocent death to the penitent sinner.

Cf. Jn 1:14

Rm 5:5

Cf Jn 14:30

He put his faith and charity into his heart, the saving confession of himself into his mouth,* and his body and blood into his hand. In this way he presents him to God the Father as His own, a culprit yet redeemed. With the sin of the presumer condemned and the sin of the penitent destroyed, he restored him, pleasing and acceptable, to a part in the sacrifice of his justice.

    This is the redemption which you have sent, O Lord, to your people. This is your justice, about which your poor man cries to you daily from the ends of the earth, 'Deliver me in your justice'.* This is your work, about which the prophet requests, 'O Lord, make your work true'.* Your work is made true for us when we sacrifice to you this your sacrifice. When we remember with the sure sacrament of faith and a pious affection of heart what you have done for us, faith, as it were, receives it with its mouth, hope chews it, and charity cooks into salvation and life the blessed and beatifying food of your grace. There you show yourself to the soul which desires you, accepting the embrace of her love and kissing her with the kiss of your mouth.* As happens in a loving kiss, she pours out to you her spirit, and you pour in your spirit, so that you are made one body and one spirit when she receives in this way your body and your blood. There the conscience is not only cleansed from dead works, but is filled and strengthened with the fruits of life and of the spirit to serve the living God,* when the justice of the law is completely fulfilled in her. Just as you somehow showed yourself to us even to the point of being despised, so also your sons promise and devote themselves to you even to the point of being despised themselves.

    'For God sent his Son in the likeness of sinful flesh', in real flesh, but not in sinful flesh. The first man was not created in sinful flesh because no sin of his parent preceded him, but we are born in sinful flesh because his sin precedes us. Christ, in order to condemn sin of sin, appeared that way: in the likeness of sinful flesh. The likeness of sinful flesh was in

Cf. Rm 10:10

Ps 70:2

Cf. Hab 3:2

Cf. Sg 1:1

Cf. Heb 9:14

Christ, because death can only result from sin, and certainly his body was mortal. Unless it were mortal, it could not die. Thus death is called sin, because it is caused by sin, just as we speak of the greek tongue or the latin tongue, not as a part of the body, but as that which is produced by a part of the body. So, the Lord's death is sin, because it was caused by sin, since he took flesh from stuff which had deserved death because of sin. Mary [born of Adam,] was dead on account of sin, and the Lord's flesh from Mary was dead on account of sins to be destroyed.[5] Mary was a virgin not knowing man's embrace; she was without the heat of concupiscence, for it was in order to avoid this heat that it was said to her, 'The Holy Spirit shall come upon you, and the power of the Most High shall overshadow you.'* The Virgin Mary, therefore, did not bed [with a husband] and conceive, but she believed and conceived, and the Lord was born mortal for mortals. Why mortal? Because he was in the likeness of sinful flesh, not in sinful flesh. What are the marks of sinful flesh? Death and sin. What are the marks of the likeness of sinful flesh? Death without sin. If he had sin, his flesh would have been sinful. If he did not have death, there would not have been the likeness of sinful flesh. That was the way the Saviour came. He was mortal and died, but he killed death,[6] and condemned sin of sin. By means of the sin of the presumer, as I have said, he condemned the sin of the penitent sinner, and by the death of his own flesh he killed the death of the soul in us. In the law the sacrifice for sin was called sin. Therefore, being himself the sacrifice for sin, he condemned and destroyed all sin in us. This is the justice of the law which is not fulfilled by the law, but through him who came not to destroy the law, but to fulfil it,* Jesus Christ our Lord. In this way, therefore, **the justification of the law** is fulfilled in us, **who do not walk according to the flesh, but according to the spirit.*** To walk according to the flesh means to pursue the concupiscences of the flesh. To walk according to the Spirit is by the help of grace not to obey concupiscences.* After grace

[PL: ex eadem]

Lk 1:35

Mt 5:17

[PL: Not to walk according to the flesh means, by the help of grace, not to obey concupiscence.[

has been received a conflict with the flesh remains, because iniquity has been blotted out, but weakness remains.

NOTES

1. Migne's text lacks this greek word on PL 180:611; in the MS it occurs on fol. 151ᵛ. The word meant is *anamarteton*, which also occurs in Cassian, *Conference* 23, title as *De anamarteto*, and in the body of the text of Cassian, Chapter 7, *anamarteti, id est, inpeccantiae*. This is William's use of the word. This difference between the MS reading and Migne's text may indicate two different MS sources for William's text.

2. William's point may be easier to understand if note is made of the fact that in Latin the words for 'covet' in 'You shall not covet', and for 'concupiscence' are *concupisces* and *concupiscentia* respectively, two words from the same root.

3. The ungrammatical expression, *Quia bonum est mors*, is added after *Absit* in the verse which is otherwise identical to the Vulgate text. No authority has been found for this addition. The pauline text in MS 49 on fol. 7ᵛ has the Vulgate reading. A search of the Beuron microfilms of the Vetus Latina readings for Rom 7:13 revealed nothing. This is apparently a scribal error and does not appear in the PL.

4. This and two other statements in the *Exposition on Romans* might indicate William's lack of adherence to a belief in the Immaculate Conception. In Book 3 under Rm 5:12 William says, 'The Saviour alone appeared without sin.' And later in Book 4 under Rm 8:3-4 he says 'Mary, born of Adam, was dead on account of sin . . . '. Cf. Bernard, *Ep* 174.

5. 'The likeness of sinful flesh was in Christ' down to here is Augustine, *Ennar on Ps 34;* PL 36:335. Florus refers to this passage, PL 119:296.

6. 'Mary was a Virgin . . . ' down to this point is from Florus, PL 119:296-297. No earlier source is given.

BOOK FIVE

CHAPTER EIGHT Continued

Rm 8:5-7

VERSES FIVE THROUGH SEVEN. **Those who live according to the flesh mind the things of the flesh; but those who live according to the spirit mind the things of the spirit.** Wisdom hates malice. What is wisdom except a taste for good? What is malice except a taste for evil?[1] Those who relish or have a feel for the things of the spirit or of the flesh are those who find either good or evil tasty and sweet to their hearts. They are the ones who walk according to the spirit or according to the flesh. The text adds, **For the prudence of the flesh is death.** Prudence is properly compared to taste, for just as taste discerns what is savory in foods, so prudence weighs what is expedient. If in this it only seeks what pleases the flesh, it is the prudence of the flesh, and this is the death of the soul. For, just as the soul is the life of the body, so God is the life of the soul, and whatever the soul seeks lower than God is death to it. The prudence of the spirit is to seek its own life, which is God, and the peace which is in God. This peace cannot exist in him who minds carnal things, because as we have said, wisdom hates malice, and the wisdom of the flesh is hostile to God, for it is not subject to the law of God, nor can it be.

What does this mean: nor can it be? It is not man, or flesh, or spirit, or any nature which cannot be subject to the law of God, but the prudence of the flesh which cannot be. The defect cannot be subject, but the nature can. It is as if you said that limping is not included in the idea of normal walking, nor can it be. The foot can be, but limping cannot. Remove the limping and you will see normal walking. As long as limping is present there is no normal walking; likewise, as long as prudence of the flesh is present there is no subjection to God. Let the prudence of the flesh disappear and man can be subject to God. The expression 'the prudence of the flesh is hostile to God' should not be understood as though this enemy could harm God. It is an enemy by its resistance, not by its ability to inflict harm. What prudence of the flesh harms is the person in whom it exists, for it is a defect and harms the nature in which it inheres. So although it cannot be subject to the law of God insofar as it is a defect, it does not escape the order imposed by God's law insofar as it inheres in a nature. God knows well how to impose order in his creation, even on the evils that exist outside his order. He does not impose order on defect but on defective nature. Therefore, the text continues:

Rm 8:8

VERSE EIGHT. **And they who are in the flesh cannot please God.** Those who trust in the flesh, who follow its lusts, who dwell in them, who are delighted by their pleasures and who see a blessed and happy life in their attainment, these people are in the flesh and cannot please God. The expression 'those who are in the flesh' should not be understood to mean those living in this flesh, in which many live who have merited to please God. They were not in the flesh, although they lived in flesh. They carried the flesh but were not carried by it. Therefore, the Apostle adds, **But you are not in the flesh.** He speaks to the people of God, to the Church of God; he wrote to the Romans, but he spoke to the universal Church. He spoke to the wheat, not to the chaff; he addressed himself to the hidden mass and not to the visible straw. Let each one know in his own heart if he is part of the wheat.

Rm 8:9

VERSE NINE. **However you are not in the flesh, but in the spirit, provided that the Spirit of God dwells in you,** if you are delighted with the law of God according to the interior man. This is the meaning of the expression 'provided that the Spirit of God dwells in you', for if you presume on your own spirit, you are still in the flesh. Thus, you are not in the flesh if you are in the Spirit of God. If the Spirit of God withdraws, man's spirit falls again into the flesh by its own weight. It returns to carnal deeds, to carnal desires, and the last state of that man is worse

Lk 11:26

than the first.* Therefore, have free will in such a way that you implore help. 'You are not in the flesh.' Is this by your own strength? Far from it. How then? 'Provided that the Spirit of God dwells in you.' **Now if any man does not have the Spirit of Christ, he does not belong to him.** Therefore, let a weak and defective nature not boast or puff itself up, or claim power for itself, because if any man does not have the Spirit of Christ, he does not belong to him. The Spirit of Christ is the Spirit of God; the same Spirit belongs to the Father and the Son. But behold, with the help of his mercy we have the Spirit of Christ, and know that the Spirit of God is in us by the delight we take in justice and by the true Catholic faith. But what about this mortal flesh? What about the law fighting against the law of the mind? What about that groan, 'Wretched man that I am'? Listen.

Rm 8:10-11

VERSES TEN AND ELEVEN. **If Christ is in you, although the body is dead because of sins, the spirit is life because of justice.** The body, he says, is dead, not because of earthly frailty but because of sin. He says very carefully that the body is dead, not that it is mortal. For, before it was changed into that incorruption which is promised in the incorruption of the saints, it could have been mortal although it would not die, just as our body can be subject to sickness without being sick. Is a man's flesh capable of being sick even if by some accident he dies before he becomes sick? So, that body was already mortal, but a change into eternal incorruption was to remove that mortality if justice, that is, obedience, remained in man. What was mortal did not die except by reason of sin. The change that will take place in the resurrection will not only remove that death which occurred because of sin, but also that mortality which the animal body had before sin. The Apostle does not say, 'He will give life to your dead bodies', although he had used the word 'dead' before, but he says, **He will give life to your mortal bodies,** so that they will not only not be dead but will not be mortal either, when what is animal shall rise as spiritual, and this mortal body shall put on immortality and shall be absorbed by life.* When he described the grace of the present time and said that the body was dead because of sin—since the reward for sin, i.e., the necessity of death, remained in it as long as it was not yet renewed by the resurrection—and that the spirit was life because of justice—since we sigh toward the justice of faith according to the inner man when renewal has begun, although we are still burdened with the body of this death—nevertheless, so that human ignorance might have something to hope for in regard to the resurrection of the body, the Apostle said that even that which he said was dead in the present life because of the reward of sin would be brought to life in the future world as the reward of justice, and not merely in such a way that what was dead would be alive, but that from being mortal it would endure as immortal. Notice the brilliance of the Apostle's knowledge. Whatever he says here he says to dissuade men from thinking that they derive little or no benefit from the grace of Christ because they must die a bodily death. They should note that the body still bears the punishment of sin which was contracted in the condition of death, but that the spirit already has begun to live on account of the justice of faith, although it* had been killed in man by a kind of death from infidelity. Do not, therefore,

I Cor 15:44,55

PL: the body

think that it is a small gift that Christ is in you, and that your spirit by justice lives now in your body which is dead because of sin, and for the same reason do not despair of the life of the body itself. **If the Spirit of him who raised up Jesus from the dead dwells in you, he shall bring to life also your mortal bodies because of his Spirit which dwells in you.** He even says how it is that life converts death into life by killing it.

Rm 8:12-13   VERSES TWELVE AND THIRTEEN. **Therefore, brothers, we are debtors, not to the flesh, that we should live according to the flesh, for if you live according to the flesh you will die. But if by the Spirit you put to death the deeds of the flesh you will live.** What does this mean except that if you live according to death, you shall totally die, but if by living according to life you give life to death, you shall totally live? Therefore, brothers, having received help, the help given to us from above by the arm of the Lord, that is, having received the Holy Spirit, 'we are debtors, not to the flesh that we should live according to the flesh,' but that we should have love, and that by it we might be able to perform good works, for faith cannot operate except by love. 'For if you live according to the flesh, you will die.' He said earlier that the prudence of the flesh is death, not because the flesh is bad, but because it is bad to live according to the flesh. 'If by the Spirit you put to death the deeds of the flesh you will live.' This is our task in this life, to put to death the deeds of the flesh by the spirit, to afflict them daily, to diminish them, rein them in and slay them. The deeds of the flesh mean carnal concupiscences. Not to consent to them is great praise; not to have them is perfection. But lest anyone trust in the strength of his own spirit, he adds:

Rm 8:14   VERSE FOURTEEN. **All who are influenced by the Spirit of God are sons of God.** To be influenced is something more than to be directed. He who is directed does something and he is directed in order that he may do it rightly. But he who is influenced is scarcely understood to do anything himself. And yet the grace of the Saviour gives so much to our wills that the Apostle does not hesitate to say, 'All who are influenced by the Spirit of God are sons of God'. The sons of God are influenced to do what should be done and, when they have done it, they give thanks to him by whom they were influenced, because they acted as they should; namely, with delight and love of justice, and they rejoice over the sweetness that the Lord gave them 'so that the earth should yield her fruit'.* The Apostle gives the name of helper to the one who influences, because he also does something. The sons of God are, therefore, those who are influenced by the Spirit, not by the letter; they are those whom the Spirit excites, enlightens and helps, not those whom the law commands, threatens and makes promises to.

Cf. Ps 84:13

Rm 8:15

VERSE FIFTEEN. **For you have not received the spirit of bondage again in fear** as on Mount Sinai, **but you have received the spirit of adoption of sons,** so that, in a wonderful but true way, we slaves might not be slaves. That is, we are slaves with a chaste fear which characterizes a slave entering into the joy of his Lord; we are not slaves with a fear of being cast outside, which characterizes a slave who does not remain in the house forever.* Sons serve, and yet they are free, and for this reason they bear the name of children. The same Spirit is both the spirit of servitude and the spirit of liberty; the former works on tablets of stone, i.e., on hearts hardened in fear, but the latter works on the tablets of the heart in charity. But what is slavery in fear? No one who acts unwillingly acts well, even if what he does is good, because the spirit of fear is in no way profitable where there is no spirit of charity. If the commandment of God is accomplished in the fear of punishment and not the love of justice, it is accomplished in a servile way, and therefore is not accomplished. 'But you have received the spirit of adoption.'

Cf. Heb 3:3-6

A father usually rejoices in an only son who will alone possess everything and has no one with whom to divide the inheritance. Not so God the Father. He had an only Son, but was unwilling to have only one, and so he sent him into the world so that he might have adopted brothers. The Only-begotten came and took on himself the sins with which we were involved, lest the grace of adoption be impeded by them. **In whom we cry: Abba, Father!** Of these two words, one is taken from the law and the other from uncircumcision. Those who cry out seek something. What do they seek except that for which they hunger [and thirst:] namely, justice?* The only Son of God gave his slaves the power to become sons of God* and he admonished them to ask, seek, and knock so that they might receive, find, and have the door opened to them.* In him we cry out, that is, in him who pours forth charity in our hearts, without which anyone who cries out does so in vain.

[PL omits]
Cf. Mt 5:6
Cf. Jn 1:12

Cf. Mt 7:7-8

Rm 8:16

VERSE SIXTEEN. **For the Spirit himself gives testimony to our spirit that we are sons of God.** No soul at all capable of reasoning is so perverse that God does not speak in his heart. Ask your heart* if it is full of charity. Ask your soul if it is influenced* by fear or by love. He who pours forth charity in your heart bears witness to your spirit as to what is done in it. The Spirit himself testifies about himself. How? Do you wish to hear now? Listen to him by whose gift you receive the Spirit, if you have him. 'If anyone loves me he will keep my commandments.'* If love and the delight of justice move you to keep the commandments of God, that is the testimony of the Spirit of God dwelling in you. If you are such, you are a child and a son; all that the Father has is yours. The Spirit of adoption inspires in you the love of the Father. In the Spirit you cry out to the degree that you love, because he is the love and the cry in which you cry, 'Abba, Father'. If you invoke the Father with a son's affection, the Holy Spirit, the author of grace, insinuates your spirit into himself, and by this effect bears witness that you are a son of God.

viscera
aguntur

Cf. Jn 14:15,23

Rm 8:17

VERSE SEVENTEEN. **And if sons, heirs also;**

heirs indeed of God, and joint heirs with Christ. When the Lord Jesus Christ died on the cross, we who are his sons were made his heirs, as he himself said, 'The children of the bridegroom cannot fast as long as the bridegroom is with them'.* We are called heirs because he left us possession of the Church's peace through the faith of the temporal dispensation which we possess in this life; as he himself said, 'I give my peace to you; I leave you peace'.* We shall be made joint heirs with him when death is absorbed in victory at the end of the world. For then 'we shall be like him, because we shall see him as he is'.* We shall not obtain the inheritance by the death of his Father, for he cannot die, and moreover he is our inheritance, as Scripture says, 'The Lord is the portion of my inheritance'.* But because we were called as little children and not yet fit to contemplate spiritual things, divine mercy accommodated itself to our lowly thoughts, so that whatever we did not see plainly and clearly, however much we tried to see, that very thing, which we saw in an enigma,* dies when we began to see face to face. Rightly therefore is it said that that which is taken away dies, for 'when that which is perfect has come, that which is incomplete shall be done away with'. Therefore, to some extent and in an obscure way the Father dies in our regard, and he becomes our inheritance when he is possessed face to face. It is not that he dies, but that our imperfect vision of him is destroyed by perfect vision. And yet if that imperfect vision did not nourish us, we could not be made worthy for that other complete and direct vision.

But if the text is to be understood in regard to our Lord Jesus Christ, we cannot be joint heirs with him unless he also is an heir, that is, unless he is understood to be an heir in his body, which is the Church. We are joint heirs with him, although the Church is composed of us, just as we are called sons of his mother, although she is also composed of us.

It can be understood simply that we are heirs of God inasmuch as we are made firm possessors of his glory, and we are co-heirs with Christ inasmuch as Christ, the glorified man, deigns to have us share and participate in

margin:
Cf Lk 5:34
Cf. Jn 14:27
1 Jn 3:2
Ps 15:5
Cf. 1 Cor 13:12

his glory. For the whole Christ will receive the inheritance. 'Inheritance' comes from the word 'to inhere'.² We who are the members of his body should hope for an inheritance by which we shall obtain the good which never passes, and shall avoid the evil which has no end.

If, however, we suffer with him, that we may also be glorified with him Since Christ prepared the inheritance for himself by his own blood and mortal passion, it is necessary that those who wish to be fellow heirs with him be heirs of the passion as well. 'For because he himself has suffered and been tempted, he is able to help those who are tempted.'* *Heb 2:18*
The mere memory of his passion should be enough to strengthen us to endure all things for him. Those insults and scourges, that ignominious garment, the face struck and spat upon, the crown of thorns, and to omit much more, his cross and death meditated on, what will these things not effect in us? What about the magnitude of the rewards promised? Therefore, the text continues:

Rm 8:18

VERSE EIGHTEEN. **For I reckon that the sufferings of this time are not worthy to be compared**—for the sufferings have an end, but the promised gifts have no end; the sufferings can be calculated, the rewards are beyond calculation—**with the glory to come,** with the great multitude of the sweetness of God, which he has hidden for those who fear him, and which he will perfect in those who hope in him.* *Cf. Ps 30:20*
He will so reveal it to us that it will be fulfilled in us. In this life the reckoning of consolations is 'according to the multitude of sorrows',* but in that life there is no *Cf. Ps 93:19*
reckoning. What is the glory we expect but to see God and to associate with his holy angels?

Rm 8:19

VERSE NINETEEN. **For the expectation of creation waits for the revelation of the sons of God.** That which suffers pain in us because we mortify the deeds of the flesh, when we hunger or thirst through abstinence, when we refrain our lustful pleasures through charity, when we patiently endure tearing injuries and spiteful stings, while we labor for the harvest of mother Church, neglecting and denying our own pleasures, whatever in us grieves in this struggle is a creature. The body and soul grieve, for they are assuredly creatures, and they await the revelation of the sons of God; that is, they wait to see when* their call to that glory to which they are called will appear. The Only-begotten Son of God cannot be called a creature, since all things that God has made were made through him; but we are distinctly called creatures before that revelation of glory, and we are distinctly called sons of God, although we merit this by adoption. For he is the Only-begotten Son by nature. Therefore, 'the expectation of creation', that is, our expectation, 'waits for the revelation of the sons of God', that is, when what has been promised shall appear, and when what we are now through hope will be manifest in reality. 'For we are sons of God, and it has not yet appeared what we shall be. We know that when he appears, we shall be like him, because we shall see him as he is.'* It is the very revelation of the sons of God that the expectation now awaits. Creation does not wait for the revelation of some other nature which is not creation; but creation as it is now, while it is, awaits what it will be. It is as if it were said that a painter was at work, with the colors near him and prepared for his work, and that the expectation of the colors is awaiting the manifestation of the image. Not that they will then be different or that they will be something other than colors, but only that they will have a different dignity.

PL: how

1 Jn 3:2

Rm 8:20

Qo 1:2-3
Gen 3:19

VERSE TWENTY. **For creation was subject to vanity.** This is the same as the text, 'Vanity of vanities and all is vanity. What gain has a man for all his labor that he has under the sun?'* To the same man it was said, 'In labor you shall eat your bread'.* 'Creation was made subject to vanity, not willingly.' 'Not willingly' was well added. Man sinned willingly but he was not condemned willingly. The willing sin was to act against a precept of the truth; the penalty of sin was to be subject to deceit. Creation was not subject to vanity willingly, **but by reason of him who made it subject, in hope,** that is, because of the justice and clemency of him who does not leave sin unpunished, and who does not will the sinner to be beyond healing. We can understand the text in a higher sense. Creation—that is, man himself—since he already lost the seal of the image because of sin, remained merely a creature, and that creature who is not yet called by the perfect form of sons, but is only called a creature, shall be liberated from the slavery of death. The expression 'that creature shall be liberated' makes it understood to be in the same category as ourselves. There should be no despair about those who are not yet called sons of God but are only creatures since they have not yet believed, because they will believe and will be freed from the servitude of death, just as we were who are now the sons of God, although it has not yet appeared what we shall be.

Rm 8:21-22 VERSES TWENTY-ONE AND TWENTY-TWO. **It shall therefore be delivered from the servitude of death into the liberty of the glory of the sons of God.** That is, even they will be turned from slaves into freedmen, and from being dead men they will become glorious in the perfect life possessed by the sons of God. Another meaning can be given to the name of creature. Every creature is summed up in man: not that all the angels and superlative virtues and powers are in him, or heaven and earth and sea and all that is in them, but because every creature is partly spiritual, partly animal, and partly corporeal.[3] To begin from the lower things, the corporeal creature is distended through space; the animal gives life to the corporeal; the spiritual rules the animal, and rules it well, when the spiritual subjects it to the rule of God. When it transgresses his precepts, then it becomes involved in labors and distresses through the very things which it could rule. Thus, every creature is in man, because he understands with the spirit, and feels with the soul, and is moved bodily through space.

Every creature groans and suffers in man. The Apostle did not say 'all creatures' but 'every creature', as if someone should say, 'Men who are healthy see the sun, but not all men see it.' So in man every creature exists, because man understands, lives, and has a body; but not all creatures are in him, because besides him there are angels who understand and live. There are also bodies which live and exist, and there are bodies which only exist; yet to live is better than not to live, and it is better to understand than to live without understanding.

And is in labor. Therefore, it is said, 'A woman when she is in labor has sorrow; but when she has given birth, she no longer remembers the anguish for joy.'* Since man in his misery groans and suffers, every creature groans and suffers even till now.

Jn 16:21

Even till now is rightly said because even if some are already in Abraham's bosom, and even if the robber who entered paradise with the Lord on the same day he believed has ceased to suffer, yet even till now all creation groans and suffers. For all creation exists in those men who are not yet freed, because of man's spirit, and soul, and body.

Rm 8:23

VERSE TWENTY-THREE. **And not only** does all creation groan and suffer, **but also we ourselves.** That is, not only do the body and soul and spirit suffer in man because of the difficulties of the body, but also we ourselves, not counting our bodies, groan in ourselves. And he spoke well in saying, **we who have the firstfruits of the Spirit,** meaning those whose spirits are offered to God as a sacrifice, and who are seized by the divine fire of charity. These are the firstfruits of man, because truth first obtains the spirit and by means of it seizes the rest. The man who says, 'With the mind I serve the law of God, but with the flesh the law of sin,'* has offered his firstfruits to God, as has the one who says, 'I serve God in my spirit.'* Also, the one of whom it is said, 'The spirit indeed is willing, but the flesh is weak'.* But the burnt offering has not yet been offered, for he says, 'Unhappy man that I am, who shall deliver me from the body of this death?'* and because the following words still apply to such men; 'He shall give life to your mortal bodies

Rm 7:25
Rm 1:9

Mt 26:41

Rm 7:24

Rm 8:11 because of his Spirit which dwells in you'.* The burnt offering will take place when death is absorbed in victory, when it will be said, 'O death, where is your

Cf. 1 Cor 15:55 struggle? O death, where is your sting?'*

Then the Apostle says that not only every creature, that is, the soul together with the body, **but even we ourselves who have the firstfruits of the Spirit,** that is, we souls who have already offered firstfruits, our minds, to God groan in ourselves, aside from the body, **waiting for the adoption, the redemption of our body,** so that even the body, receiving the benefit of the adoption of the sons of God, might manifest that we are wholly liberated sons of God with every sort of trouble put behind us.

Rm 8:24-25 VERSES TWENTY-FOUR AND TWENTY-FIVE. **For we are saved by hope. But hope that is seen is not hope. For who hopes for what he sees? But if we hope for that which we do not see we wait through patience.** What does he await through patience? The health, that is, redemption of his body. He rejoices that he is redeemed, but he is not really redeemed yet. He is secure in hope, but groans in hope that he might arrive at the reality. He was awaiting health of body, because he did not have the health that hunger and thirst destroy if they are not relieved. We are already redeemed, but we are saved in hope, because we await what we hope for; we do not yet have it. In our Head our flesh is saved in reality and not merely in hope, and we groan that this has not yet been accomplished in us. Since it is promised, we hope for it; and when it is deferred, we await it with patience. Therefore, this groan is excusable, for faith excuses it, hope emits it, and charity strengthens it. The holier a person is and the more filled with holy desire, the more abundantly does he weep over this in his prayers. The firstfruits of the Spirit and the expectation of divine adoption cause this. The fact that we have come to such misery is the punishment of sin, and the punishment is more drawn out than the guilt, lest the guilt be thought small if the punishment also ended with the guilt. Thus temporal punishment retains its hold on man either to show the misery that is due, or to correct an unstable life, or to exercise needed patience; this is true even of the man whom guilt no longer holds liable to eternal damnation. This condition deserves tears but not censure.

'For we are saved by hope', because the full adoption of sons will bring about the redemption even of our bodies. We already have the firstfruits of the Spirit, and therefore are in reality already sons of God. As for the rest, just as we are saved in hope and renewed in hope, so we are also sons of God. Because we are not yet saved in reality, we are not yet fully renewed, and we are not yet sons of God but sons of the world. We have already begun to be similar to God by possessing the firstfruits of the Spirit, and yet are still dissimilar through the remnants of our oldness. The whole sinner will pass into adoption, so that if you seek his place you will not find it. In the meantime let us hope* for what we do not see. Our hope is our lantern. As long as we do not see and yet hope, it is night but the lantern shines. But if we neither see nor hope, it is night and the lantern does not shine. What could be more wretched than such darkness? But the word of God which is daily spoken to us is a continuous infusion of oil to keep our lamp from being extinguished.

PL: we hope

Rm 8:26

VERSE TWENTY-SIX. **Likewise the Spirit also helps our infirmity. For we do not know what we should pray for as we ought.** Whatever prayer obtains or seeks to obtain is obviously a gift of God; if it were within one's power, it would not be asked for. But prayer itself is placed among the gifts of grace, when the Apostle says that 'we do not know what we should pray for', unless we are helped by the Spirit, lest the merit of praying should be thought to have precedence so that grace would not be given gratuitously, in which case it would not be grace if it were rendered as something owed. **The Spirit asks on our behalf and groans,** because he inspires in us the interior disposition to ask and to groan. But his help is expressed in such a way that he himself is said to do what he makes us do. Just as without the spirit of faith there is no belief and without the spirit of hope there is no hope, and without the spirit of love there is no love, so without the spirit of prayer no prayer is as it should be. 'One and the same Spirit does all these things.'* Those persons in whom the Spirit does not dwell are helped by him to be among the faithful; those in whom he already dwells through faith are helped by him to be among the faithful.⁴ The Spirit who intercedes for us is the very charity which he inspires in us. Since he gave it he cannot close his ears to it.⁵ Rest easy. Let charity request and God's ears are there.

1 Cor 12:11

The Apostle says, 'We do not know what we should pray for as we ought.' And what indeed, except that we may be blessed? Beatitude is defined in different ways by different people. Let our beatitude be that of which it is said, 'Blessed is the people whose Lord is its God.'* Let us ask fearlessly to be among that people so that we may come to contemplate him and live with him forever. In our tribulations which can either help or hurt us, for they are troublesome to the sense of our infirmity, we pray God that we may endure them; but we owe the Lord God this degree of devotion, that if he does not take them away from us, we should not think that he is neglecting us. Rather let us hope for more ample goods as a reward for loving patience in the face of evils.⁶ When we pray for others because we love them as ourselves, we ask for them as we do for ourselves and since the Lord God knows what should be done, he allows us to follow patiently and willingly in what he wills to do. But in all the things for which we pray, we should most firmly believe that if something happened other than what we prayed for, it must have been what God willed, rather than what we willed. In that way, therefore, 'He asks for the saints,'* that is, the Holy Spirit teaches them to ask.

Ps 143:15

Rm 8:27

But there are other spiritual types of intimate prayers by which they enjoy God about which he says, 'My children are in bed with me.'* They are unknown to us who deal with externals through the

Lk 11:7

senses of the flesh. Often in its prayer the faithful and devoted soul tries to direct the mind's gaze toward him to whom it desires to offer in the Holy Spirit the firstfruits of the Spirit and the sacrifice of its prayer, and it tries to contemplate the invisible and to see with the quivering pupil of the inner eye, but, fatigued by the difficulty, it returns to itself and takes a step up for itself out of itself. First it considers itself, if it can, and then investigates that nature which is above it, as far as it is able. But if our mind is scattered in carnal images, it is in no way able to consider either itself or the nature of the soul, because it is blinded, as if by obstacles, by the thoughts by which it is enticed. Therefore, the first step is to recollect itself; the second is to see what it is like when recollected; the third is to rise above itself and give itself to the contemplation of its invisible Maker. But it can in no way recollect itself unless it first learns to restrain the images of earthly and heavenly things from the eyes of the mind. It must learn to spit out and trample upon whatever comes to its mind from the sense of sight, of hearing, of smell, of touch and of bodily taste, so that it can seek its true self, as it is without these elements. When it thinks about these things, it reflects inwardly upon certain kinds of bodily shadows. All these things are to be rejected from the mind's eye with a discreet hand so that the soul can consider itself as created beneath God and above the body. After the soul understands its small measure and is not disturbed with itself but is recollected and elevated and knows that it transcends all bodily things and has moved from the understanding of itself to an understanding of its Maker, then the understanding of God begins to operate in it as differently from its own understanding as the nature of uncircumscribed light differs from the nature of the soul.[7] What the soul understands it grasps; but in this case, in an unusual way, it does not grasp but is grasped. Something sensible happens to it which only enlightened love is permitted to feel, a certain sweetness, not one which love has merited, but which, once tasted, causes love, something which is not known and sensed, the most

	solid substance of things hoped for, a most certain
Cf. Heb 11:1	evidence of things that appear not,* the faithful testi-
	mony of the Lord to the christian faith bestowing
Cf. Ps 18:8	wisdom on the little ones.* This is felt, this is relished

by the little, tranquil one on whom the Spirit of God rests, so that the things which pertain to the flesh and to the world or to any creature, become so insipid for him that he would like to die while this is permitted to continue. He prays for what he does not know, since he does not know what he is experiencing. For it is the Spirit which desires and asks on his behalf, and the Spirit makes him experience what as yet he does not know, and the Spirit makes him ask and desire that which he does not know through his senses.

Rm 8:27	VERSE TWENTY-SEVEN. And he who searches the hearts knows what the Spirit desires, that is, what he causes to be desired. He will fulfil it when his prom-
Jn 8:28	ise is fulfilled: 'Then you will know that I am he.'* Asking one thing of the Lord, seeking one thing, seek-
Cf. Ps 26:4,8	ing his face, searching for his face,* he throws away,

rejects and reproves whatever occurs to his thought. He knows that this is not what he seeks, although he does not yet know just what that thing is. There is in him a certain kind of learned ignorance taught by the Spirit of God which helps our infirmity.[8] The Spirit humbles man by exercising man, and by humiliation forms and conforms man to the countenance which he seeks until, renewed to the image of him who created him, he begins through the unity of similarity to be a son who is always with the Father, to whom all the Father's possessions belong, and to whom, while others come and go, it is said, 'You remain here with

Deut 5:31	me.'* Meanwhile let him who seeks seek. Let him walk in the light of God's face, and let his judgment
Cf. Ps 16:2	come forth from God's countenance,* so that the following text may be fulfilled in the meantime:
Rm 8:28	VERSE TWENTY-EIGHT. We know that for those who love God all things work together to good, for those who are called according to his purpose.

When the Apostle said, 'We know that for those who love God all things work together to good', he knew that some loved God but did not remain in that good to the end, and so he quickly added, 'for those who are called according to his purpose'. For these persevere in the love of God right to the end. Even if for a time they turn away, they return to bring their initial goodness to completion. Then the Apostle adds the following to show what it means to be called according to his purpose:

Rm 8:29-30

VERSES TWENTY-NINE AND THIRTY. **For, whom he foreknew he also predestined to be conformed to the image of his Son, that he might be the firstborn among many brothers. And those whom he predestined he also called** according to his purpose. **Those whom he called he also justified, and those whom he justified he also glorified.** He foreknew, he predestined, he called, he justified. All these things are already brought to pass, because all men are already foreknown and predestined, and many are already called and justified. 'And he glorified them', which he placed at the end, should be understood as that glory of which he said, 'When Christ appears, who is your life, you also shall appear with him in glory'.*

Col 3:4

This has not yet come to pass, just as those two, 'he called' and 'he justified', have not yet happened to all of whom they were said. For, even to the end of the world many shall be called and justified.

The author used verbs in the past tense about future things as if God had already done what he had decided from all eternity should be done. Therefore, the prophet Isaiah says, 'He made those things which shall be'.* Those who in God's most provident order have been foreknown, predestined, called, justified and glorified, are already sons of God, and cannot completely perish, and I am speaking not only about those who are not yet reborn but even of those not yet born. For such lovers of God all things work together to good, and that is absolutely all things, to such an extent that even if some of them wander and go astray, this itself turns to their profit, since they

Cf. Is 44:7, 41:22

return more humble and wiser. They learn that even in the life of justice they should rejoice with fear, not claiming to their own virtue the power to remain faithful, and not saying in their abundance, 'I shall never be moved'.* Rather they ought to rejoice in the Lord with fear, lest they perish from the just way in which they have begun to walk* while they assign their gifts to themselves. The Apostle used these words in the text, 'With fear and trembling work out your salvation', and showing why with fear and trembling he said, 'For it is God who works in you both to will and to accomplish, according to his good will'.* Although the death of the flesh originated in the sin of the first man, yet the good use of the flesh produced glorious martyrs; therefore, not only death, but also all the evils of this world, and men's labors and sorrows, although stemming from the merits of sin, especially of original sin, because of which life itself has been fettered by the bond of death, should remain even when sins have been remitted. By means of them man should strive for truth, and through them the virtue of the faithful is exercised so that the new man is prepared through the New Testament for the new world amidst the evils of this world, wisely tolerating the misery that this life of condemnation has deserved, prudently rejoicing that it will come to an end, and faithfully and patiently awaiting the happiness of the future life.

When it is said that God cooperates with us it should be understood that we can perform no works unless God either causes us to will, or cooperates with us when we do will. The text, 'It is God who works in us to will',* speaks of him working in us so that we will; and the text, 'We know that for those who love God all things work together to good',* speaks of him cooperating. But how is it that all things work like this, since even those which are reckoned adverse are included?[9] Even if the enemies of the Church receive the power to afflict her bodily, they exercise her patience. If they oppose her only by their bad opinions, they exercise her wisdom, and they exercise her good will in that she may love her enemies.

Ps 29:7

Ps 2:11-12

Phil 2:12-13

Phil 2:12

Rm 8:28

'For, whom he foreknew he also predestined to be made conformed to the image of his Son, that he might be the firstborn among many brothers.' Predestination is the preparation of grace and it cannot exist without foreknowledge, but foreknowledge can exist without predestination. By predestination God foreknew what he was going to do. Therefore, it was said, 'He made those things which shall be'.* He is capable of foreknowing even what he does not do, such as those sins which are the punishment of other sins. Therefore, it is said, 'God delivered them up to a base mind and to improper conduct'.* This is not a sin on God's part but a judgment. So God's predestination for good is a preparation [for grace], as I said, and grace is the effect of that same predestination.¹⁰ This and nothing else is the predestination of the saints: the foreknowledge and the preparation of divine benefits by which whoever is freed is most certainly freed. Where do the rest remain except in the mass of perdition, by the just judgment of God?¹¹

Cf. Is 44:7; 41:22

Rm 1:28

[PL omits]

The Apostle's words that the predestined are conformed to the image of the Son of God can be understood according to the inner man. So in another place he says to us, 'Be not conformed to this world, but be reformed in the newness of your minds'.* We are conformed to the Son of God in those ways in which we are reformed so as not to be conformed to this world. The same words can also be taken in this other sense, that as he is conformed to us in mortality, so we shall be conformed to him in immortality, and this meaning pertains to his resurrection.¹² 'Those whom he foreknew he predestined to be made conformed to the image of his Son, that he might be the firstborn among many brothers.' He is firstborn from the dead, according to the same Apostle, because by death his flesh was sown in dishonor but rose again in glory.*¹³ 'Those whom he predestined he also called; and those whom he called he also justified.' That sanctification is given to the just, but so that they may be justified the call precedes and it is not based on merit but on the grace of God. 'For all have sinned and need the glory of God.'* Those whom he called 'he also justified; and

Rm 12:2

Cf. Col 1:18, 1 Cor 15:43

Rm 3:23

those whom he justified he also glorified'. The one who said, 'O Lord, you have crowned us as with the shield of your good will',* is a witness that the call is not based on our merits but on God's benevolence. God's good will precedes our good will so that he calls sinners to repentance, and these are the arms by which the enemy is assaulted, and against him the following words are spoken:

Ps 5:13

VERSES THIRTY-THREE, THIRTY-ONE AND THIRTY TWO. **Who shall make accusations against the elect of God? If God is for us, who is against us? He who spared not even his Only-begotten Son, but delivered him up for us all.** 'For if, when we were still enemies, Christ died for us, much more when we are reconciled shall we be saved from wrath through him.'* This is the unconquerable shield with which the enemy is repelled when he suggests that we despair of salvation in the midst of our tribulations and temptations.[14] The way that we tend to eternal and blessed life is first by condemning our sins, and then by living well, so that after an evil life has been condemned and a good life has been led, we may merit eternal life. According to the decree of his secret justice and goodness, God called those whom he predestined, and justified those whom he called, and he glorified those whom he justified.* Our predestination is not made in us but secretly by God in his foreknowledge; the remaining three things are carried out in us: the call, the justification, and the glorification. We are called by predestination to penance, for that was the way the Lord began to evangelize. 'Do penance, for the kingdom of heaven is at hand.'* We are justified by the renewal of mercy and the fear of judgment. Therefore, it is said, 'Save me, O God, by your name, and judge me in your strength'.* He who has already been saved is not afraid to be judged. Called, we renounce the devil through penance; justified, we are healed through mercy lest we fear judgment; glorified, we pass to eternal life. I think it is to this that the Lord's words refer when he says, 'Behold I cast out devils today and tomorrow, and the third day I am

Rm 8:33, 31-32

Cf. Rm 5:10,9

Rm 8:30

Mt 4:17

Ps 53:3

Lk 13:32 consummated.'* He showed the same thing in his three days of passion and watching. For he was crucified, buried and rose again. On the cross he triumphed over principalities and powers; he rested in the tomb; he was exalted in the resurrection. Similarly, penance crucifies, justice gives rest, eternal life glorifies.¹⁵

'What shall we say then to these things? If God is for us, who is against us?' It is as if he said, 'God is for us in predestining us; God is for us in calling us; God is for us in justifying us and God is for us in glorifying us. Therefore, if God is for us, who is against us?' He predestined us before we were; he called us when we were turned away; he justified us when we were sinners; he glorified us when we were mortal. Whoever wishes to oppose those who are predestined, called, *[PL omits]* justified [and glorified] by God wages war against the Omnipotent One. How do you prove that God is for you? 'Easily', he replies, '**because he spared not even his own Son, but delivered him up for us all.**' Therefore, let not the roar of the world terrify him for whom the Maker of the world has been delivered up. **Has he not also given us all things with him?** What 'all' is this? That will be known when this promise is fulfilled; its guarantee we already received when Christ died for us. Still you wish to know what this 'all' means? Man's spirit will have no defect under which it lies, or to which it yields, or against which it struggles even laudably, since he has been perfected with a most tranquil virtue. There he will possess extensive and precise knowledge of all things without any error or effort, for he will drink from the very fountain of wisdom with supreme happiness and without diffculty. His body will be wholly subject to the spirit, and endowed with sufficient life so that it will need no nourishment. For it will not be a natural body but a spiritual one, truly possessing the substance of flesh without the corruption of flesh. There all things will be so possessed that each single thing belongs to all, and all things belong to each one. For just as greed holds nothing without anxiety, so charity holds nothing with anxiety. All things, therefore, will be ours, since things superior to us will be ours to live by;

equal things will be ours to live with, and inferior things will be ours to control.

Rm 8:33-34   VERSES THIRTY-THREE AND THIRTY-FOUR. **Who shall make accusations against the elect of God? God who justifies; who is it who condemns?** etc. What is observed with ambiguous distinctions is to be observed also with ambiguous assertions. For, unless they are caused by the reader's carelessness, they are corrected either by the rules of faith or by reference to the text preceding or following. Of if neither of these is used as a corrective, doubts will remain, so that however the reader interprets he will not be at fault. For, unless faith restrains us, by which we believe that God will not make accusations against his elect and that Christ will not condemn his elect, we could interpret the sentence thus: 'Who shall make accusations against the elect of God?' as if the answer were, 'God who justifies'. And it is asked, 'Who is it who condemns, Christ Jesus who died?' But because it is sheer madness to believe this, the sentence should be stated in such a way that a *percunctatio* precedes and an *interrogatio* follows. The ancients used to say that there was this difference between *percunctatio* and *interrogatio*: to the former many answers could be made, but to the latter only 'yes' or 'no': The sentence will, therefore, be stated so that after the *percunctatio* by which we say, 'Who shall make accusations against the elect of God?' the following sentence will be spoken like an *interrogatio*; namely, 'God who justifies?' with the tacit response, 'No'. Again we use a *percunctatio*, 'Who is it who condemns?' and again we ask, 'Christ who died, and, what is more, who rose, who is at the right hand of God, and who makes intercession for us?' with the response in each case being 'No'.[16]

In regard to what is said about Christ sitting at the right hand of God, the divine power is shown through a human comparison. It is not that a throne is set up and God the Father sits on it and has his Son sitting with him, but that we cannot understand the Son judging and ruling, except by using our own language.

He intercedes for us by appearing to God the Father in the human nature he assumed for us.

A protestation of great love with spiritual rejoicing follows, caused by the remembrance of great benefits. 'Who,' he asks, 'will separate us from the love of God which is in Christ Jesus our Lord?'* In the Son the Father is loved; in the Son's work the Fathers' love is commended. Therefore, in another place he is called 'the Son of his love'.* Let him who possesses a feeling of love understand the words of a lover. 'Who', he says, 'and by what power, knowledge or craftiness, will separate us predestined, called, justified, and glorified; who will separate us [by the sword,] by counsel, or by example from the love of God, from faith in the beloved, from the love of the one believed in "which is in Christ Jesus our Lord,"* by whom we love to be ruled, by whom we rejoice to be saved, and whom we serve in our spirit?" Not having found who will separate us, we ask what will separate us.

Cf. Rm 8:35-39

Col 1:13

[PL omits]

Rm 8:39

Rm 8:35-37   VERSES THIRTY-FIVE THROUGH THIRTY-SEVEN. **Tribulation or distress** in soul, **famine or nakedness** of body, **the peril of death, or the sword** that slays? **As it is written, 'For your sake we are put to death all the day long. We are accounted as sheep for the slaughter.'** We are not killed nor do we die just once, but all the day long. That is, without intermission we are put to death by afflictions and torments, prepared as we are to give for you* not only our goods but ourselves, like a sheep for slaughter which is not asked for its milk or its wool, but its very life. What wonder is it if a martyr suffers for his God what an avaricious man suffers for his gold? The avaricious man gives himself to the danger of the sea, and says to his gold, 'For you I am put to death all the day long.' The martyr gives himself to torments and the sword, and says to his God, 'For you I am put to death all the day long.' The same words but a different cause. The one does it for Christ; the other for gold. Let Christ reply to his martyr, 'If you die for me, you will find me.' Let the gold answer the greedy man, 'If you die for me, you lose yourself and me.'

PL: for law

But in all these things we overcome, because of
him who has loved us. Why does the text not say,
'whom we have loved'? Because, just as no one
chooses unless he is chosen, so no one loves unless he
is loved. Our love is an affect of the human mind; the
love of God is an affect of God's grace. We are
affected when we love God, but God is not affected
when we are loved by him. Rather, his love is the
Holy Spirit, and when he deigns to give him to us,
through him he pours into our hearts the charity by
which we love him. Therefore, the Father loves us
when he enriches us with the gift of his love; we love
him when we are borne by the whole weight of our
soul toward him. This is what we owe to God alone.
When the flesh and the concupiscence of this life try
to turn this love from God to themselves, the servant
of God suffers the human temptations spoken of
above; but when the malice of spiritual wickedness
attacks the love of God in him, then he suffers the
[PL omits] [super] human temptations which follow. The text
continues:

Rm 8:38-39   VERSES THIRTY-EIGHT AND THIRTY-NINE.
**For I am sure that neither death, nor life, nor angels,
nor principalities, nor powers, nor things present, nor
things to come, nor might, nor height, nor depth, nor
any creature, shall be able to separate us from the love
of God, which is in Christ Jesus our Lord.** Let no one
therefore separate us from God by threatening death,
because the fact of our loving God is something which
cannot die. It only dies by not loving God and not
loving God is its very death, and this is nothing else
than to prefer to love and pursue something else rather
than him. Let no one separate us by promising life,
since no one separates anyone from the fountain by
promising him water. Let an angel not separate us, because when we cling to God no angel is stronger than
our mind. Let power not separate us, for if here
'power' means something which holds sway in the
world, the mind that clings to God is stronger than
the whole world. But if here 'power' means an upright
affection of the soul, then that power or virtue residing

in someone helps join us to God; if it exists in us it joins us to him. Do not let insistent troubles separate us, because we feel them more lightly as we cling more closely to him from whom they try to separate us. Do not let the promise of future things separate us, for it is God who promises whatever future good there will be, and nothing is better than God himself who is present to those who cling to him. 'Nor might, nor height, nor depth.'[17] Just as among the heavenly powers there are some who, by adhering to God through the grace of love, are identified by the name of his power in which they received a prominence above all others, so also among the spirits of the enemy's territory there are those who, clinging with fervent pride and wicked cunning to him who said, 'I will be like the Most High', are called, according to the status of each one's evil, Might or Height or Depth. Among the philosophers of this world are men who dispute vigorously, who are wise in great matters and who carefully examine profound issues. These men often try to separate simpler men from the love of God which is in Christ Jesus, our Lord.

CHAPTER NINE

Rm 9:1-5   VERSES ONE THROUGH FIVE. I speak the truth in Christ, and I am not lying, my conscience bears witness to me in the Holy Spirit that I have great sadness and continual sorrow in my heart. For I have wished that I were cut off from Christ for the sake of my brothers, who are my kinsmen according to the flesh. They are Israelites, to whom belong the adoption of sons, and the glory, the testament, the giving of the law, the service, and the promises; to them belong the patriarchs, and theirs is Christ, according to the flesh, God who is over all things be blessed forever. Amen. See the great sweetness of this well-disposed mind ascending almost to heaven in spiritual exultation over his immense joy for the progress of the Gentiles, and then suddenly descending to the abyss with sorrow of heart for the miserable defection

of his own people. It seems that having left the
others in heaven with God he returns to earth to die
for his own brothers. And as we read that the face of
Moses seemed horned when he left the face of the
Lord, and carnal people could not stand the bright-
Cf. Ex 34:35   ness of his countenance,* so Paul seems insane with
love and totally drunk with the Holy Spirit, unable to
speak sober words, but in ecstacy of mind, saying that
he wishes to be anathema from Christ for Christ, that
is, for his brothers so they might be in Christ. He
wished to be anathema from Christ's blessedness by
embracing Christ's justice, thinking it was more just
in God's sight to wish for the salvation of an entire
race than for that of his own soul alone. But while
this was a wonderful affect of self-transcending love,
a far different effect was forming in the judgment of
the justice of God; for while Paul was offering before
the just Judge the loss of his salvation, not of his love,
for the glory of God and the salvation of his brothers,
[PL omits]   he gained supreme progress in love [and salvation,] since
the salvation of some specially chosen portion of that
Cf. Rm 11:5   people was given to Paul;* nor was he defrauded of
Cf. Rm 11:26   the reward of their universal salvation,* since he
offered himself with such constant love for the salvation of them all. Love has affects and it has effects.
And although it is not apparent to men, all love's
affects find their effects with him who judges the
affects of the mind much more truly than men judge
the effects realized in works. These words of the
Apostle show his affect, since he does not wish to be
anathema from Christ by transgression, but by loving
devotion. It is the languor of a soul that loves but
cannot accomplish what it wishes. So it is the bride
Sg 5:8   in the Canticle says, 'I languish with love'.*

'I speak the truth in Christ, my conscience bears
witness to me in the Holy Spirit.' Blessed soul, whose
truth is founded in Christ, whose conscience is made
solid in the Holy Spirit, in whose conscience burns the
truth of love and in whose confession shines the love
of truth.

Rm 9:2   VERSE TWO. There is great sadness and continual sorrow. Where is that great sadness and that continual sorrow, and where can joy be? **In my heart.** Just as the Apostle serves in the Holy Spirit whomever he serves,* so he grieves in his heart for whomever he grieves.

Cf. Rm 1:9

Rm 9:3

VERSE THREE. **For my brothers who are my kinsmen according to the flesh.** These are the names of a relationship; first is what is natural, and then what is spiritual.*

Cf. 1 Cor 15:46

Rm 9:4-5

VERSES FOUR AND FIVE. **Who are Israelites,** made to see God.

To whom belong the adoption, because the Son of God was sent particularly for them.

And the glory, because to them are entrusted the words of God.

And the testament, because the Old Testament was given to them, and the New is prefigured in the Old.

And the giving of the law, which they especially merited to receive.

And the service, because the law and the prophets especially served their salvation.

And the promises about Christ.

To them belong the patriarchs, of whom Christ was born. This is the principal cause of his grief and sorrow: that the patriarchs were such in Christ's estimation that he chose to be born from them, but that the sons were such that, leaving them, he passed over to the Gentiles.

Rm 9:6

VERSE SIX. **Not as though the word of God has failed.** 'I encountered tribulation and sorrow,' says the prophet.* It is the mark of a prudent man to encounter sorrow when necessary, and to limit sorrow in due time. It is enough for the Apostle to have revealed the sorrow of his heart about the rejection of his people; immediately he finds consolation for himself, saying, 'Not as though the word of God has failed', that is, the promise made to them has not come to nothing. The true Israel shall attain God's promises. But whoever does not see through faith the God who said, 'He who sees me sees also the

Ps 114:3

Jn 14:9	Father,'* cannot be called Israel. Therefore, he says:
Rm 9:6-9 PL: vv 6, 7	VERSES SIX THROUGH NINE. **For all are not Israelites who are of Israel. Neither are they who are the seed of Abraham all children, but they who are the children of promise are accounted for the seed;** that is, those who are sons of that faith of his by which Abraham merited to receive the promise of a future inheritance. This seed was then pointed out in Abraham when, already having many sons whom the Apostle calls 'the children of the flesh', his posterity was placed in Isaac alone who was the son of the promise. As the Lord said, **'In Isaac shall your seed
PL: vv 8,9 [PL omits]	be called.* For this is the word of promise.'** [He strives to show how Isaac is not the son of the flesh but the son of God, and he returns to what was written in Genesis about him, "This is the word of
Gen 18:10	promise."*] **'According to this time will I come, and Sarah shall have a son.'** Isaac therefore was not born according to ordinary carnal birth, because Abraham was dead in his body and Sarah's womb was dead also, but he was born through the power of the promise. He is rightly called the son of God, and not of the flesh, because he was born by the visit of God and by the
Cf. Gen 18:10	word of God.*
Rm 9:10-13	VERSES TEN THROUGH THIRTEEN. **And not only she.** This reason is not only to be accepted in regard to Isaac but to Jacob also. For Rebecca as well did not give birth according to the ordinary course of carnal birth. For when she had conceived twins by lying with Isaac once after her long and tedious sterility, and when the children **were not yet born and had done nothing good or evil** among men, the divine choice fell to Jacob and it was said, **'The elder shall
Gen 25:23 Mal 1:2-3	serve the younger,'*** and also, **'Jacob I have loved, but Esau I have hated.'*** From these sayings we are taught, Paul says, that **God's purpose stands according to his choice,** and that it is **not from works but from the grace of him who calls** that 'the elder shall serve the younger' and 'Jacob I have loved, but Esau I have hated'. We are taught that it is not the children of the

flesh but the children of God who are counted as his seed, since Isaac is chosen from many sons, and of two sons the younger is chosen for adoption as God's son; and so it is true that the promises of God hold, not in the carnal children, but in the children of God,[18] and that the divine purpose abides according to his choice, not from works but from the grace of the one who calls, and not on carnal children but on the children of God. Paul in explaining this thought used the testimony of a prophet living much later, saying, 'Jacob I have loved but Esau I have hated', so that
[PL omits] what existed in divine predestination [through grace] before the children were born should be openly understood later through the prophet. For what did he love in Jacob before he had done anything good, except the free gift of his own mercy? And what did he hate in Esau before he was born or had done anything evil, except original sin? For God would not love justice in Jacob, because he had done nothing just, neither would he hate in Esau the nature which he himself had made good. Since the Apostle had proposed an astonishing matter in that he could rightly say that God loved one and hated the other before either of them were born or had done anything good or evil, he addressed the consternation of his hearer by proposing a question to himself, saying:

Rm 9:14 VERSE FOURTEEN. **What shall we say then? Is there injustice with God? Certainly not.** This was the place where it could be said, 'God foresaw their future works when he predicted that the elder would serve the younger.' But the Apostle does not say this. Rather he wished his words to avail to the commendation of the grace and glory of God, lest anyone should dare to preen over the merits of his own works. And when he has said, 'Certainly not' to the suggestion that there could be injustice with God, as though we had asked him 'How did you prove this, when you assert that the elder shall serve the younger and not from works but from the one who calls them?' the Apostle says:

Rm 9:15-16	VERSES FIFTEEN AND SIXTEEN. 'I will have mercy on whom I will have mercy, and I will show
Ex 33:19	mercy to whom I will show mercy.'* Therefore, it is not a question of who wills or who runs but of God who is merciful. Where are merits now? Where now are works, either past or future, either done or to be done by the vigor of the will? The Apostle made a plain statement commending gratuitous, that is, true grace. About grace itself the Apostle dealt sufficiently, and therefore made mention of the sons of the promise. Only God accomplishes what God promises. Recommending the children of the promise, he showed that they were first signified by Isaac, Abraham's son. The divine work appeared more clearly in him who was born from sterile and aged organs, and not in the usual course of nature, so that it might be shown among the sons of God that it is by divine, and not human, effort that they are sons of God, and so that in the vessels suited for destruction because of condemned material the vessels made out of the same material and chosen for honor might recognize what divine mercy generously gave them.
Rm 9:17-18	VERSES SEVENTEEN AND EIGHTEEN. For the Scripture says to Pharaoh, 'To this purpose I have raised you up, that I might show my power in you, and that my name might be declared throughout all
Ex 9:16	the earth.'* God would create no angel or man whom he foreknew would be evil unless he knew equally how to use him for the benefit of the good, and so to adorn the course of the ages with contrasting elements like a beautiful song. It was obviously to the benefit of the vessels of mercy that the name of God should be declared throughout all the earth. Pharaoh served their interests, as the outcome of the event showed. So in regard to both possibilities the Apostle concludes, **Therefore, he has mercy on whom he will; and whom he will, he hardens.** And the one who does this is he in whom there is no iniquity. He shows mercy by his free gift; he hardens justly according to merit. But let haughty and unfaithful pride or the guilty excuse of those under punishment still speak out:

Rm 9:19-20 VERSES NINETEEN TO TWENTY. **Why does he then find fault? For who resists his will?** Let him say this, and then let him hear the answer man should receive. **O man, who are you that you reply to God?** Let him hear this and not despise it. But if he does despise it, let him know that he is hardened in this very act of contempt. But if he does not despise it, let him so believe himself to be helped as not to despise it. But he is helped gratuitously, and he is hardened because he deserves it. How will these men excuse themselves? In the manner in which the Apostle makes a brief objection to himself as though in their words, 'Why does he then find fault? For who resists his will?' If they are not ashamed to contradict, not us, but the Apostle, with this excuse, then why do we tire of repeating the Apostle's answer?

Rm 9:20-21 VERSES TWENTY AND TWENTY-ONE. **O man, who are you to reply to God? Shall the thing formed say to him who formed it, 'Why have you made me thus?' Or has not the potter power over the clay, to make from the same lump,** rightly condemned, of course, **one vessel unto** undue **honor** on account of his merciful grace, **and another unto dishonor,** on account of his angry justice? In regard to justice and grace, the same can rightly be said both of the guilty on who is freed and of the guilty one who is condemned, 'Take what is yours and go. I will to give to this man what is
Cf. Mt 20:14-15 not owed. Is it not lawful for me to do what I will?'*

NOTES

1. Compare Bernard, *Sermon 85, On the Canticle*, Section 8-9.
2. The source for this etymologically incorrect definition has not been found. See A. Ernout and A. Meillet, *Dictionnaire étymologique de la langue latine* (Paris, 1959) for articles on *haereo* and *heres*.
3. This tripartite view of man is found in Paul, I Thess 5:23; Augustine, *Certain Propositions on the Epistle to the Romans;* PL 35: 2074; Origen, *On Roms,* PG 14:866.
4. The discussion of this verse down to this point is taken from Augustine, *Letter to Sixtus* 194.16-18; PL 33:879-880. This passage is referred to by Florus, PL 119:300.
5. The previous two sentences are from Augustine, *Sermon 6 on the Epistle of John* 8; PL 35:2024. Also see Florus, PL 119:300.
6. This paragraph down to here is from Augustine, *Letter 130;* PL 33:503.
7. The term *lumen incircumscriptum* is found in Gregory the Great, *Homily 37 On the Gospels;* PL 76:1275.
8. These sentences, including the expression *docta ignorantia,* are from Augustine, *Letter 130.28;* PL 35:505.
9. The previous two sentences are from Augustine, *Grace and Free Will 17.33;* PL 44:901. Florus refers to it, PL 119:300.
10. This paragraph down to this point is from Augustine, *Predestination of Saints* 10.19; PL 44:974-975. Also Florus, PL 119:301. In the pauline text in MS 49, fol. 9r there is a marginal gloss on Rm 8:28: *Augustinus. Praedestinatio gratiae est preparatio. Gratia vero ipse est effectus.*
11. The previous two sentences are from Augustine, *Gift of Perseverance 14.35;* PL 45:1014. Also Florus, PL 119:301.
12. This paragraph down to this point is from Augustine, *City of God 22.16;* PL 41:778. Also Florus, PL 119:301.
13. The previous two sentences are from Augustine, *Trinity 14.18.24;* PL 42:1055. Also listed in Florus, PL 119:301.
14. 'That sanctification is given to the just . . . ' down to this point is Augustine, *Enarration on Ps 5.17;* PL 36:89. Also, Florus, PL 119: 301.
15. 'The way that we tend to eternal . . . ' down to here is a long passage from Augustine, *Enarration on Ps 150.3;* PL 37:1962-1963. Also, Florus, PL 119:301.
16. The entire discussion for this verse to this point is Augustine, *On Christian Doctrine* 3.3.6; CC 32:79-80. Florus, PL 119:302.

17. This paragraph down to this point is Augustine, *Catholic and Manichaean Ways of Life* I. 11, 19. PL 32:1319.

18. 'For Rebecca as well did not give birth . . . ' down to this point is Origen, *On Roms*, PG 14:1142-43.

BOOK SIX

CHAPTER NINE Continued

Rm 9:22-24

VERSES TWENTY-TWO THROUGH TWENTY-FOUR. What if God, willing to show his wrath and to make his power known, endured with much patience vessels of wrath fit for destruction, that he might show the riches of his glory on the vessels of mercy, which he has prepared for glory, even those whom he has called, not only from the Jews, but also from the Gentiles? This question is implicitly attached to, 'Who are you to reply to God?' so that with this sentence added to the previous words the meaning is: If God, wishing to show his wrath, endured the vessels of wrath, who are you to reply to him? Not only did he will to make his power known, but also, as it follows in the text, to make known the riches of his glory in the vessels of mercy which he has prepared for glory. For what profit is it to vessels fit for destruction that God endures them with patience so that he may destroy them in an orderly manner and use them as an instrument of salvation for those upon whom he has mercy? But this is of great profit for those for whose salvation the wicked are thus used. Notice, as much explanation is given to man as is due to him. It is as if the Apostle said, 'Who are you to reply to God, if God, willing to show his wrath and to demonstrate his power, while supremely good himself, can use for good even the wicked, in so far as they are wicked not by divine establishment but by a nature spoiled by iniquity of will, a nature which was created good by God the Creator?' He endured with much patience vessels of wrath fit for destruction, not because the sins of angels or men were necessary for him, for whom no one's justice is necessary, but in order to make known the riches of his glory in the vessels of mercy, not so that they should exalt themselves for their good works as if they were done by their own effort, but so that they should understand humbly that unless the free, undeserved grace of God helped them, they would be repaid according to their merits as they see repaid others who are made of the same material as they. The rest of men—not belonging to this group and whose souls and bodies were fashioned by the goodness of God, and also whatever else their nature possesses aside from the defect which is inflicted on them by the audacity of a haughty will— were created by a provident God to show what the free will of a deserter can do without grace. In their just and deserved pains, the vessels of mercy, who are separate from that other mass of people not by the merits of their works but by the free grace of God, learn what has been given to them, so that every mouth should be stopped* and so that whoever glories should glory in the Lord.*

Cf. Rm 3:19
1 Cor 1:13

The blessed Apostle reminds us with as much succinctness as authority why the Creator chose some for damnation and not for grace. For he says that God, willing to show his wrath and to demonstrate his power, endured with much patience the vessels of wrath fit for destruction, in order to make known the riches of his glory toward the vessels of mercy. Previously he had said that God was like a potter making from the same clay some vessels for honor and some for dishonor. It would rightly seem unjust that the vessels of wrath were made for perdition unless all the clay was condemned from the time of Adam. That some are made into vessels of wrath from their birth results from the punishment due them; that some are made into vessels of mercy by being born again results from grace which is not deserved. God, therefore, shows his anger, not of course a disturbance of soul as is the case among men, but a just and fixed resolve to punish, because from the stock of disobedience is produced a progeny of sin and punishment. As is written in the book of Job, 'Man born of a woman, living for a short time, is filled with wrath.'* A vessel is said to be of that thing of which it is full. Therefore, they are called vessels of wrath. God also showed his power by which he uses well even the evil, giving them many natural and temporal goods and accommodating their malice to prod the good and to admonish these by comparison with them, so that the good might learn to give thanks to God because they are separated from the wicked not by their own merits, which are part of their common makeup, but by the mercy of God.

Cf. Job 14:1

This is especially clear in regard to infants. Of those infants who are born again through the grace of Christ and, ending their life while still young, pass into eternal and blessed life, it cannot be said that they are distinguished by their free will from other infants who, without this grace, die in the condemnation which is common to men. If those alone were created from Adam who were to be recreated through grace, and no other men were born except those who are adopted as sons of God, the benefit given to the unworthy would lie hidden because just punishment would not be rendered to any of those coming from that condemned stock. But since God endured with much patience the vessels of wrath fit for destruction, he not only showed his wrath and demonstrated his power by punishing and using the wicked for good, but he also made known the riches of his glory toward the vessels of mercy. A man who is freely justified learns what is given to him when he is separated from a condemned man not by his own merit but by the glory of the most generous mercy of God, for he also could have been condemned with equal justice. God willed so many to be born whom he foreknew would not belong to his grace that they are incomparably more numerous than those whom he deigned to predestine to the glory of his kingdom as sons of the promise. He did this that he might show from the very multitude of the rejected how completely unimportant to the just God is the number of those who are justly condemned, and that those who are redeemed from that condemnation might understand that the damnation which they saw rendered to so large a part of mankind was deserved by the whole of mankind. This condemnation applies not only to those who have by the desires of an evil will added many other sins to original sin, but also to many infants who are snatched out of this light without the grace of the Mediator, bound only by the bond of original sin. That whole mass would receive the just condemnation it deserves had not the potter, who is not only just but merciful, made out of it some vessels for honor, according to grace, not according to what is owed, when he helps the little ones who cannot be said to have any merits, and anticipates the older ones so that they can have some merits.[1] Therefore, let the one who has been gathered in compare himself to those left behind, and let the elect compare himself with the rejected. Let the vessels of mercy compare themselves with the vessels of wrath, and let them see that from the same material some vessels are made for honor and others for dishonor. Let one who has been liberated learn from one not liberated what was just for him also, had grace not helped him. For unless the debtor is hung, someone whose debt has been forgiven is less grateful.

A profound question has led us into deep waters, but it has not taken us to the bottom, because although man is rebuked for replying to God, as if the clay were to replay to the potter, the holy Apostle does not forbid questioning by those of whom he says elsewhere, 'The spiritual man judges all things'.* And especially this text, 'Now we have received not the spirit of this world, but the Spirit that is of God, that we

1 Cor 2:15

1 Cor 2:12 — may know the things that are given us from God.'* He forbids questions by those made of earth and clay who are not yet reborn or nourished, and who bear the image of the first earthling made of the earth. Because he was unwilling to obey Him by whom he was made, he relapsed into that from which he was made, and deserved to hear, 'Earth you are and unto earth you shall return'.* Rightly are such men held back.

Gen 3:19

For if a beast were able to speak and could say to God, 'Why did you make him a man and me a beast?' would you not justly burn with anger and say, 'Beast, who are you to reply to God?'

Therefore, God prepared vessels of mercy and called them both from the Jews and from the Gentiles, because one throng of wicked sinners comes from Adam and to that throng both Jews and Gentiles belong if grace is removed.

Rm 9:25-26

VERSES TWENTY-FIVE AND TWENTY-SIX. As he says in Hosea, 'I will call that which is not my people my people and her who has not obtained mercy one who has obtained mercy. And it shall be that in the place where it was said to them, "You are not my people," they shall be called sons of* God.'† The apostles understood this prophetic testimony as pertaining to the call of the Gentiles, the people who did not formerly belong to God, and they considered the Gentiles spiritually among the sons of Abraham and rightly named Israel for that reason, and they recalled the corner stone and the two walls meeting it, one from the Jews and one from the Gentiles.* The Apostle seems to return to comforting his sorrow, because just as there is one mass of the condemned composed of Jews and Gentiles, so there is one Church of the elect taken from both peoples. Therefore, the example taken from Hosea applies to the Gentiles, while the one added from Isaiah applies to the Jews, for the Gentiles were not the people of God but were made the people of God. Not having obtained mercy they did obtain it.

*PL: the living
†Hos 1:10; 2:24*

Cf. Eph 2:14, 20

'But it shall be that in the place,' says the Apostle. What place is that? Could it be Judaea, or Rome? Far from it. Judaea is the more worthy place, and Rome the more sublime place where it is suitable, and possible, for God to speak. Here the place is the mind of man, his sense of reason, the principal element of his heart. There under the action of God the conscience worthy of being condemned says to the sinful people, 'You are not my people.' But to those in whom charity is poured forth in their hearts through the Holy Spirit who is given to them, the Holy Spirit himself gives testimony 'that they are the sons of God.'* Isaiah cries out, that is, clearly announces, and tells what the Holy Spirit is doing for Israel and says:

Cf. Rm 5:5, 8:14

VERSE TWENTY-SEVEN. **Though the number of the children of Israel be as the sand of the sea, it is a remnant that shall be saved.*** The prophet foresaw that very many from Israel would be like the sand of the sea in their sterile justice, their hardness of heart, and their inordinate and diffused number, and so would be vessels of wrath fit for destruction, not having confidence in their life,* but crucifying the Lord of glory;* but the remnant would be like the stars of heaven, participants in the heavenly glory. Both aspects of this had been announced to Abraham, 'So your seed shall be like the sand of the sea, and like the stars of heaven'.*

Rm 9:27

Is 10:22

Cf. Deut 28:66
1 Cor 2:8

Gen 22:17

VERSE TWENTY-EIGHT. **For he completes his reckoning and cuts it short in justice, for it is a brief reckoning that the Lord shall make upon the earth.** It is a brief reckoning and one cut short in the justice about which the Lord spoke in the gospel: 'You shall love the Lord your God with your whole heart and your neighbor as yourself; on these two commandments depends the whole law and the prophets.'* Or else it is a summary of the faith by which believers are saved without the innumerable observances with which that multitude was oppressed in a servile way. That the salvation of the remnant is to be reckoned as grace is shown by the subsequent testimony spoken in the person of those who have believed through circumcision:

Rm 9:28

Mt 22:37, 40

PL: through grace

Rm 9:29	VERSE TWENTY-NINE. **If the Lord of Sabaoth had not left us a seed, we would have fared as Sodom,**
Is 1:9	**and would have been like Gomorrha.*** Cast over the earth, they were multiplied like a seed. Or else the seed is understood as that grain of wheat which by the passion of death fell into the ground, and dying
Cf. Jn 12:25	brought forth much fruit.* We have been made, they say, as Sodom (whose people merited destruction for being lewd with guests), when, sacrilegious toward our brother, the Lord of glory, we could not escape the danger of perdition except by the blessing of the holy seed cast upon the earth. Then showing that the Gentiles obtained justice through faith, the Apostle goes on, saying:
Rm 9:30–33	VERSES THIRTY THROUGH THIRTY-THREE. **What then shall we say? That the Gentiles, who did not pursue justice, have attained justice, even the justice which is of faith. But Israel, by pursuing the law of justice, has not arrived at the law of justice. Why not? Because they did not seek it by faith, but, as it were, by works. For they stumbled at the stumblingstone, as it is written, 'Behold, I place in Sion a stumblingstone and a rock of scandal; and all who**
Is 8:14, 28:16	**believe in him shall not be confounded.'*** The faith of Christ is to believe in him who justifies the wicked, to believe in the Mediator without whom no one is reconciled to God, to believe in him who says, 'Without me
Jn 15:5	you can do nothing.'* But this faith is not attained by the man who ignores God's justice, that is, the justice which God gives who justifies the wicked, and wishes to establish his own justice as performed by the strength of his own will, to which God could give grace according to merits, and does not will that first should come the grace of God which causes man to have the justice which he believes he makes for himself. Therefore, men of this type are said to pursue justice, which they think they attain by their own efforts as though it were fleeing from them. This is the case with the Jews who pursue the law of justice as though it justified by works. But the Gentiles do not pursue justice, and yet attain it, finding it close to

them, since the grace of faith already asked for it for them, and they find it lodged in their hearts by the natural law. The Gentiles who did not pursue justice, which is proper to the law which is carried out in fear of punishment not in love of justice, and which man makes, not God, have attained the justice of God, the justice of faith. But Israel by pursuing the law of the letter, which it thought, or presumed to be, the law of justice, has not come to the law of the spirit, which is truly the law of justice, because they sought it not by faith, but, as it were, by works, as though they were their own justice, and so they stumbled at the stumblingstone. He who believes in him will not have his own justice which is from the law, although the law is good, but will fulfil the law itself, not with his own justice, but with that given by God; and thus he will not be confounded. For 'love is the fulfillment of the law'.* And from what source is this love diffused in our hearts? Not indeed from us, but through the Holy Spirit who is given to us.*

Rm 13:10

Rm 5:5

We should know that in the prophet Isaiah this testimony is written, 'Behold, I place in Zion a foundation, a costly stone, a choice corner-stone, and he who believes in him shall not be put to shame'.* But the Apostle inserted into this testimony of the prophet 'a stumblingstone and a rock of scandal' taken from another place, in which is written, 'And you shall not come against him as against a stumblingstone, neither as against the falling of a rock'.* Taking from each place what seemed suited to his statement, he fitted them together for his own purposes.

Cf. Is 28:16

Cf. Is 8:14

Why Christ the Lord, who is the way and the truth and the life,* is called here a stumblingstone and a rock of scandal should not be an offence or scandal to anyone. For those who were in Sion walking in paths that were not good were quickly running on the road to ruin, fostering each other in evil, because, as the prophet says, 'the sinner is praised in the desires of his soul, and the unjust man is blessed'* and so the Lord came and began to rebuke their evil ways, saying, 'Woe to you, Pharisees,' etc.* and he became to them a stumblingstone and a rock of scandal by not

Jn 14:6

Ps 9:24

Mt 23:13 ff.

being silent about their evils, and he began to block the road to perdition by rebuking them.² Not only to them, but to all the wicked, Christ is a stumblingstone. Whatever Christ says is bitter to them, but whoever has believed in him shall not be put to shame. He who glories in himself will be put to shame, because he will not be found without sins. He will be put to shame not for a day, nor for an hour, but forever. Whoever you are, if you do not wish to stumble, take hold of yourself, hinder yourself; take up your justice, take that justice which is from God. Although you are called a Christian, you stumble on him if you deny his grace. It is a smaller thing to stumble against Christ hanging than sitting in heaven. Let there be justice, but let it be from grace. Have it from God; let it not be your own. 'Let your priests be clothed with justice,'* he says. It is received like a garment, it does not grow like hair. The Apostle preaches this to you; God gives this to you. Groan, cry, believe in order to obtain it.

Ps 131:9

CHAPTER TEN

Rm 10:1

VERSE ONE. **Brethren, the will of my heart, and my prayer to God is for them unto salvation.** The will does not suffice by itself to be moved to believe the truth, without being helped by the grace of God. Therefore, although the Apostle preached the gospel to them with earnestness, he was not satisfied unless he also prayed for them that they might believe. Otherwise they could not attain salvation. Therefore, he prays for those unwilling to believe so that God may effect in them the will to believe.

Rm 10:2

VERSE TWO. **For I bear them witness that they have a zeal for God, but not according to knowledge.** 'I know,' he says, 'I am well aware; I was one of them, I was that way myself.' He then shows what he means by zeal or emulation 'not according to knowledge'.

Rm 10:3

VERSE THREE. **For they, not knowing the**

justice of God, and seeking to establish their own, have not submitted themselves to the justice of God. He says this of the Jews who, relying on themselves, rejected grace and therefore did not believe in Christ. He says they wish to set up their own justice, the justice which comes from the law, not because the law was set up by them, but because they set up their own justice in the law which comes from God, when they believed themselves able to fulfil that same law by their own strength, ignoring the justice of God— not that by which God is just, but that which is in men from God. This is the sum of the great knowledge of man: to know that by himself he is nothing, and that whatever he is is from God and through God.

Rm 10:4

VERSE FOUR. **For the end of the law is Christ, that everyone who has faith may be justified.** But faith is distinguished from works, just as elsewhere it is said that man can be justified by faith without the works of the law.* And there are works which seem good without the faith of Christ, but are not good, because they are not referred to him, the end, by which they might be good. 'For the end of the law is Christ.' Therefore, the Lord in the gospel was unwilling to distinguish faith from works, but said that faith itself was a work. Faith it is which works through love.* He did not say, 'This is your work', but 'this is the work of God, that you believe in him whom he sent.'* A man's faith, therefore, belongs to Christ, because it comes from him, and every work of faith must be referred to him because it comes from him, for he is the end of the law and of all justice. Every perfection is in him, and the hope of charity and of faith extend to nothing beyond him.

Rm 3:28

Gal 5:6

Jn 6:29

Rm 10:5

VERSE FIVE. **For Moses wrote that the man who does the justice which is from the law shall live in it.*** He does not say, 'The one who does it shall live in the law', so that you can understand that in this verse the law has been used in place of the works themselves, and that those who did them lived in them; otherwise they would feed crows on the cross.

Lev 18:5

He says, therefore, that he who performs justice shall not be stoned, shall not be killed. His reward shall be not to die.

Rm 10:6-7

[PL omits]

VERSES SIX AND SEVEN. But the justice which is of faith speaks thus, 'Say not in your heart, "Who shall ascend into heaven?" that is, to bring Christ [down; or "Who shall descend into the abyss?" that is, to bring Christ back] from the dead." The justice which derives from the law of deeds is the deeds themselves, and its profit and reward is not to die and not to be punished. It is very different with the justice which derives from faith. That demands only the heart's true faith and the mouth's free confession, not sought out by human reason but received with a simple and voluntary assent of the mind. Faith is the voluntary assent of the mind to what must be believed in religion. In religion the man with a faithful and sober mind does not scrutinize the human element in Christ with the senses of divine wisdom or by the reasoning of human science, in order to ask that an understanding of the divine element in Christ be brought down from heaven for him, or that Christ be recalled out of the abyss for him from the common fate of the dying, but he simply believes what divine authority sets down to be believed and freely confesses what truth presents to be confessed, and so by his humble belief he progresses to an understanding of the faith he has received and to works which are done through love.³ For so it is written in Deuteronomy, from which this example is taken, 'This commandment that I enjoin on you today is not above you, nor far from you. It is not in heaven, so that you say, "Who shall ascend for us into heaven and receive it for us so that we can hear and do it?" Neither is it beyond the sea, so that you say, "Who shall cross over and receive

Deut 30:11-13   it for us?" '*

Rm 10:8-9
Deut 30:14

VERSES EIGHT AND NINE. 'The word is near you, in your mouth and in your heart.'* This is the word which we preach, for if with your mouth you confess the Lord Jesus and believe in your heart that

God has raised him up from the dead, you shall be saved. Although in an unfamiliar situation there is some difficulty in believing an unusual miracle, nevertheless, in anyone who faithfully confesses that Jesus is the Lord, and believes that he does not belong to the common run of those who die, God, who 'resists the proud and gives grace to the humble',* through love of the spirit enlightens the affection of faith and offers understanding so that what he believes is made sweet to his heart, and it becomes glorious for him to confess what he knows he believes most beneficially. By believing, he is saved, not in order to live during the present like that doer of the law who lives in his own justice or in the justice of his own works, but in order to live with the life of God by doing his works through love, and to receive perpetual glory in the future. For the true justice of faith has a double reward of bliss. Here by the utterly certain argument of experience man gets a taste of the substance of things to be hoped for,* and there he receives what he believed, the most manifest verity of eternal happiness. Because of this, man glories here in troubles, in which a conscience of holy patience is a promise and pledge of future blessedness. Therefore, situation should be compared with situation, justice with justice, life with life: on the one hand, that of the slave, enclosed in the mill of hard necessity, who lives as long as he performs his servile chores; on the other hand, that of the son of grace, for whom to serve is to live, and to serve pleasingly is a great grace, and to serve freely is great glory, and whose reward is eternal life.

Jas 4:6

Cf. Heb 11:1

Rm 10:10

VERSE TEN. **For with the heart we believe unto justice; but, with the mouth confession is made unto salvation.** Although the justice of faith by which we believe with the heart unto justice is a clear matter, it is not vain to add 'with the mouth confession is made unto salvation'. Nearly all of those who denied Christ before their persecutors, did they not hold in their hearts what they believed about him, and yet perish by not confessing with their mouth unto salvation, unless they regained life through repentance? Who would be so vain as to think that the apostle Peter esteemed the Lord in his heart the same way he denied him with his lips? Why, speaking truth in his heart, did he punish with such bitter weeping the lie he drew from his lips, unless he saw it was a great disaster not to have confessed with his mouth unto salvation what he really believed in his heart unto justice? For just as truth is unprofitable on the lips if it is not also in the heart, so truth is unprofitable in the heart if it fails to appear on the lips when confession is demanded.

Rm 10:11
Is 28:16

VERSE ELEVEN. **For Scripture says, 'Whoever believes in him shall not be put to shame.'*** Some do not blush to confess that Christ is the Word of God, the strength of God, the wisdom of God, but they blush to confess that he was born, died and was buried. How shall the sick man be cured if he is ashamed of his medicine? But let him choose the time, for now is

Cf. Qo 3:2-8

the time for choosing.* When he who was despised for our sakes comes in marvelous splendor, he who was judged for us will judge; he who was slain will raise up; he who was dishonored will honor; and then whether Jew or Greek—for there is no distinction— everyone who believes in him will not be put to shame.

Rm 10:12

VERSE TWELVE. **For there is the same Lord for all,** because he is not the God only of the Jews but

Cf. Rm 3:29

also of the Gentiles,* rich to fulfil the desires of all who call upon him.

Rm 10:13

VERSE THIRTEEN. **For whoever calls upon the name of the Lord shall be saved.** The name of the Lord is invoked by one who desires to be his slave; anyone desires to be the Lord's slave who understands his name. They understand his name who experience in themselves his dominion. They are the ones who recognize in themselves the grace of God, and are not ungrateful; and thus, calling upon the name of the Lord, they are saved. So faith in Jesus Christ the Lord obtains for us salvation, both inasmuch as it is begun here in hope, and as it will be given in reality. What the Apostle says, 'he shall be saved', should be taken in the sense of 'saved from fever' or 'saved from pestilence', because it is not the healthy that need a physician, but the sick. Therefore, if salvation is promised to all who call upon him, and there is no distinction between Jew and Greek, then all should call upon him.

Rm 10:14-15   VERSES FOURTEEN AND FIFTEEN. **How then shall they call on him in whom they have not believed?** The Teacher of the Gentiles seems here to be speaking about the Gentiles, and to be refuting those who thought that the gospel should be preached only to the Jews and not to the Gentiles. Wishing to show that the gospel applied not only to the Jews but to the Gentiles as well, he set down the previous text from the prophet, 'For everyone who calls upon the name of the Lord shall be saved,'* and then adds, **How shall they call on him in whom they have not believed? Or how shall they believe him of whom they have not heard? And how shall they hear without a preacher? And how shall they preach unless they be sent?** But they have been sent, and they have preached, **as it is written, 'How beautiful are the feet of those who bring tidings [of peace and] of good things.'*** We should not desist from planting and watering just because God gives the increase;* by this path the discourse returns to grace. Unless grace provides [preachers,] and preachers make believers, there will be no one to call out and be saved. This is why the feet are beautiful of those who preach the gospel of peace, of those who bring glad tidings of good things. The peace is that by which we are reconciled to God by the remission of sins; the good things are those promised to the sons of grace; and the beautiful feet are those which leave us beautiful footsteps to tread in, for the cultivation of the soul, for love of God and for contempt of the world. Yet the evangelists are sent forth, but few are found to obey. Therefore, a complaint is voiced, using the words of the prophet, saying:

Joel 2:32

[PL omits]
Is 52:7
Cf. 1 Cor 3:7

[PL omits]

Rm 10:16 Is 53:1	VERSE SIXTEEN. **'Lord, who has believed our report?'*** What we have heard from you we have announced to them, but there are few who obey us. All this profusion of words proceeds to this end, that the Apostle pursues his great sadness and continuous sorrow of heart, due to the blindness of his own people, which he cannot conceal. He acts on their behalf as far as the truth and justice of God do not prevent him, for the Apostle cannot resist them even though the obstinancy of stubborn malice is resisting him. Therefore, united to God, he condemns the many blind, obdurate men among them, but as a remedy for his sorrow he embraces the few chosen ones among them.
Rm 10:17	VERSE SEVENTEEN. **Therefore,** he says, in regard to them, that is, the few, **faith comes by hearing, and hearing by the word of God.** He glories in that the zeal of the preachers has borne fruit in at least a few of them. Then he takes away all excuse from the rest, saying:
Rm 10:18 Ps 18:5	VERSE EIGHTEEN. **Have they not heard? Indeed, they have. 'Their sound has gone forth into all the earth, and their words unto the ends of the whole world.'*** If all have heard, then have they also. If the nations dwelling at the ends of the earth have heard, then how can the Jews excuse themselves, dwelling in the center of the world where salvation was accomplished?
Rm 10:19 Deut 32:21	VERSE NINETEEN. **But I say, 'Has not Israel known?'** As if he says, 'But I shall say, "Why has Israel not known"?' And not I, but first Moses before me; and in him God says, **'I will provoke you to jealousy by that which is not a nation; by a foolish nation I will anger you.'*** He is saying, as it were, 'By withdrawing from you the grace that you reject, I will permit you to be drawn away into jealousy and envy, which you will feel toward a nation which you have not even dignified with the name nation until now. It is no longer a nation, that is, it is ceasing to be a

nation, changing from a natural creature of its own error into a new creature of faith. I will cast you into anger from which envy is never missing against a people hitherto foolish, having no wisdom about God, but now superior to you in the knowledge of God.' Therefore, envy is the chief cause why Israel has not known. When the younger son was feasting and rejoicing with his father, the older son refused to enter.* Isaiah dares to predict the call of the Gentiles in rejection of the Jews, although he knew that he would die for confessing God and the truth of the word of God. He said:

Lk 15:28

VERSE TWENTY. 'I was found by those who did not seek me; I appeared openly to those who did not ask about me.'* Behold, by his most manifest grace the Lord God foreknew the future, and yet we believe that he predicted the infidelity of the Jews but did not cause it, as the expression about 'provoking to jealousy' might seem to suggest. God does not force men to sin because he already knows their future sins. It is their sins that he foreknows, not his own, and not the sins of someone or other, but of the very persons in question. If the sins which he foreknew to be theirs were not theirs, he would not really foreknow them. But because his foreknowledge cannot be deceived, it is not some other person, but the very persons whom God foreknows will sin who do sin. Therefore, the Jews committed sin, which he did not compel them to do, for sin displeases him; yet he foretold that they would sin because nothing is hidden from him. If they had willed to do good and not evil, they would not have been forbidden; and it would have been foreseen that they would do this by him who knows what each one will do, and what will be returned to each one for his work. This has concerned the rejection of the Jews.

Rm 10:20

Is 65:1

What shall we say about those by whom he was found, even though he was not sought? What indeed, except that which is said by him who had the spirit of God: 'His mercy shall anticipate me'.* If you, whoever you are who are one of them, first brought some-

Ps 58:11

thing of your own, and by this first good thing of your own merited the mercy of God, he does not anticipate you. But what did you do in order that you might exist? What activity did you engage in so that you might be and call upon God? If you did anything in order to exist, you existed before you existed. But if you were nothing at all before you existed, you did not merit existence.

But God made you exist; and did you make yourself exist as good? If God gave you existence and someone else gave you goodness, then he who gave you goodness is surely better than he who gave you mere existence. But he was found by those who did not seek him, because his prevenient grace opened their senses, and he appeared plainly to those who did not ask about him. What is the result of all this? The power to become sons of God is given to men. Let them give thanks because power is given; let them pray lest weakness succumb. Let not excessive confidence in his own will raise anyone up in pride so that he says, 'Why shall I ask of God not to be overcome by temptation, since this lies within my own power?' Let no one's excessive distrust of self cast him into negligence so that he says, 'Why shall we try to live well, since this is in God's power?' Rather let the whole world be subject to God. Let him who is drawn follow; let him who is not drawn pray that he may be drawn. The text continues:

Rm 10:21

VERSE TWENTY-ONE. **But to Israel he says.** The preceding is for the Gentiles, the following for Israel. The former spoke of the acceptance of the Gentiles, the latter of the rejection of the Jews. **All the day long have I spread my hands to a people that believes not, but contradicts me.*** The Lord says, 'Let the children be filled'.* For 'I was not sent except to the lost sheep of the house of Israel'.* All day long—that is, all during the time of his dwelling with men—the Lord spread out his hands as though embracing the Jewish people. Toward them principally he directed his miraculous works, denoted by 'hands', and his zeal for teaching, by which he tried to

Is 65:2
Mk 7:27
Mt 15:24

draw to him, with both hands so to speak, those who did not believe but rather contradicted. And as though someone answered, 'Where are the promises made to Israel?' the Apostle added immediately:

CHAPTER ELEVEN

Rm 11:1-2 VERSES ONE AND TWO. **I say then: Has God cast away his people? Certainly not. For I also am an Israelite of the seed of Abraham, of the tribe of Benjamin. God has not cast away his people, whom he foreknew.** But to show that the remnant was left by the grace of God and not by the merits of their works, he added:

Rm 11:2-7 VERSES TWO THROUGH SEVEN. **Do you not know what scripture says about Elijah, how he calls on God against Israel? 'Lord, they have slain your prophets, they have overthrown your altars; and I**
1 Kgs 19:10 **alone am left, and they seek my life.'*** But what does the divine answer say to him? **'I have kept for myself seven thousand men who have not bowed their knees**
1 Kgs 19:18 **to Baal.'*** So also at the present time there is a remnant saved according to the election of grace. And if by grace, then no longer by works; otherwise grace is no longer grace. What then? What Israel sought he has not obtained; but election has obtained it; and the rest have been blinded. The Jews were the people of God; to them belonged the adoption, and the glory,
Cf. Rm 9:4 and the testament, and the giving of the law.* To this people first came all the sacraments which promised the Saviour. What then? Is all that condemned? Far from it. The winnowed mass lies on the threshing floor; the straw lies outside. All that you see which pertains to the deceitful Jews is straw. Those who were foreknown and predestined were not rejected.

The text says, 'I have kept for myself'. What is the meaning of these words? 'I have chosen them, because I saw that their minds did not trust in themselves or in Baal. They are not changed; they are as I made them.' 'So also at the present time, there is a remnant saved according to the election of grace.' Beware of pride, Christian. Although you imitate the saints, always assign everything to grace, because it is grace and not your merit that causes some remnant to exist in you, for the prophet was speaking of the remnants themselves. If you presume on your merits or works, then grace is no longer given to you, but a reward is owed to you. 'If by grace, it is not now by works; otherwise grace is no longer grace.'

What does the phrase mean, 'according to the election of grace'? We were evil, and we were chosen to be good through the grace of the one choosing us. For grace did not find merit, but made merit. 'What then? What Israel sought, he has not obtained.' What did Israel seek and not obtain? The Apostle had already said that 'by pursuing the law of justice, Israel has not arrived at the law of justice.'* Why? 'Because they sought it not by faith, but by works.' Israel pursued the law of works, and seeking justice in it, did not obtain it; but the elect both of the Jews and the Gentiles obtained it in the law of grace, in the law of faith, in the law of the spirit of life. 'The rest', because they were unwilling to believe when they could have, 'were blinded', that is, made unable to believe. Because they sinned with their will, they were also punished in will, so that because they knowingly said true was false, they were afterwards unable to understand truth itself. This is not due to simple ignorance but to envy motivated by evil.

Rm 9:31-32

VERSE EIGHT. Therefore, God has given them the spirit of compunction. This compunction is the punishment inflicted on a condemned conscience, about which the Apostle said above, 'But to those who are contentious, he will give wrath and indignation,' etc.* For condemned to the hell below, they first suffer in this world a hell of conscience, not having the sadness* which is according to God, or the repentance which works toward a lasting salvation, but a diabolical desperation which produces eternal death. It is not clear from where this scriptural testimony is taken, unless perhaps it is from Isaiah, where

Rm 11:8

Rm 2:8

PL = justice

Is 6:9-10

he says, 'Go and say to this people, "You will hear with the ear and not understand; seeing you will see and you will not see." For their heart is grown coarse,'* so that their inner eyes are shut tight and their ears are deaf, and they can no longer see or hear, since they were unwilling when they could.

Rm 11:9

Ps 68:23

VERSE NINE. **And David says, 'Let their table be before them as a snare, and a trap, and a stumblingblock, and a recompense to them.'*** The table of the Jews is the writings of the Old Testament, on which various platters taken from Moses and the prophets are placed. These become a snare to them because, caring nothing for spiritual things, they think that only carnal things are promised to them in Scripture. Why the phrase 'before them'? Because they knew their own iniquity and yet tenaciously persevered in it, and their presumption of soul was so strong that even though the snare was open before them, they still fell into it. So the text continues:

Rm 11:10

VERSE TEN. **'Let their eyes be darkened that they may not see.'** Because they saw to no purpose, it befell them that they could not see. This saying is a prophecy, not a desire; it is said not to bring it to pass, but because it will come to pass. 'Let it be to them a stumblingblock,' because they stumbled when they saw that the Lord could suffer. **And bow down their backs** so that those who were unwilling to know heavenly things may now know only earthly ones. Therefore, they were unhappily expelled from the place that they killed Christ to save, and they were dispersed throughout the world. Wherever the Church spreads, they are present and by their own scriptures they are a testimony to us that we have not fabricated the things that are preached about Christ, but that these are found in the books of the Jews. When these blind men do not believe our Scriptures, therefore, then their own scriptures, which they read blindly, are fulfilled in them.

Rm 11:11

Cf. Prov 24:16

Cf. Is 24:20

VERSE ELEVEN. **I say then, have they so stumbled that they should fall? God forbid.** There is a fall by which the just man falls seven times and rises,* and there is a fall in which he who falls does not rise again,* just as Lucifer fell from heaven in a fall of everlasting despair. The Apostle says: God forbid that Israel has fallen in this way, since the meditation of the law persists in it still, as well as a zeal for God, although not according to knowledge. For the fall of the Jews has a resurrection, and their turning away a conversion. How? He continues and says: **But by their offence salvation has come to the Gentiles, that they may emulate them.** For the fall has not been found wholly useless, because where they fell others have arisen. For this reason he wished to designate their fall by the milder term of 'offence'. Their offence is the salvation of the Gentiles, so that they may emulate them; that is, just as now the Gentiles are found among the Jews and are saved among them, so the Jews when they finally recognize the truth will emulate the Gentiles to their own salvation.

VERSE TWELVE. **Now if their offence means riches for the world, and their diminution riches for the Gentiles, how much more will their fulness mean?** The offence of the Jews means the riches of the world, because in their offence the Lord's portion has become the whole world, although at first in the constitution of the boundaries of the world only Jacob was made his allotted inheritance.* 'But if their diminution means riches for the Gentiles, how much more will their fulness mean?' What was lessened and removed from the Jews was added and attached to the Gentiles. And it is well that the fulness has been given to the diminution, because as long as Israel remains in unbelief, the fullness of the Lord's portion cannot be called complete. Israel will complete it by its own conversion.

Cf. Deut 32:9

Rm 11:13-14

VERSES THIRTEEN AND FOURTEEN. **And I**

say to you, Gentiles, as long as I am the Apostle of the
Gentiles, I will honor my ministry, if in some way I
can provoke to emulation those who are my flesh,
and can save some of them. By exercising vigilant
care and continuous solicitude about teaching the
Gentiles, and by showing forth the Gentiles' upright
manner of life, the Apostle provoked the Israelites,
who saw this, to emulate those who were progressing.
And this was a great glorification of his ministry, to
arouse one person to progress by the progress of
another.

Rm 11:15

VERSE FIFTEEN. **For if the loss of them is the
reconciliation of the world, what shall the receiving of
them be, but life from the dead?** If the casting away
of that people afforded reconciliation to the world, if
the grace among them was such that when it was taken
from them and given to the Gentiles it filled the whole
world, it cannot be estimated what the world would
receive from their reconciliation. 'What shall the
receiving of them be, but life from the dead?'[4] Now
in the meantime, while people progress from death to
life, various stages of progress are announced, but then
it will be perfection itself. Then, at the end of the
world, will come the general acceptance of the Jews,
when in all the faithful will take place that celebrated
resurrection by which mortality shall put on immortality and corruption shall put on incorruption.

Rm 11:16

VERSE SIXTEEN. **For if the sample is holy, so
also is the mass; and if the root is holy, so are the
branches.** God created the holy patriarchs as an olive
tree; from them the people of God flowered. This tree

PL: was pruned for was not cut off but* from it were broken off proud
branches, the blasphemous Jewish people. But the good,
useful branches remained: the holy apostles. That is a
sample, for a sample is a small amount taken from
something to test the whole. That is why the Apostle
says, 'If the sample is holy, then the mass can be made
holy'. As the root is, so are the branches. In every
tree the nature of the branches reflects the holiness of
the root; and any sample of the fruit reflects the

quality of the whole crop. Therefore, the fruit and the branches manifest the natural holiness of the root. If you were unnaturally grafted from somewhere, whatever sanctity you possess you would have as a favor of the grafter and from the richness of the root. So, the text continues:

Rm 11:17-18   VERSES SEVENTEEN AND EIGHTEEN. **And if some of the branches were broken, and you, a wild olive, were grafted on to them, and made partaker of the root and of the richness of the olive tree, do not boast against the branches.** He says that some branches were broken off from the root of the patriarchs because of unbelief, and the wild olive was grafted to share in the richness of the olive, speaking of the Church of the Gentiles. And who grafts a wild olive onto an olive? The olive is usually grafted onto the wild olive; we never see the wild olive grafted onto the olive. Anyone who does that will find the fruit not of the olive, but of the wild olive. For what you graft on is what grows and bears the fruit. The fruit grows from the grafted shoot, not from the root. The Apostle shows that God by his omnipotence has caused the wild olive to be grafted onto the root of the olive in such a way that it bears olives and not wild fruit. He relates this to God's omnipotence, saying, 'If some were made branches,* and you, a wild olive, were grafted onto them, and made partaker of the root of the richness of the olive tree, do not boast against the branches'. Do not boast because you were grafted, but fear least you be broken off for infidelity as they were broken off. A proud olive it was, worthy of being broken, that said, 'We are not born in slavery; we have one father, Abraham'.* Listen to a wild olive worthy of being grafted: 'I am not worthy that you should come under my roof'.* It was a foreign centurion who said this. Of him the Lord said, 'I have not found such faith in Israel'.* I did not find in the olive tree what I found in the wild olive. Therefore, let the proud olive be cut down and the humble wild olive be grafted. See the Lord cutting off and grafting. "Many shall come from the East and the West, and shall sit

PL: If some of the branches were broken,

Cf. Jn 8:33, 39, 41

Mt 8:8

Mt 8:10

*PL adds: Isaac and Jacob
†Mt 8:8-11
[PL omits]
Mt 8:12

down with Abraham* in the kingdom of heaven."† [You have heard the Lord grafting; hear him cutting off, 'For the sons of the kingdom will be cast into exterior darkness'.*] Let us not therefore proudly boast against the broken branches, but rather think by whose grace and great mercy and in what root we have been grafted, so that 'we be not highminded, but consent to the humble'.*

Rm 12:16

Rm 11:18

VERSE EIGHTEEN. **But if you boast, you do not support the root, but the root you.** For you have nothing which you have not received.* But if you are insolent about the breaking of the branches, you do not support the root, but the root which you insult supports you. To such insolent men the Apostle says:

Cf. 1 Cor 4:7

Rm 11:19-20

VERSES NINETEEN AND TWENTY. **You say then, 'The branches were broken off, that I might be grafted in.' Well, because of unbelief they were broken off; but you, stand by the faith.** The natural branches were cut off because of the pride of unbelief. Stand by the faith, so that faith may be reputed to you as justice and be fulfilled in you, not because your merit demands it but because a favor was promised by the Lord. **Be not highminded, but fear.** Grace contains its own kind of fear, and this fear is commanded even for those who live by faith, who are the heirs of the New Testament and have been called to freedom. To be highminded is to be proud. Wickedness does not delight this fear, even if impunity is offered. The soul fears only this: to lose the grace through which sin displeases it. He who is highminded and therefore does not fear is fearless in a ruinous way. What good does he love who loves fearlessness for its own sake? A person can persuade himself of this, not rightly, but monstrously. For such a man, because he loves fearlessness, attempts great crimes in order to practice what he loves. Therefore, what can be found in the worst of men should not be considered a great good. So let a Christian fear before perfect charity casts out fear.* For the man making progress fear diminishes as he approaches the homeland toward which he is moving.

Cf. 1 Jn 4:18

Those still on pilgrimage should have the greater fear; as they approach, they should have less fear, and none at all when they arrive. But fear also leads to charity, and perfect charity casts out fear.

Rm 11:20-21   VERSES TWENTY AND TWENTY-ONE. **Therefore, be not highminded but fear. For if God has not spared the natural branches, fear lest perhaps he also not spare you.** For he resists the proud, but gives grace
Jas 4:6   to the humble.*

Rm 11:22-24   VERSES TWENTY-TWO THROUGH TWENTY-FOUR. **See then the goodness and severity of God: the severity for those who are fallen; but the goodness of God, for you, if you abide in goodness.** Scripture wholesomely recommends not only the goodness of God but also his severity, because it is useful to love God and to fear him. Although the holy patriarchs live in its root, the unfaithful pride of the natural branches is broken off by the just severity of God, and the faithful humility of the wild olive is grafted on by the grace of divine goodness. Whoever you are who are grafted, see the goodness and severity of God, as the text says. All physical matter, although undoubtedly of one nature, through accidental qualities produces different physical objects, such as men, animals, trees and grass; in just the same way, although all rational beings have one nature equally endowed with freedom of choice, yet each one's own movements, approved by free choice, lead the soul subject to them either to virtue or to lust, and either form the soul to the beauty of a good tree (according to the antecedent grace of God) or else deform it into a bad tree through its own fault. Therefore, in order to show that a tree becomes good and is not born good, the Lord says, 'Either make the tree good and its fruit
Mt 12:33   good, or make the tree evil and its fruit evil.'*

Otherwise you shall be cut off, and they, if they no longer abide in unbelief, shall be grafted on. For God is able to graft them on. And if you were cut off from the wild olive tree, which is natural to you, and were grafted unnaturally onto the good olive tree, how

much more shall those natural branches be grafted onto their own olive tree? For just as external accidental forces form physical nature into different appearances, as has been said, so the grace of God either forms the rational soul into an olive tree, as it were, from its beginning, or makes a wild olive tree pass over into a true one; or else an abuse of free choice acts against this. God can be equally effective both with the true olive tree of the Jews, and the wild olive tree of the Gentiles.

Rm 11:25

VERSE TWENTY-FIVE. **I would not have you ignorant of this mystery, brethren, lest you be wise in your own conceits, that partial blindness has afflicted Israel, until the full number of the Gentiles come in, and so all Israel will be saved.** It is dangerous to rejoice over another's ruin; insolence is a sign of one's own imminent destruction. Fearful for the weaker of the gentile disciples, the Apostle reveals to them this hidden mystery about the salvation of the Jews, lest they think that the Jews are altogether alienated from God, both because partial blindness has afflicted Israel, and because the very fullness of the Gentiles cannot be completed without the general conversion of the Jews. But the Gentiles are wise in their own conceits. Neglecting to fear God's hidden judgments while they judge others, they estimate their own merits as a kind of guarantee of their own salvation. Blindness has afflicted Israel because of its own sins, so that the full number of the Gentiles might enter. When they have entered, the Jews' blindness must cease. How this shall be done the Apostle adds, saying:

Rm 11:26-27

VERSES TWENTY-SIX AND TWENTY-SEVEN. **There shall come out of Zion he who shall deliver and turn away ungodliness from Jacob, and this is my covenant with them when I take away their sins.** He shall come out of Zion of whom it is written, 'Out of Zion the loveliness of his beauty,'* who shall deliver the full number of the Gentiles from the enemy's possession, and take away ungodliness from Jacob so that they shall no longer envy the Gentiles, but com-

Cf. Is 59:20

Ps 49:2

pete with them in goodness.

'And this is my covenant with them when I take away their sins.' The Apostle adds something of his own which is not contained in the prophet: 'when I take away their sins', because, just as it is said about the Gentiles that the wickedness of the Amorites and of the inhabitants of Gomorrah was not yet filled up,* so until that time the wickedness of the Jews shall not be filled up or taken away. What is that full quantity of Gentiles before the wickedness of the Jews will be removed, and who is 'all Israel' that shall be saved—these are hidden elements of the mystery which the Apostle wished partly to be known and which he permitted partly to be unknown. For from the first humble coming of the Lord blindness has afflicted Israel. At the second coming all Israel shall be saved. Well known in the words and hearts of the faithful is the knowledge that the Jews will believe in the Lord Jesus before the judgment at the end of time, through the exposition of the law to the Jews through Elijah, the great and wonderful prophet. It is hoped that he will come before the arrival of the Judge; and he is being kept alive in the flesh until that time. He will expound spiritually the law which the Jews now observe carnally. 'And he shall turn the heart of the fathers to the children',* that is, with the result that the children understand the law as did their fathers, the prophets, among whom was Moses. For the heart of the fathers is turned to their children when the father's understanding is communicated to the children, and the heart of the children is turned to their fathers when the children feel the same as their fathers did.

Cf. Gen 15:16

Mal 4:6

Rm 11:28-29 VERSES TWENTY-EIGHT AND TWENTY-NINE. **As regards the gospel they are enemies for your sake; but as regards election they are most dear for the sake of their fathers.** What does it mean that they are enemies as regards the gospel for your sake, except that their enmity, by which they killed Christ, profited the gospel, as we see? And this, the Apostle shows, comes about by God's disposition, for he well knows how to use even the wicked. Not that the vessels of wrath bring him any profit, but he uses them well so that they profit the vessels of mercy. The wicked have the power to sin, but by their sinful malice to accomplish this result or that is not in their power, but in the power of God who so divides the darkness and orders it that, even in what they do against the will of God, only the will of God is accomplished. We read in the Acts of the Apostles that they were praying in the midst of persecution and after some other words said, 'There assembled in this city against your holy child Jesus, whom you anointed, Herod and Pilate and the people of Israel, to do as much as your hand and counsel decreed to be done.'* Behold what is meant by the words 'enemies for your sake as regards the gospel'. God's hand and counsel predestined as much to be done by the Jewish enemies as was necessary for the gospel for our sakes. *[Ac 4:27-28]*

But what is the meaning of the following sentence, 'But as regards election, they are most dear for the sake of their fathers'? Can the same people be enemies and also most dear? Far from it. Although enemies and most dear are contrary to each other, they can both pertain to the same Jewish people and to the same carnal seed of Israel, although not to the same men. Some of them belong to Jacob's limping and others to Israel's blessing.* The Apostle explained this meaning more openly above, where he said, 'That which Israel sought he has not obtained; but election has obtained it; and the rest have been blinded'. When we hear the expression 'election has obtained it,' we should understand those who are most dear for the sake of their fathers, to whom these things were promised. They were not called with the call spoken of in the words, 'Many are called, but few are chosen',* but with the call by which the elect are called. *[Cf. Gen 32:26, 31]* *[Mt 20:16]*

Thus, the text continues, **For the gifts and the calling of God are without repentance,** that is, they are firmly fixed without change. Those who belong to this calling are all 'taught by God';* and none of them can say, 'I believed so I might be called'. The grace of *[Is 54:13]*

God anticipated them all, because they were called so they might believe. All those who are taught by God come to the Son, because they have heard and learned from the Father through the Son who clearly says, 'Everyone who has heard and learned from the Father comes to me'.* None of these perish, for of all that the Father has given him he has lost nothing.* 'For the gifts and the calling of God are without repentance.' They are those of whom it is said, 'that you should go and should bring forth fruit and that your fruit should remain'.* By these words he shows that he gave them not only justice, but also perseverance in justice.

Jn 6:45
Cf. Jn 17:12, 18:9

Jn 15:16

Rm 11:30-31   VERSES THIRTY AND THIRTY-ONE. **As you in times past did not believe, but have now obtained mercy through their unbelief, so they now have not believed for your mercy, that they also may obtain mercy.** Here the Apostle reveals the deeper cause of the unbelievers' unbelief. Just as the Gentiles, who formerly did not believe, were not entirely abandoned but were unnaturally grafted from the wild olive tree onto the true olive on the occasion of the breaking off of the natural branches, so after the dispensation of the fullness of the Gentiles has been fulfilled, the Jews themselves will attain mercy. In this the Apostle wishes to show the goodness of God by which he effects the salvation of some through the unbelief of others.

Rm 11:32   VERSE THIRTY-TWO. **For God has consigned all men to unbelief, that he might have mercy on all.** Misunderstanding these words, some give themselves delusive comfort, but the context of the passage indicates whom he means by 'all men'. The Apostle is dealing with the Jews and the Gentiles, of whom God has consigned to infidelity all whom he has foreknown and predestined to conform to the image of his Son, so that being put to shame in penitence for the bitterness of their unbelief, and having turned in belief to the sweetness of the mercy of God, they might cry out in the words of the psalm, 'O how great is the multitude of your sweetness, O Lord, which you have hidden for those who fear you, which you have wrought for those who hope in you,'* and not in themselves. He has mercy on all the vessels of mercy; but of what 'all' is the Apostle speaking? Of those whom God has predestined, called, justified, and will glorify* from the Gentiles and from the Jews. Not of all men, but of all these men God has left none abandoned.

Ps 30:20

PL: glorified

Rm 11:33-36

VERSES THIRTY-THREE THROUGH THIRTY-SIX. O the depth of the riches of the wisdom and knowledge of God. How incomprehensible are his judgments, and how unsearchable his ways. For who has known the mind of the Lord? Or who has been his counsellor? Or who has first given to him that recompense should be made him? For from him, and through him, and in him are all things. To him be glory forever. Amen. First is given a profound judgment about the free, and not unjust, grace of God based on no preceding merits, which does not so much disturb us when it is given to the unworthy, as when it is denied to others equally unworthy. Why does election call this one and not that one? The Apostle is here knocking at the door of one of the Almighty's secrets and because he cannot be admitted within by knowledge, he humbly stands outside the door by humble confession, and what he cannot comprehend inside through understanding he praises outside through fear.[5] And let us therefore give thanks insofar as he has deigned to manifest his judgments to us; insofar as he has hidden them, let us not murmur against his counsel, but believe that his is very beneficial for us. For not in vain was it said, 'Your judgments are a great abyss'.* Frightened at the depth of that abyss, the Apostle exclaimed: 'From it come the riches of his glory on the vessels of mercy which he calls to adoption, and he wills to make known those riches even through the vessels of wrath fit for destruction.' The divine ways which can be investigated are those of which the psalm sings, 'All the ways of the Lord are mercy and truth'.* Mercy, because he

Ps 35:7

Ps 24:10

Rm 9:18 — has mercy on whom he will,* not in justice but in merciful grace; and he hardens whom he will, not in unfairness but in the truth of punishment. This
Cf. Ps 84:11 — mercy and truth have so met each other* that neither does mercy impede truth by which the worthy man is punished, nor does truth impede mercy by which the unworthy is freed. Are there, therefore, no merits for the just? There are merits, indeed, because there are just; but there were no merits to make them just. They were made just when they were justified. We have a very small capacity for discussing the judgments of God and their justice, and we should believe that even as nothing is impossible for him, so there is no injustice in him when he resists the proud and gives
Cf. Jas 4:6 — grace to the humble.*

'O the depth.' This depth is not the one which separates heaven and earth, because both heaven and earth are temporal and local, but it is the distance separating God from every temporal and local creature, which all creatures are. The depth of the wisdom of God is not attained by any creature's sense, nor understood by its intellect. In that depth are made all things; and although all things are made in it, those that sin do not defile it, for 'no defiled thing comes into it, although it reaches everywhere by rea-
Wis 7:24-25 — son of its purity'.*

Since God is wise and begets wisdom from himself, it is asked whether he is wise by himself for himself, or through that wisdom which he begets from himself; and also, whether he is wise in the same way as he speaks, for he speaks through the Word which he begot. But if the Father who begot wisdom is wise by that wisdom, his existence is not the same as his wisdom; it is a quality and not his Begotten Son. Also supreme simplicity is not there. But that certainly cannot be the case, because in the Father there is surely supremely simple essence. Therefore, being and wisdom are the same for him. But if being and wisdom are the same for him, the Father is not wise through that wisdom which he begot; otherwise, he did not beget wisdom, but wisdom begot him. What are we saying when we say that being and wisdom are the same for him, except that he is wise by that by which he is? Therefore, the cause of his being wise is the cause of his being. So the Father is wisdom itself, and the Son is called the wisdom of the Father as he is called the light of the Father. That is, just as the Son is light from light and both are one light, so the Son can be understood as wisdom from wisdom, and both are one wisdom. Therefore, there is one being, because here being is the same as wisdom. What being wise is to wisdom, and being able is to power, and being eternal is to eternity, being is to essence. And because in that simplicity being wise and being are not distinct, wisdom is the same as essence. Therefore, the Father and the Son are at the same time one essence and one magnitude, one truth, and one wisdom.[6]

These things and things of this sort which pertain to God no one knows except the Spirit of God, who is in God through unity of nature so that there is nothing in God which his Spirit cannot know through their natural unity. This fullness of knowledge is possessed only by the natural unity through which his Spirit is so in God that he is by nature one God with him. The Spirit of God is so in God and is one God with him that he does not have one person with him, as a man's spirit, which is in him, has with a man, for then there would be one person in the Trinity.

God the Trinity is of one and the same nature and substance, and is not less in each person than in all of them. The Trinity is not greater in all the persons than in each of them, but it is as much in the Father alone, or in the Son alone, as in the Father and the Son together, and as much in the Holy Spirit alone as in the Father and the Son and the Holy Spirit together. The Father did not diminish himself to produce the Son from himself, but he begot another self from himself in such a way that he would remain whole in himself, and yet be as great in the Son as in himself. Similarly the Holy Spirit, a whole proceeding from a whole, does not excel that from which he proceeds, but is as great with his source as from it. He did not diminish his source by proceeding from it, nor increase it by adhering to it.[7] And all of these are not

one in a confused manner, nor are they three
separately. Although they are three, they are one;
though they are one, they are three.⁸ These are the
riches of the wisdom of God, because to know God
the Father and Jesus Christ whom he has sent is eter-
Jn 17:3   nal life.* No one knows the Father but the Son, and
no one knows the Son except the Father and he to
Cf. Mt 11:27   whom he wills to reveal him.* He wills to do so
through the Holy Spirit. The Holy Spirit is the will of
the Father and the Son.⁹

    The providence or knowledge or judgments of
this wisdom affect an individual soul as much as a
[PL omits]   city, [and a city as much as a nation,] and a nation
as much as the whole multitude of the human race,
for the Lord so regards individuals as if he left aside
everyone else, and so regards the whole as if he left
aside the individuals. This is the meaning of the sentence, 'Who has known the mind of the Lord?' He
who fills all things by his administration rules them
by fulfilling them; neither is he absent from all when
he attends to one, nor is he absent from one when he
attends to all. By means of his natural power he
operates all things with tranquility.

    The Son is from the Father, with the result that he
exists and is coeternal with the Father. If the image
perfectly matches that of which it is the image, it is
made equal to the original, not the original to it.
Where there is such agreement, there is both fundamental equality and radical similarity, with total
absence of divergence, of inequality, of dissimilarity;
and the image corresponds exactly to that of which it
is the image. Here is the most excellent and highest
life, in which understanding and living are not two
different things; but understanding, living, and being
are all identical. One is all, just like a perfect word to
which nothing is lacking, or some art of the wise,
almighty God, full of all the unchangeable living
essences; all things are one in it, just as it is one from
the one with which it is one. In this [art] God knows
all the things which he made through it; and therefore, when times cease or succeed each other, nothing
ceases or changes in God's knowledge. For created

things are not known by God because they are made; but, on the contrary, they are made changeable because they are known unchangeably by God. This is that inestimable depth of the riches of the wisdom and knowledge of God.

But that unspeakable embrace of the Father and the Image is not without fruition, charity and joy. In the Trinity the Holy Spirit is that love, delight, happiness or beatitude, if indeed he is worthily mentioned in any human term. He is not begotten, but is the sweetness of the Begetter and the Begotten, flooding with great generosity and richness over all creatures according to their capacity, so that they may hold to their order and agree to their stations.[10] Whoever sees this even partially, even in a mirror and an enigma, let him rejoice. Insofar as he sees this, he 'knows the mind of the Lord', and let him give thanks. Whoever does not see this, let him tend through piety toward seeing, toward loving. Let him not be an evil counsellor, tending to calumny because of blindness, and wishing to correct the order of supreme equity according to the whims of his own will. All creatures either hold to this order, or do not escape it, even if they do not agree to the places assigned them by God.

The text continues: 'Who has first given to him, that recompense should be made him?' It is in one tone of voice that you say to a man, 'You are indebted to me because you made me a promise', and in a different tone, 'You are indebted to me because I gave you something'. When you say, 'You are indebted to me because I gave you something', the favor proceeded from you, and it was loaned, not given. When you say, 'You are indebted to me because you made me a promise', you gave nothing and yet you make a demand. It is the goodness of him who promised which will give, lest his pledged word turn into bad conduct. For he who deceives is evil. But do we say to God, 'Make a return to me because I gave to you'? What did we give to God, when everything good that we are and have we have from him? Therefore, we gave him nothing.[11] This is how we can press our claim on the Lord our God, 'Give what you promised because we did what you ordered, and even this you did, because you helped us in our labor'. See what God first gave to you, what he did for you, when he predestined you who did not yet exist. As the Apostle says, 'He calls those things that are not, as those that are'.* If you were already in existence, you would not have been predestined. Unless you turned away, you would not have been called. Unless you were wicked, you would not have been justified. [Unless you were earthly and wretched, you would not have been glorified.] What then shall we return? 'To him be glory', because we did not exist when we were predestined; because we turned away when we were called; because we were sinners when we were justified. For all these things let us give thanks to God, lest we be ungrateful.

'For from him, and through him, and in him are all things. To him be glory forever. Amen.' Religion ties us to the one almighty God, because no creature is interposed between our mind (by which we understand the Father) and the truth (that is, the interior light through which we understand him). Therefore, let us also venerate that truth which in no way is different in him and with him, which is the form of all things which are made by him and which strive toward him. Therefore, it is clear to spiritual souls that all things are made through this form which alone provides what all things seek. All these things would not be made by the Father through the Son, nor would they be kept within their limits, unless God existed to a supreme degree and denied to no nature the goods which could come from him. And in regard to the good, he gave permanence to some things to the degree that they wanted, and to others to the degree that they were capable of.

Therefore, it behooves us to cherish and to preserve the Gift of God, equally immutable with the Father and the Son, and of one substance, the Trinity, one God from whom we are, through whom we are, in whom we are. From him we departed, to him we became unlike, from him we were not permitted to perish. He is the principle to whom we return, the

Rm 4:17

[PL omits]

form which we follow, the grace by which we are reconciled. He is the one Creator by which we were created, the likeness by which we are reformed to unity, and the peace by which we cling to unity.[12] This is the only thing which we should enjoy, the Holy Trinity, if indeed it is a thing and not the cause of all things, if indeed it is a cause. An appropriate name which is suitable for such excellence cannot be found, unless it is somewhat acceptable to say the Trinity, one God, from whom, through whom, and in whom are all things. Thus, it is the Father, and the Son, and the Holy Spirit; and each one of them singly is God, and together they are all one God. Each one of them singly is the full substance, and together they are all one substance. Yet the Father is not the Son nor the Holy Spirit; the Son is not the Father nor the Holy Spirit; the Holy Spirit is neither the Father nor the Son. The same eternity, the same immutability, majesty, and power belong to the three. In the Father is unity, in the Son is equality, and in the Holy Spirit the connection of unity and equality. And these three are all one on account of the Father, and equal on account of the Son, and connected through the Holy Spirit.[13] Therefore, the sentence, 'From whom are all things, through whom are all things, and in whom are all things', should not be taken in a confused sense. And not to many gods, but, 'to him be glory forever. Amen'.

NOTES

1. The previous paragraph and this one down to this point are Augustine, *Letter 190.3;* PL 33:859-861. Florus refers to this section, PL 119:305.
2. The previous paragraph and this one to here are Origen, *On Roms;* PG 14:1155.
3. 'It is very different with the justice . . . ' William here condenses a gloss from fol. 10ᵛ of MS 49.
4. This paragraph down to here is Origen, *On Roms;* PG 14:1190.
5. This sentence is attributed to Gregory the Great in a gloss on fol. 12ᵛ of MS 49. The exact reference has not been found.
6. 'But if the Father who begot wisdom . . . ' down to here is Augustine, *Trinity 7.1.2;* PL 42:934. Also, this passage is used in *Enigma;* CF 9:82-83.
7. This paragraph down to here is based on Augustine, *Letter 170.5;* PL 33:749. It occurs in *Enigma;* CF 9:92.
8. The previous two sentences are from Augustine, *Letter 170.5;* PL 33:749. They also occur in *Enigma,* CF 9:105.
9. The equation of the Holy Spirit with the will of the Father and the Son is Augustinian. See later in this same section where the Holy Spirit is called the love, delight, happiness, and sweetness of the Trinity. Cf. *Enigma;* CF 9:114-115.
10. The previous paragraph and this one down to this point are from Augustine, *Trinity 6.10.11;* PL 42:931. This passage is referred to by Florus, PL 119:311. The last sentence, for the most part, occurs in William's *Enigma;* CF 9:116.
11. This paragraph down to here is Augustine, *Sermon 158.2.2;* PL 38:863. Florus refers to it, PL 119:311.
12. The previous paragraph and this one down to here are Augustine, *On True Religion;* PL 34:172. Also, Florus, PL 119:311.
13. 'This is the only thing which we should enjoy . . . ' down to here is Augustine, *On Christian Doctrine 1.5;* PL 34:21. Also, Florus, PL 119:311.

BOOK SEVEN

CHAPTER TWELVE

Rm 12:1-3   VERSES ONE THROUGH THREE. **Therefore, I beseech you, brethren, by the mercy of God, to present your bodies as a living sacrifice, holy, pleasing unto God, your reasonable service.** True sacrifice is every good work that is done in order that we may cling in holy union to God, that is relative to that good end by which we may be truly blessed and happy. Therefore, mercy itself is not sacrifice if not done for God, for sacrifice is a godly thing. For this reason man himself, when consecrated and devoted to the name of God, is a sacrifice insofar as he dies to the world in order to live to God. Our body also, when we chastise it by temperance as we should, and do it for God's sake, is a sacrifice, and to this the Apostle exhorts us in this text. Therefore, if the body (although the soul uses it as an inferior, as a servant or a tool) is a sacrifice when its right and good use is referred to God, how much more will the soul itself become a sacrifice when it refers itself to God in order to be burned up with the fire of his love and so to lose the form of worldly concupiscence, and be reformed and subject to him as an immutable form, thus pleasing him because receiving of his beauty? The Apostle proceeds to add this, saying: **And do not be conformed to this world; but be reformed in the newness of your sense, that you may ascertain what is the good, and the acceptable, and the perfect will of God.** Since works of mercy are true sacrifices, whether they are performed for us—as it is said, 'Have mercy on your own soul, pleasing God'*—or for our neighbors—provided these works are referred to God—and since works of mercy are done for no other reason than that we may be freed from misery and become blessed, and this is not done except by that good of which it is said, 'It is good for me to adhere to God'* so it is that [the city of God,] the whole congregation and society of the saints, is offered as a universal sacrifice to God through the high priest, who also offered himself for us in his passion according to the form of a slave, so that we might be the body of such a head; and he offered this form, and he was offered in this form, because in it he is mediator, priest, and sacrifice.[1] 'That you may ascertain what is the good and the acceptable and the perfect will of God.'

In three ways we merit to know the will of God:[2] by being still and seeing that he is God;* by firmly believing that every word of God is true, for 'unless you believe, you will not understand';* and by fulfilling the word and will of God according to our strength. One will of God is good, another acceptable, and another perfect. The will of God is good when is fulfilled the saying, 'I desire mercy and not sacrifice',* that is, when we show ourselves cheerful in works of mercy and eager in bodily asceticism, in those done for God. The acceptable will of God is cleanness of heart. His perfect will is when we are deformed from the world in action and affect and are conformed to God. In bodily asceticism reasonable service is required; in purity of heart, a newness of spiritual perception* that in no way serves the oldness of the flesh or of the letter. Reasonable service means that just as we yielded our members to serve uncleanness and iniquity unto iniquity, so now we yield our

Si 30:24

Ps 72:28
[PL omits]

Cf. Ps 45:11

Is 7:9 (LXX)

Hos 6:6

sensus

members to serve justice unto sanctification.* *Cf. Rm 6:19* Through this we merit newness of perception and receive the grace of the spirit of understanding. Through it we come closer to the likeness of God and regain his image, which we partially, but not totally, lost by acting in a contrary manner. If we had lost the whole image nothing would have remained, and so it would be said, 'Although man passes as an image, in vain is he troubled.'* *Cf. Ps 38:7* But if we had lost nothing at all of the image there would be no reason to say, 'Be reformed in the newness of your perception.'

The soul cannot reform itself as it could deform itself, for no one can be continent unless God grants it.* *Wis 8:21* This reformation consists of two things, prohibition and command. The general prohibition is, 'You shall not covet',* *Cf. Rm 7:7* and the general command is, 'You shall love'.* *Cf. Mt 22:37* This is what is meant by not being conformed to the world but conformed to God. The former pertains to not-coveting, and the latter to loving. The former to continence; the latter to justice. The former to turning away from evil; the latter to doing good. By not coveting we are stripped of oldness, and by loving we put on newness. This will be accomplished in us by the love of God which is poured forth in our hearts, not through us, but through the Holy Spirit who is given to us.* *Cf. Rm 5:5*

When our affections are restrained from the love of the world, and when not being conformed to the world has become a reality in us, then renewal in the newness of our perception will follow immediately. We shall no longer imitate our neighbor as a model,* *genus* and live by the authority of a better man, for God did not say of man, 'Let us make man according to a model', but 'Let us make man according to our image and likeness'.* *Gen 1:26* The result will be that we ourselves shall finally begin 'to ascertain what is the good and acceptable and perfect will of God'. When a man is renewed in mind and perceives the will of God with understanding, he does not need another man to show him how to imitate his own model, but with God himself showing him, he ascertains what is the will of

God and his good pleasure.

For I say, by the grace that is given me. What I say to you I do not say through human wisdom, but through the grace which is given to me. 'For to one is given the word of wisdom, and to another the word of knowledge.'* The effect of the word of knowledge is that what is said is clear and therefore pleases; the effect of the word of wisdom is that what is said has savor and therefore moves us. 'I may be rude in speech, yet not in knowledge,'* he says. It is clear therefore that the Apostle received the grace of the word of wisdom and of knowledge, but he confesses himself unskilled in verbal embellishment. When the preaching of the truth is carried out in truth and grace, it transforms the whole manner of the speaker, his face, voice, and words, and forms them into proper and clear tools, so that what our Lord says is plainly carried out: 'It is not you who speak, but the Spirit of your Father who speaks in you'.* There is a great difference between one who speaks with a wisdom for words and one who speaks through grace, and far different are their results. Therefore, the Apostle restrains his hearers from the emptiness of worldly wisdom.

He says: **Not to be more wise than is fitting, but to be wise unto sobriety.** He is speaking to the proud branches of the wild olive, to which he had said above, 'Be not highminded, but fear'.* Anyone who has not received grace in regard to the word of doctrine and the nature of profound knowledge and yet seeks to boast, although he is less than wise, wishes to be wiser than is fitting. 'But be wise unto sobriety.' Virtue is contrary to sin, and whatever is not virtue is sin. But if anything is either added to virtue or subtracted from it, that is sin according to the judgment of the ancient philosophers.[3] Here the Greek text does not have the word 'sobriety' but 'temperance',[4] indicating that we should maintain temperance in everything that we do, say, or feel.

As God has apportioned a measure of faith to each one. Behold, an open confession of that grace which the Apostle is vehemently commending: the

1 Cor 12:8

2 Cor 11:6

Mt 10:20

Rm 11:20

measure of faith, without which it is impossible to please God,* by which the just man lives,† which works by love,** and before which and without which no one's works are to be counted good, for 'all that is not of faith is sin'.* He says God has distributed this faith to each man. For 'there are diversities of graces, but the same Spirit'.* It is clear that we cannot love Christ or keep his commandments without the Holy Spirit. The less we have received him, the less we can do; the more we have received him, the more we can do. And therefore he is promised not only to those who do not possess him, but even to those who do possess him. The Only-begotten alone has not received him in a measured way, 'because in him dwells all the fullness of divinity'.* That the Only-begotten Son is equal to the Father is not a matter of grace but of nature; but that a man was taken up into unity with the only-begotten person is a matter of grace, not of nature. To the rest of men he is given in measure, as God has divided to everyone the measure of faith. Now, the Spirit himself is not divided, but the gifts are divided by the Spirit. Therefore, he he adds:

*Heb 11:6
†Rm 1:17
**Gal 5:6

Rm 14:23

1 Cor 12:4

Col 2:9

Rm 12:4-5

VERSES FOUR AND FIVE. **For as in one body we have many members, but all the members do not have the same function, so we, though many, are one body in Christ, and individually members of one another.** The man who strives for more power than he has received tries to exceed the limitations placed on him. But the man who does not heed the limits of his capacity sets his foot on a precipice. We are instructed by our bodily posture, and it is most disgraceful not to imitate what we are. The foot sees by means of the eye, and the eyes walk by means of the foot, and thus all the members support one another and become one by agreeing with each other. Therefore, the text says, 'individually members of one another.' Different gifts are possessed for this very purpose.

Rm 12:6

VERSE SIX. **And having different gifts, according to the grace that is given us.** These gifts are the gifts of the Holy Spirit by whom they are given, and these gifts are brought to each one until the proper measure of his perfection is complete. They differ for different people so that the unity of the body is build from a diversity of members.

Either prophecy according to the reasoning of faith This prophecy is that which the Apostle Paul teaches, not that which says, 'Thus says the Lord'. For 'the law and the prophets lasted until John'.* Not that even later there was a lack of prophets who predicted the future, laid bare secrets, and foretold things not present, when and where it pleased him whose gifts these are; but in the age of grace, after all that the prophets prophesied has shone forth, prophecy now belongs in the order of miracles and is not to be sought except when just cause demands it. It is to be given, however, by the giver of gifts when and where he judges it necessary. It is this prophecy about which the same Apostle says, 'He who prophesies speaks to men for their edification, exhortation and comfort'.* Is it not certainly prophecy when contempt of the present and an appetite for the future is preached? Therefore, the sons of the prophets in the company of Elijah and Elisha were said to lead a prophetic life,* which we now call eremitic. If this is carried out rightly both in teaching and in manner of living, either in the church or in the desert,[5] it is the most important of the gifts, provided it is truly lived according to the 'analogy of faith', for this is what the Greek text has.[6] But often pestilences are found in the cathedras of the churches,* and vipers' dens in the desert, when they try to be wiser than is fitting and do not proceed according to the analogy, that is, the right rule, of faith and the pious sobriety of the Church. There is also the discernment of the spirits of prophecy and the knowledge of the hidden meaning of the scriptures, and the ability to bring forth at the right time new and old things from the good treasure of the heart. By the word 'doctrine' which follows in the text is to be understood simple edification. 'Exhortation' means gentle moral instruction.

Lk 16:16

1 Cor 14:3

Cf. 1 Kgs 19:21, 2 Kgs 6:1

Cf. Ps 1:1

Rm 12:7-16	VERSES SEVEN THROUGH SIXTEEN. After prophecy is listed ministry, because as prophecy is necessary in spiritual matters, ministry is necessary in temporal affairs.

Anyone who gives, with simplicity; that is, let him give in simple charity, asking nothing further.

Anyone who rules, let him rule **with concern;** not with worldly concern, but with that about which the Apostle says, 'My daily concern for all the churches'.* And explaining what that is, he says, 'Who is weak and I am not weak? Who is scandalized, and I am not on fire?'*

2 Cor 11:28

2 Cor 11:29

Anyone who shows mercy, let him enhance his work of mercy with the grace of cheerfulness. To teach and to exhort seem to pertain to prophecy, but to give with simplicity, to rule with concern, to show mercy with cheerfulness seem to pertain to ministry. What follows is common to all.

Let love be without dissimulation. Hating evil, clinging to good. Note the purity of this holy teaching. In love a simple inner disposition is needed. It is not enough to turn away from evil and do good, unless there is hatred for evil and love for good.

In the phrase which follows, **Loving the charity of the brotherhood mutually,*** pay attention to the Apostle's meaning as he instructs others about his meaning. For what is the charity of the brotherhood except the charity of charity? What does it mean to love the charity of the brotherhood, except to love the love of love? This is absolutely so. If we really love our brothers, we love both our brothers and the brotherly love in us.

Cf. Rm 12:10

The two things which follow apply to the discipline of this same love; that the honor which anticipates one another might stir up mutual charity, and that they be solicitious in heart and not lazy in work. In the duties of this charity let them be **fervent in spirit, serving the Lord.** That is, let them serve the Lord with fervor of spirit.

Let them **rejoice in hope** and, therefore, be **patient in tribulation,** and for this reason, **persevering in prayer.** We must persevere in prayer lest the enemy snatch prayer away, or negligence lose it.

We should help in everyone's needs, but in the case of the saints we should even share in their needs, so, if necessary, we can suffer need with them. We should not only show hospitality, but even pursue it, for guests are to be urged and encouraged. **Bless those who persecute you;** bless them with your mouth, and **do not curse** them in your heart. **Rejoice with those who rejoice** over the good progress of those who rejoice rightly, and **weep with those who weep** with the compassion of fraternal charity over penitence for sins.

Agree with one another, consenting to the humble for this purpose, not talking together, but consenting together,[7] because the very mind of humility must be put on. This cannot be if you would savor lofty things. Note that in regard to what is common the Apostle used the word 'agree', but in regard to what is lofty and above others, the word 'savor' because whatever reveals his loftiness usually savors sweetly in the heart of a proud man. This normally happens to those who are great in their own eyes, but whom he adds:

Rm 12:16-17 VERSES SIXTEEN AND SEVENTEEN. **Be not wise in your own conceits.** In all these things and for the sake of all these things, if a person does you some evil, **to no one render evil for evil. Providing good things, not only in the sight of God, but also in the sight of all men.** Our conscience we owe to God, to our neighbor our reputation. The fact that he says 'all men' signifies that we owe good example even to those who are outside.

Rm 12:18 VERSE EIGHTEEN. **If it be possible, as much as is in you, be at peace with all men.** It would be difficult to be at peace with everyone, even if they corrected everything that should be corrected, but sometimes by dissimulating in certain matters, exterior peace should be sought in such a way that there is no interior withdrawal from the peace of God.

Rm 12:19 VERSE NINETEEN. **Revenge not yourselves,**

dearly beloved. He calls them 'dearly beloved' as if to soothe them, when he invites them more urgently to humility and patience. The simplicity of a holy soul finds it sweet to keep its vindication for God, lest, as it struggles to defend itself, it lose the practice of patience and sometimes act against God's scourges. **But give place to wrath.** To give place to wrath is not to resist the wrathful man, but to expose oneself and all one's things to his anger. **For it is written, 'Revenge is mine, I will repay,' says the Lord.*** We should wish our persecutors corrected rather than punished, and if vengeance is carried out against them in this world, we should not take delight in the punishment of the enemy whom we do not hate, but in the justice of God whom we love.

Deut 32:35

Rm 12:20-21   VERSES TWENTY AND TWENTY-ONE. **But if your enemy is hungry, feed him; if he thirsts, give him drink. For, doing this, you shall heap coals of fire upon his head.** Some say about enemies that it is enough not to hate them, but we are debtors even to love, because they provide what the Lord speaks of in 'Blessed are those who suffer persecution'.*[8] But whoever does good to his enemy in order to heap coals of fire on his head, that is, in order only to bring him to confusion, is himself an enemy. But let us do simply and with a good motive what pertains to us, and it will follow that they will be put to shame and perhaps even be converted. Even if this does not happen in the heart of him to whom it happens, it should be in the intention of him who does it. If he perseveres in doing this, he will not be overcome by evil as though he became evil through an evil intention, and so there would be two evil men; but he will conquer evil by good, and so there will be two good men.

Mt 5:10

CHAPTER THIRTEEN

Rm 13:1   VERSE ONE. **Let every soul be subject to higher powers.** If those in power are good, they nurture us; if they are evil, they tempt us. But let us love to be

|[PL omits]| nurtured and let us not avoid being tempted. For both are from God. Therefore, let us be subject to God and not as to men. This subjection [of the lover] originates in love; but just as those who fear owe love to those who terrify them from a position of power, so those who terrify must know that they owe love to those who fear them.

And whatever powers exist are ordained by God. Men's malice can have an eagerness to harm, but it cannot have the power to harm, unless it is given from above. Power is sometimes given to the wicked, but under God's control, so that the patience of the just can be proved and the iniquity of the evil can be punished.

Rm 13:2

[PL omits]

VERSE TWO. **Therefore, he who resists a power resists the ordinance of God. And they who resist acquire for themselves damnation.** However, if the power commands what God prohibits, then, Christian, spurn power [because of power]. For it threatens punishment, but God threatens hell.

Rm 13:3-4

VERSES THREE AND FOUR. **For princes are not a terror to good work, but to evil. Do you wish not to fear power? Do what is good, and you shall have praise from it. For it is God's minister to you for good.** If you do good and the power is good, you shall have praise from it by its own judgment. If the power is bad, then even if you are punished and slain, you shall have praise from it, by its very ferocity.

But if you do what is evil, fear; for he does not bear the sword in vain. There is a proper time to fear; namely, when a bad conscience deserves punishment. For it is bad to sin, but much worse not to fear punishment when one is in the wrong. A secular judge fulfills the greatest part of God's law, for he is the minister through whose ministry are punished crimes which God does not wish to be punished through the bishops and prelates of the Church.[9] Therefore, the Apostle says, **For he is God's minister.**

Rm 13:5

VERSE FIVE. **Therefore, you must be submissive,**

because he who so orders so wills, **not only for wrath, but also for conscience's sake,** not only to avoid offending men, but also to have a good conscience toward God who so ordained. For, just as being angry is not without sin, so provocation to anger is not without sin.

|Rm 13:6|
|Cf. Mt 17:25|
|[PL omits]|

VERSE SIX. Therefore, by the authority of the Lord himself, since you are children and free,* you do [not] pay tribute, but you give it, since you will receive it again from him whose precept and example in this matter you hold. **For they are ministers of God, serving unto this purpose,** and servants should be paid their salaries. Therefore, the Lord prescribed

Cf. 1 Cor 9:14

that the ministers of the gospel live from the gospel.*

VERSE SEVEN. **Render therefore to all men their due.** To whom does the Apostle say this? To those who trusted in Christian holiness and liberty, and thought they were exempt from serving the public vanity, which creation serves both willingly and unwillingly. Unwillingly, because creation yearns for the glory of the sons of God and for the expectation of its blessed liberty; willingly, on account of

Cf. Rm 8:18-25

him who subjected it in hope.* Therefore, also according to the counsel of the Apostle, if it can be

Cf. 1 Cor 7:21

free, it uses the opportunity more.* 'Render therefore their due,' he says, just as you fulfill what is required if you faithfully cause to be your debtor in obedience him to whom you do not refuse to be debtors.

Tribute to whom tribute is due; revenue to whom revenue is due. Every son of the kingdom is a stranger on the earth dwelling in a foreign land as long as he is in the world. But one wishes to defile the laws of hospitality if he wishes to violate the laws of the land where he is.

Fear to whom fear is due; honor to whom honor is due. It is stupid madness to want to fear no one because of an arrogant holiness, and it is the shallowest sort of pride to wish to honor no one. Fear is owed to high power, honor is owed to humble service, and love to benevolence.

Rm 13:8

VERSE EIGHT. **Owe no man anything but to love one another.** Passing from the higher powers to the grace of a life in society, the expert on God's law, just as he orders that whatever is owed according to the world's law should be paid, so in regard to the law of charity decrees that nothing is owed except the debt of charity alone, which is owed all the more, the more it is paid, and which is possessed even more by being paid. For he who loves makes a debtor out of him whom he loves. Love itself demands a debt, so that we who serve fraternal charity help as much as we can him who rightly wishes to be helped, and still we continually remain debtors to charity. Charity is owed even if it has been given, because there is no time when it should not be given. When it is faithfully rendered, charity itself causes us to owe nothing else besides it.

See how through charity the Apostle reduces all things to unity. In the faith of Christ there is no distinction between Jew and Greek, between slaves and free men, between ruler and subject; insofar as all are of the faith all are one in Christ Jesus. And if [faith] does this, through which one walks justly in this life, how much more perfectly and completely will that vision accomplish this when we see face to face? Now, although they have the firstfruits of the Spirit, which is life on account of the justice of faith, yet because the body is still dead because of sin, this difference of race, of status, or of sex, although removed by the unity of faith, still remains in this mortal existence, and the apostles command that this order be maintained throughout the course of this life. They even give very sound rules on how the faithful are to live together in light of these differences of race or status, and the Lord himself already enjoined, 'Render to Caesar the things which are Caesar's.'*

[PL: in faith]

Mt 22:21

Then the Apostle comes to the common, mutual love which pertains to life in society; this he so praises and approves that he says the whole law is fulfilled in the love of neighbor alone. Thus he says, 'Owe no man anything but to love one another. For he who loves his neighbor has fulfilled the law'.

Rm 13:9	**VERSE NINE. For 'You shall not commit adultery. You shall not kill. You shall not steal. You shall
Ex 20:13-17	not bear false witness. You shall not covet.'* And if there is any other commandment, it is summed up in
Lev 19:18	this statement, 'Love your neighbor as yourself.'*** One can ask why the Apostle mentioned only love of neighbor, by which he said the law is fulfilled. Why, unless because men can lie about love of God, since they are more rarely tried in regard to it? But in regard to love of neighbor, they are more easily convicted of not having it when they act badly toward men. The result is that he who loves God with his whole heart, his whole soul, and his whole mind, also loves his neighbor as himself, because he whom he so loves orders this. If he loves himself for himself, he does not refer himself to God; he is turned toward himself with the result that he cannot be turned to anything unchangeable. Therefore, he enjoys himself with a certain disadvantage, because he is better off when he wholly clings and is bound to the unchangeable good than when he is loosed from it and even left to himself. So if you ought not love yourself for your own sake but for the sake of him wherein the goal of your most proper love lies, another man should not be angry if you also love him on account of God, for this is the divinely constituted rule of love. He says, 'You
Lev 19:18	shall love your neighbor as yourself.'*

We should love God with our whole heart, our whole soul and our whole mind, so that we direct all our thoughts, our whole life and our whole understanding toward him from whom we have those things which we direct toward him. When he said 'with your whole heart, your whole soul, your whole mind', he left no part of our life aside which might be excluded to give room, so to speak, for the enjoyment of anything else. Whatever presents itself to be loved should be taken with our whole soul there where the entire thrust of love rushes. Therefore, whoever rightly loves his neighbor should influence his neighbor also to love God in this way. Thus loving him as he loves himself, he refers all of his and his neighbor's love to that love of God which allows no rivulet so to be directed away from it that it is diminished by its outpouring.

Rm 13:10 VERSE TEN. **Love of neighbor does no evil. Love therefore is the fulfilment of the law.** By 'neighbor' every man should be understood, because there is no one to whom evil should be done. For who does evil to him whom he loves? Love, and you cannot but do good to him whom you love. Perhaps you strike him, but you do it for discipline's sake, because love of that love does not permit you to neglect the undisciplined one. In some way different and contrary fruit appear so that sometimes hatred caresses and love rages. Charity therefore does no evil, but accomplishes every manner of good, because the fulfilment of the law is charity by which God and neighbor are loved. And on these two commandments

Mt 22:40 depend the whole law and the prophets.* Rightly is he guilty of all, who acts against that on which all depend; no one sins except by acting against that.

'Love therefore is the fulfilment of the law', not
[PL omits] that love by which men love themselves [as men],
but that which the Lord distinguished from other
Jn 15:12 loves saying, 'As I have loved you'.* Why has Christ the Lord loved us except that we might be able to reign with him? So that we might fulfill the law therefore, let us distinguish our love from that of others who do not love themselves for this purpose, because they do not love. They love themselves who love themselves in order to possess God. Therefore, let them love God in order to love themselves. This is not the love of everyone; there are few who so love
Cf. 1 Cor 15:28 themselves that God is all in all.*

Rm 13:11 VERSE ELEVEN. **And know this: that it is now the hour for us to rise from sleep. For now our salvation is nearer than when we first believed.** Up to now the Apostle has been engaged in moral teaching. Now he hastens the pace, pressing the matter, rebuking the idle, rousing sleepers, emphasizing the passage of time which is paramount in every undertaking. Every sleepy, lazy person is roused by the brightness of the coming day, and his inertia is rebuked by the splendor of the rising sun if it finds him sleeping. Understanding and love are senses of the rational soul. When in a man's heart these senses are alert to the Lord his God, they are awake. They slumber or sleep when they grow lazy and listless in their hunger for the delights of temporal things. Since those who sleep sleep at night, as day appears he rouses the sleepers to be alert and says, 'It is now the hour for us to rise from sleep'. What hour? It is the morning of grace, when the dark night of infidelity has passed, and there is expected that illumination in which the thoughts of the heart will be revealed, and then each one will have his praise from God.* We are placed on this pilgrimage in this light of faith, which is daylight compared to the darkness of unbelievers,[10] but night compared to the light in which we shall see face to face; and we must rise from sleep, and adapt our life to the future life, which is closer now than when we first believed; as the Lord says, 'When you see these things come to pass, know that the kingdom of God is at hand'.* Therefore, because we should be lovers of eternity and of unity, desiring to cling to our one Lord God, we should turn our soul away from the multitude of things that are born and that die.

Cf. 1 Cor 4:5

Lk 21:31

Rm 13:12-13 VERSES TWELVE AND THIRTEEN. **Let us therefore cast off the works of darkness, and put on the armor of light,** so that we walk honorably **as one should walk in the day.** By walking honorably we are in the daylight compared to unbelievers. The Apostle subsequently shows what the works of darkness are, what should be cast away, what is not fit to be done in the light of faith, and what the clear light of truth rebukes.

Not in reveling and drunkenness, not in debauchery and licentiousness. The most disgraceful kind of drunkenness usually accompanies extravagant banqueting, and what does banqueting entail except immodest and foul debauchery? What except contentions and envy? Those who walk honorably as in the day do the following: They take care not to make provision for the flesh in its concupiscences. They do nothing by contention and envy, but hasten to put on the Lord Jesus Christ, that is, wisdom and justice and sanctification and the other virtues. He who puts these into his affection is believed to have put on the Lord Jesus. The text continues:

Rm 13:14

VERSE FOURTEEN. **And make no provision for the flesh in its desires.** The flesh is to be cared for, but not in its desires. Hunger and thirst are like diseases, and they kill like a fever unless nourishment is supplied like medicine. Since this medicine is available through the consolation of the gifts of God, for heaven and sea and earth minister to our infirmity, this misfortune is called delight. But temperance teaches that we should approach food as we do medicine. But the snare of concupiscence lies in wait for us in the very transition by which we pass from the distress of want to the calm of fullness. The transition itself is a pleasure, and there is no other way to pass except where necessity compels us. And although health is the cause of eating, a perilous enjoyment attaches itself like a lackey, and often tries to run ahead so that what is thought to be done for the sake of health is done for pleasure. And the same measure does not fit both of them, for what is enough for health is too little for pleasure. And often it is uncertain whether necessary concern for the body is seeking support or whether a willful desire for deceit is asking for help. And the unhappy soul is delighted at this uncertainty, and with it prepares a defense and an excuse, rejoicing that it is not clear how much is needed for the maintenance of health; and under the pretext of health it hides the business of pleasure.[11] For we are forbidden not to care for the flesh, but for its desires. Those who succumb to them live miserably. But those who have undertaken war against them will not have peace as long as the flesh lusts against the spirit.

CHAPTER FOURTEEN

Rm 14:1

VERSE ONE. **As for the man who is weak in faith, welcome him.** After the Apostle has repressed the wantonness of desire in caring for the body, he also prescribes the mode of self-restraint necessary for those gathered from among the Jews and the Gentiles into one church, who seem to cause division on account of different foods. He brings them back into the unity of peace by restraining the scandals arising among them from this cause, and by restraining their rash judgments of one another. For, the Jews even with the light of the gospel abstained from the foods forbidden in the law, and could not be so quickly torn away from the old custom of the law, and therefore were believed by the Gentiles to remain Jews. But the Gentiles with freer and more confident faith partook of all things with thanksgiving, not even refraining for the sake of conscience from food offered to idols, and so were thought by the weaker brethren especially the Jews to eat the food of idols. In this way they caused divisions and judged each other, and seemd to split

[PL omits] the unity. [The Apostle teaches that the actions of those who are strong in faith must be moderated for the sake of those weak in the faith.] The Apostle teaches that each one is still to be left to his own opinion for the sake of peace, because sometimes something by which conscience is hurt, even if only a little or hardly at all, is to be tolerated, lest one fall into what imperils salvation. Therefore, he commands that he who is weak in faith, or sickly in making judgments regarding food, should be taken and not rejected; that is, he is to be moved to better things by word and example and patience. He forbids disputes about others' thoughts as long as what is done and why it is done remain hidden because of the blindness of this mortal life.

Rm 14:2

VERSE TWO. **For one, that is, one more firm in faith, believes that he may eat anything,** but another who has not reached this measure of faith thinks that is not allowed him. Let such a man be left to himself for the time being. **Let him eat vegetables,** let him receive ordinary food until he has grown strong for better things by the use and improvements of his faith.

Rm 14:3

VERSE THREE. **Let not one who eats despise him who abstains,** as though he were still a Jew. **And let one who abstains not judge him who eats,** as though he knowingly ate an offering to an idol, or as if he ate out of greed what was forbidden by the law. **God has welcomed him,** whether he eats or does not eat, for God is the cause of his eating or his not eating. In regard to the use of food we should know that there is no justice in abstaining or in eating, but in the equanimity of tolerating scarcity, and in the temperance of not destroying ourselves by abundance, and of taking or not taking in an opportune way those things whose greedy consumption, not whose use, is to be restrained. It makes no difference at all what food you take to help the body in its necessities, as long as you suit your food to the people with whom you must live. Nor does the quantity you consume matter much, since we see some whose stomachs are soon filled, and yet who open their mouths eagerly, impatiently and in a way completely unbecoming for that little amount of good that satisfies them. Others require a little more to satisfy them, but they tolerate scarcity with more patience and can quietly look at a feast set right before them and not touch it, if at the time there is some need or necessity. It is less a question of what or how much food someone takes to suit himself or to take care of the needs of his health, than a question of the ease and serenity of soul with which he can go without food, when it is required or necessary to go without, so that in the soul of the Christian is fulfilled what the Apostle says, 'I know how to abound and how to suffer hunger'.*

Phil 4:12

Num 11

They were not like this who desired to eat flesh, although manna rained on them from heaven.* They were disgusted with what they had, and what they did not have they impudently asked for, as if they could not better have asked, not that the food that was missing should be supplied for their indecent appetite, but that the food which was there should be improved by the removal of their distaste. For when evil delights us and good does not, we should instead ask God that good delight us than that evil be granted us. It is not evil to eat meat, since every creature of God is good,[12] but it was no small offence to reject what wisdom gave, and to ask for that which greed sought, although they did not ask but murmured because it was missing. But in order that we might know that at fault is not God's creation, but rather contumacious disobedience and inordinate greed, the first man found death not because of pork but for the sake of an apple;* and Esau lost his birthright not for a chicken, but for lentils.* So, beware of rash judgment in this matter. Thus, the text continues:

Gen 3
Gen 25:34

Rm 14:4

VERSE FOUR. **Who are you to judge another man's servant?** 'Judge' is here taken for 'condemn' or 'hold in low esteem'. Not that the Apostle forbids all judgments to the faithful, since he says elsewhere that the world and even angels are to be judged by them,* but he is warning them that it is dangerous to judge about hidden matters. Everyone who judges in matters of this sort should beware of two things: a hidden cause, and ignorance of how the one judged might be in the future, even when at the time it seems right to judge him. Those who love to nag their brother, but not correct him, do not notice this.

Cf. 1 Cor 6:2-3

For his own master he stands or falls. And he shall stand; for God is able to make him stand. The Apostle added, 'God is able to make him stand', lest the one standing should arrogate his perseverance to himself. Therefore, he who gives perseverance can make those standing stand firm, or even restore those who have fallen.

Rm 14:5

VERSE FIVE. **For one man judges between one day and another day, and another man judges every day the same.** The Apostle says, 'Who are you to judge the servant of another?' Does he mean man or God? There is one, man, who judges the day placed between yesterday and tomorrow; that is, he has the ability to judge only the present. There is another, God, who judges every day, who knows about him who sins, what the disposition of his will was before the occurrence of the sin, what he intended by the sin, and what change he might undergo after the sin. To the one who has this knowledge of the sinner and the sin must be left the judgment of the sinner. We must realize that a quick judgment is to be feared in matters which should be left to individual choice, and in matters about which we know nothing; but concerning those acts in which God is clearly offended, it is dangerous to defer judgment. An exception may perhaps be made for the person who, doing the same thing, himself lacks the confidence to criticize, for it might be said to him, 'First cast the beam out of your own eye, and then you will see to cast the speck out of your brother's eye'.* Therefore, let neither man be judged by the other, but let him who is aware of God in his own work abound in that awareness, that is, in God.

Mt 7:5

Rm 14:6

VERSE SIX. **He who savors the day**, that is, he who takes delight in the work of a conscience which is like the day, **savors it in honor of the Lord**, that is, his continence is something sweet to him in the Lord. **And he who eats eats in honor of the Lord**, as long as he eats motivated by faith, and glorifies God, the author of his faith. Therefore, both he who eats and he who abstains eats or abstains in honor of the Lord, because both give thanks to God. Each of them does what he does for the Lord, because each of them acts in praise of him. A good work is done piously, rightly, and justly when it is done in praise of him by whom it is allowed to be done. Whoever makes progress in this affect does whatever he does for the Lord; that is, he does it in praise of him from whom he received the ability to do it. This is the source of the thanksgiving which is celebrated by the intimate ministry of the faithful.

Rm 14:7-9

VERSES SEVEN THROUGH NINE. **For none of us lives for himself, and no man dies for himself.**

Whether we live or die, we are the Lord's. For whether we live or die, no one should live or die for himself, but for the glory of him whose we are. Living, we serve him; and [dying, we shall not perish]. For if you who never cease his praises can never cease to belong to him, you can fear that, although you are his while you live here, you will not be his when you die. But the Apostle says that 'whether we live or die, we are the Lord's,' because he redeemed us with the price of his blood. And how can the dead lose his dead slave, when his death is your ransom? Therefore, when the Apostle had said that whether we live or die, we are the Lord's, in order to indicate the cost he said, **For to this end Christ died and rose again, that he might be Lord both of the living and of the dead.** Therefore, the kingdom of death shall not be able to hold him for whose sake he died who is 'free among the dead'.*

[PL: we shall never die]

Ps 87:6

Rm 14:10

VERSE TEN. **But why do you judge your brother, or why do you despise your brother?** As though he says, 'Why do we judge each other when we have the Lord judging us?' For deeds whose motives are unclear should be interpreted in the more favorable light. The text, 'By their fruits you shall know them,'* is said of those public actions which cannot be done with a good conscience, like defilements, or blasphemies, thefts, drunkenness, etc. Of these we are permitted to judge, as the Apostle says, 'For what part do I have with judging those who are without? For we judge those who are within'.* But in regard to the different types of food, any kind of human food can be taken indifferently with a good conscience and simple heart without the vice of concupiscence, and therefore the same Apostle forbids those who refrain from eating meat and drinking wine to judge those who do. For although they were men, they wished to pass judgment on the secrets of the heart, which God alone judges, on those things which can be done with a simple good conscience, although they can also be done with a bad conscience. Therefore, it is rash to judge, and especially to condemn, those acts whose

Mt 7:20

Cf. 1 Cor 5:12

motives we do not know, because they can be done with either a good or a bad intention. But the time will come to judge these, when the Lord 'will bring to light the hidden things of darkness, and will make manifest the counsels of hearts'.*[13] Therefore, the text continues, **For we shall all stand before the judgment seat of Christ.**

1 Cor 4:5

Rm 14:11

Is 45:24

VERSE ELEVEN. **For it is written, 'As I live,' says the Lord, 'every knee shall bow to me, and every tongue shall confess to the Lord.'*** The judgment seat of Christ is the divine power of his wisdom, by which Christ, seated on himself, arranges and judges all things. For him to sit in judgment means that nothing can escape the keen judgment of his scrutiny. ' "As I live," says the Lord.' This is not an oath, but a testimony to the truth, as if he said, 'Just as I truly live, for whom life and being are the same and from whom is all life, so I speak truly, for whom to speak truly is to be truly, and from whom is all truth.' This testimony to life and to truth is proper only to him who so lives from himself that all life is also from him, and who so exists that whatever truly exists is from him. The unique nature of the divine essence is to be understood in the word 'I', and the truth of the essence of life is to be understood in the word 'live'. Every knee is bent to him, because the strength of his power will appear as an object of adoration to all, when there is no one who can hide himself from his heat,* and when it is clear to everyone that they are exposed and that no one can escape the sight of truth which penetrates all things. For before him who alone truly exists, a man will seem to confess that he does not exist who ceases to exist to the extent that by his grievous offenses he withdraws from him from whom whatever is exists. Therefore, the Apostle says that we who are to be presented to such a fearful judge should no longer judge one another rashly.

Ps 18:7

Rm 14:13

VERSE THIRTEEN. **But judge rather in this way,** that is, discern and observe with your rational judgment lest by bad example **you put a stumblingblock** or a sorrowful scandal in your brother's way, whether he be a Jew or a Gentile. SCALON in Greek[14] or *scandalum* in Latin is something against which the foot strikes. Our road is the doctrine of the gospel, and Christ is the road's end; the foot which carries us along this road is the affection of the mind which naturally tends toward what is in front, but it quickly stumbles when it transgresses through vice. On this road there are wayfarers: blind pride, envy which sees, humility which does not see, and charity which does see. The road contains both good and bad, but the end discriminates between them. Blind pride does not see where it is going and refuses to be led. Envy thinks to itself that it sees, and judges that all whom it does not lead are going astray, though it does not wish to lead anyone. These often scandalize, and are scandalized by each other. Often they so stumble as to fall, and when they have fallen they rarely and with difficulty succeed in rising again. Humility, unseeing, holds out its hand to be led, and of it is said, 'Cursed be he who places a stumblingblock in front of the blind man'.* Charity, seeing, chooses, as it were, to move less in its progress, in order not to desert humility. The Apostle wanted those to whom he preached justice, peace and joy in the Holy Spirit to be like this. For such people avoid scandalizing in every way, and they themselves are not easily scandalized.

Cf. Lev 19:14

Rm 14:14

VERSE FOURTEEN. I know and am confident in the Lord Jesus, that nothing is common of itself; but for him who considers anything common it is common. Nothing is common by itself, that is, according to his faith, except for him who, lacking faith, thinks something is common. It is not common in its nature which God indeed created good, but it is rendered common, that is, unclean for one who eats without faith. For just as the offerings made to idols, which were unclean, were rendered clean by the conscience of those who used them with faith, so those things which were clean were made unclean by the estimation of those who used them without faith. This remark was made for the Jews who refused to touch food forbidden by the law, and sinned by not eating. The following is for the Gentiles who asked no questions* and took everything, even when the weak were scandalized, and so sinned by eating. The Jews should have avoided the sins or vices which they were ordered to avoid through the law symbolically as various kinds of foods; [but according to the dictates of grace and faith they should have received the foods] which God created to be received with thanksgiving.* The Gentiles should have restrained themselves from foods that were permitted according to faith, but which scandalized brothers weaker in faith. The habit acquired through the long practice of the law could not be removed from the Jews easily or quickly, and it was to be tolerated in them for the time being in the hope of correction. What was permitted by the liberty of faith, but which was of little or no use, should have been avoided by the Gentiles for the time being, because it was not expedient, given the danger of their brothers' ruin. Therefore the text continues:

1 Cor 10:25-27

[PL omits]

Cf. 1 Tim 4:4

Rm 14:15

VERSE FIFTEEN. **For if because of your food your brother is grieved, you no longer walk according to charity. Do not destroy with your food him for whom Christ died.** For a proper reason we should sometimes avoid what is licit, but we are not commanded to do what is illicit for any reason.

Rm 14:16

VERSE SIXTEEN. **Let our good not be spoken of as evil.** What is this good of ours? It is the good proper to Christ's disciples, of which he himself says, 'By this shall all men know that you are my disciples, if you have love for one another'.* Just as the disciples of Christ are distinguished by the sign of mutual charity, so when charity is neglected the entire brilliance of the christian religion seems to be obscured. Then this wonderful teacher proclaims the mystery of the kingdom of heaven in order to restrain the faults of the present time by the authority of a future mystery, and in order to establish the form of the Church. He says:

Jn 13:35

Rm 14:17	VERSE SEVENTEEN. **For the kingdom of God is not food and drink.** As if he said, 'Why do we deal so much with food when we are hastening to the kingdom of heaven? For there, just as they do not marry, and are not given in marriage, so they neither eat nor
Cf. Mt 22:30	drink, but are like the angels of God.'* Thus, with a most perfect and clear teaching the Apostle establishes that there is no need of food and drink in the kingdom of heaven, but that there is justice and peace. And because fleshly joy usually accompanies food and drink, he adds here **joy, but in the Holy Spirit.** These things effect the kingdom of heaven in us here, but in the future they lead us where these same things are possessed more certainly and more firmly. There is justice in work; peace is in the heart or conscience; joy is in the Lord. Whoever has these
Cf. Lk 17:21	things already has the kingdom of God within him.*
Rm 14:18-19	VERSES EIGHTEEN AND NINETEEN. **For he who in this way serves Christ pleases God and is ap-**
[PL omits]	**proved by men.** [He who serves Christ in the Holy Spirit pleases God and is approved by men] in justice, and he dwells harmoniously with himself in peace. **Let us pursue the things of peace** outside because of the disposition of peace that we enjoy within; and from a disposition for justice **let us keep the things that are edifying.** What does justice demand more clearly than that we not destroy on account of food the work of Christ's redemption in our brothers?
Rm 14:20	VERSE TWENTY. **All things are indeed clean, but it is evil for a man to eat with offence,** because he wounds the conscience of inner justice if the soul of his brother is endangered by that with which he refreshes himself.
Rm 14:21	VERSE TWENTY-ONE. **It is good for a man not to eat flesh or to drink wine, or to do anything whereby your brother is offended, scandalized or weakened.** Flesh and wine: one of these God permitted to human concupiscence, and the other was devised by the curiosity of that concupiscence. Neither of them is natural.

Jn 6

Therefore, when the Lord satisfied those men in the desert, there was no talk of drink, since what was natural was ready at hand at the sea of Tiberias.* It is good therefore to restrain oneself especially from those things which are not required by the necessities of life so much as by the concupiscence of the flesh, and from those things in which our brother finds offense; for when he is disturbed as though wanting to withdraw from the faith not knowing what he believes, he is scandalized and saddened, or weak in faith he does not actually withdraw but begins to doubt.

Rm 14:22

VERSE TWENTY-TWO. **You have faith? Keep it to yourself** where no one can take it away from you, and keep it for God who approves it, and not for the weak man who is scandalized. In this way we pursue the things of peace. For the children of the world inveigh against peace while each one seeks what is his own, but the sons of the kingdom of heaven pursue peace even when it flees from them, and pursue it with danger, with labor, with loss of goods, and sometimes even with hunger. While by true and certain faith all the Gentiles are cleansed from contamination through acknowledgment of the faith, so also every food is made clean by word and by prayer, but because what is good becomes evil through the offence to the eater, let restraint be practised toward what is licit but not expedient.

Blessed is he who does not condemn himself in that which he allows. Which is the same as saying, 'Blessed is he who performs his good deed such that others are not scandalized by it'. A man condemns himself in what he allows and makes himself liable to judgment and condemnation[15] when he neglects the salvation of his weak brother while clinging to what he himself approves of. This cannot be avoided here. For if the one who is strong in faith believes he can eat everything, and the weak one eats everything following the example of the strong one, and yet does not possess the faith of the one whose act he imitates, the one who eats without faith is condemned; the one who by his example urged him to do it is condemned for his act.

Rm 14:23 VERSE TWENTY-THREE. **For, all that is not from faith is sin.** For not only every act, but the entire life of infidels is sin. Even where morals are excellent, virtue is false when recognition of unchangeable truth is lacking. For, as has been said already and should be said often and firmly believed, excellent works are done by men, but faith is worked in man, and without faith no good works are done by any man,[16] because whatever is not from faith is sin. Therefore, the one who does not eat with faith sins, but the one by whose example the weak one sins condemns himself. What cannot be improved must be taken care of in its present state.

CHAPTER FIFTEEN

Rm 15:1 VERSE ONE. **We who are stronger ought to bear the infirmities of the weak,** not that they may always be weak, but that they may be cured on their own terms. For it is better to alleviate a dangerous sore by ointments and massages until it is brought by the patience of a wise physician to the point where it can fester without danger than to worsen it by thoughtless treatment. **And not please ourselves.** As a certain man of God said, the reward of those who please themselves is the pleasure they give themselves. Neglectful of fraternal charity, they do not seek to please their brothers to a good end, but to please themselves according to the judgment of their own will.[17] The text thus continues:

Rm 15:2-3 VERSES TWO AND THREE. **Let every one of us please his neighbor unto good, for edification.** For Christ, when he saw it was time to build up the salvation of all for the sake of the public good was unwilling to please himself with a love that was private, but said, 'Father, if it be possible, let this chalice pass
Mt 26:39 from me. Nevertheless, not as I will, but as you will.'* The reproaches of those who reproached God the Father for Christ's passion saying, 'Let him now deliver him if he wishes for he said, "I am the Son of

Mt 27:43   God",'* fell upon him when they did to him what they wanted.

Rm 15:4   VERSE FOUR. **For whatever was written was written for our instruction, that through patience and the comfort of the scriptures we might have hope.** Therefore, we read the books of the prophets and of the apostles which harmonize with each other, in order to bring our faith to mind, to console our hope and to exhort our charity, and by this harmony we arouse ourselves from the torpor of this mortal life as with a heavenly trumpet, and we provoke ourselves to the rewards of our heavenly calling. The Apostle then notes that all the good things which we can have, whether in our nature or in our actions, in morals, or in virtues, are gifts of God and not from ourselves, and thus he concludes with a prayer:

Rm 15:5-6   VERSES FIVE TO SIX. **May the God of patience and of comfort grant that you be of one mind toward one another, in accord with Jesus Christ, that with one mind and one mouth you may glorify the God and Father of our Lord Jesus Christ.** Just as God is our salvation because he bestows salvation, and he is our refuge because we take refuge in him, so he is the God of patience and consolation because we are patient because of him and look for consolation only from him. For patience and consolation are not from the scriptures, although sometimes they are through the scriptures. Our patience is not only from him, but, as

Ps 70:5   the prophet says, he is our patience.* He is our consolation also, because he consoles by means of himself alone the one who loves him. When does he console him except when he gives him the gift of being of one mind with him? When we are of one mind with one another, what is as good, what is as pleasant? Is this

Ps 132:1   not brothers dwelling together in unity?* This is in accord with Jesus Christ who said, 'This is my com-

Jn 15:12   mandment, that you love one another'.* Then infusing the sap from the good root into the grafted branches, he says, 'just as I have loved you'. May all carnal affection and love that does not tend toward

unity be far from Christ's disciples. All this is so that believing with one mind in your heart unto justice,* and confessing with one mouth unto salvation,* you may glorify God who creates all things, and renews and restores what is old through his Son. 'Let your good works shine before men, that they may see and glorify your Father who is in heaven.'* This is the honor by which God is to be honored by us. But he himself is our honor, to whom the prophet says, 'Your friends are made exceedingly honorable, O God.'*

_{Rm 10:10}
_{Rm 10:10}

_{Cf. Mt 5:16}

_{Ps 138:17}

_{Rm 15:7} VERSE SEVEN. **Therefore, receive one another, as Christ has received you, for the honor of God.** We shall not love each other unless we receive each other. We receive each other when we see our brother suffering need, and do not close our heart to him,* but receive him into the bosom of charity. We receive each other when the Jew does not judge the Gentile, or the Gentile the Jew, but we are made one body and one spirit to the honor of God, just as Christ received us, repelling neither, rejecting neither because of his race. The Apostle shows that Christ received both, saying:

_{Cf. 1 Jn 3:17}

_{Rm 15:8-9} VERSES EIGHT AND NINE. **For I tell you that Christ Jesus was the minister of circumcision, for the sake of the truth of God to confirm the promises made to the patriarchs, and so that the Gentiles might glorify God for his mercy.** One wall comes from circumcision, attaching itself to the corner stone; but that stone would not make a corner unless it received another wall from the Gentiles.* The wall from the Jews properly pertains to truth, and therefore the Apostle says, 'for the sake of the truth of God to confirm the promises made to the patriarchs'. The wall from the Gentiles pertains to mercy, about which the Apostle says, 'that the Gentiles might glorify God for his mercy'. Thus, in Christ 'mercy and truth have met one another'.*

_{Cf. Eph 2:14-20}

_{Ps 84:11}

But it was not right to take the children's bread and cast it to dogs, unless the dogs, humbled to collecting crumbs which fell from the Lord's table, and exalted through that humility and made men, merited to approach the table itself.* To the Jewish people he gave such honor that the glory of his presence dwelt in their land. There he was born, there he lived, and from there he began to preach because 'out of Sion is the loveliness of his beauty'.* From there the apostles were sent to them first. The patriarchs were there; from there the prophets came. Coming from the seed of Abraham he was made manifest there, sent to them, their apostle, as he himself said, 'I was not sent but to the sheep of the house of Israel.'* For this reason the Apostle calls him 'the minister of circumcision', that is, of the Jews. But the Gentiles are to glorify God for his mercy, **as it is written, 'Therefore, will I confess to you among the Gentiles, and will sing to your name'.*** The Son says to the Father, 'Through me the Gentiles will confess to you, and you will be known more widely through their good way of life.' This confession is one of praise. By saying 'I will sing', he means the new song which he sings in us; by his grace we also sing. Therefore, he says elsewhere, 'Singing in your hearts to the Lord'.* This joy is inside where the voice of love sings and is heard by him who is praised by that voice. To love freely with the whole heart, the whole soul and the whole strength is this song.[18] The Holy Spirit says again in the canticle of Deuteronomy:

VERSES TEN THROUGH TWELVE. **'Rejoice, Gentiles, with his people.'*** **And again, 'Praise the Lord, all Gentiles; and magnify him, all peoples.'*** **And again Isaiah says, 'There shall come a root from Jesse, and he who rises up to rule the Gentiles, in him the Gentiles shall hope.'*** Jesse is interpreted as 'he is for me'. In Christ's coming, the man who believes says 'he is for me', because he who says to Moses 'I am who am'* is present to the one who believes in God. He shall rise up to be both man and more than man, not having sin, and not coming through sin by the common law of birth, and taking away the sin of the world. Therefore, the Apostle adds the following prayer, since the Gentiles shall hope in him with good reason:

Rm 15:13	VERSE THIRTEEN. *May the God of hope fill you with all joy and peace in believing, that you may abound in hope and in the power of the Holy Spirit.* This prayer seems to contain the virtues of faith, hope and charity, because it calls down on the believer the joy of a truly peaceful conscience, a full joy, and an abundance of hope and of charity, which is the virtue proper to the Holy Spirit. Our God is properly the God of hope, and the hope of those who believe in him is not put to shame; but all the gods of the Gentiles are demons and the work of their hands.
Rm 15:14	VERSE FOURTEEN. *I myself, my brethren, am sure of you, that you are full of love, filled with all knowledge, so that you can admonish one another.* Here as if in a calm harbor the sails are let down. After an ocean of such profound meanings, a gathering together of the goods of the journey is recommended, and first of all he recommends to them his own benevolence by which he brought them the things in which he knew they abounded. Then he proclaims the fullness of knowledge and love among them which is sufficient to admonish, rather than in need of admonition.
Rm 15:15-17	VERSES FIFTEEN THROUGH SEVENTEEN. *But I have written to you somewhat boldly, brethren, partly by way of reminder, because of the grace which is given me from God that I should be the minister of Christ Jesus among the Gentiles, sanctifying the gospel of God, that the offering of the Gentiles may be acceptable and sanctified in the Holy Spirit.* Somewhat boldly indeed! Unless he had proceeded from confidence in the Holy Spirit dwelling in him, a man remaining constantly in the murky darkness of ignorance would be very bold to wish to reach such deep and profound secrets of God's wisdom by discussing the law and grace, the rejection of the Jews and the call of the Gentiles, and many other things, which he says he has written about in part; because as long as we are
1 Cor 13:9	here where we know in part and prophesy in part* a full understanding of these meanings is given to no one. But he so sanctified, or better as the Greek has it,[19] he so 'made a sacrificial offering' of the gospel of

God, in which also a certain high-priestly ministry is evidenced, 'that the offering of the Gentiles may be made acceptable and sanctified in the Holy Spirit'. It is very helpful to the hearers to understand the goodwill and learning of their teacher, which is dispensed to them in his own time and manner. Therefore, he continues as though recommending the goods which he has brought, and says, **I have glory before God.** Then tempering what he said, he says **in Christ our Lord.** For although all our good pertains to the glory of him from whom grace comes, still he glories who glories in the Lord. But about what does he glory?

Rm 15:18-19

[PL omits]

VERSES EIGHTEEN AND NINETEEN. **For I do not dare speak of any of those things which Christ does not accomplish through me.** Again this is a recommendation of grace. Not what I do not do, but what Christ does [not do] through me. Christ does them, but he does them through me. Christ does them in me, but makes them appear exteriorly through me. This is what the word 'accomplish' seems to mean. At the same time it should also be understood that an awareness of holy love edifies more in preaching than does the exercise of talking, since he who teaches chooses within himself what he says.

For the obedience of the Gentiles, by word and deed, by the power of signs and wonders, in the power of the Holy Spirit When the Apostle is about to speak of the deeds and powers of signs and prodigies, he sets the obedience of the Gentiles above all things, even the word of his own preaching, ascribing all that follows more to its merit than to his labor. In the end with religious piety he assigns to the power of the Holy Spirit even the obedience of the Gentiles and whatever was accomplished by its merit and by his labor. The circumspect preacher of grace makes all things return to the place from which they emerged. Then he adds, recommending his own strenuous efforts on behalf of the gospel: **So that from Jerusalem as far as Illyricum I have filled what lies between with the gospel of Christ.**

Rm 15:20-22	VERSES TWENTY THROUGH TWENTY-TWO. I have so preached it, but not where Christ has been named, lest I build on another man's foundation. But as it is written, 'They to whom he was not spoken of shall see, and they who have not heard shall understand.'* For I did not wish to infringe on the labors of others, but I was preparing the ground for the reapers who would come by sowing the seed of the word everywhere. For this reason a long, roundabout journey greatly impeded me from coming to you, although the will was not lacking.
Is 52:15	
Rm 15:23-24	VERSES TWENTY-THREE TO TWENTY-FOUR. But now having no more room for work in these regions, and having for many years a great desire to come to you, when I begin to make my way to Spain, I hope that as I pass I shall see you and be sent on my way there by you, once I have enjoyed your company for a while. The wonderful providence of the teacher of the Gentiles! Although he wanted to labor among the Romans and was ready to do so, he did not promise, he did not intrude. But he offered them his presence, saying he was coming to Rome not because of Rome but because of Spain, lest the word of the gospel in his mouth be less precious if, like a persistent, troublesome man, he imposed upon those who were unwilling. First, announcing that he will enjoy them for a while in passing, as it were, he mentions his affection for them; then saying that he will be sent on his way by them, he gathers their love to himself. Just as it was absolutely necessary for the teacher of the Church to avoid driving away his hearers by any show of pride, so also it was necessary to avoid cheapening the word of God in his mouth by an excessive submission to humility. Therefore, it is said of Samuel that he was sought by all because 'the word of the Lord was precious'.*
1 Sam 3:1	
Rm 15:25-28	VERSES TWENTY-FIVE TO TWENTY-EIGHT. But now I shall go to Jerusalem to minister to the saints. For Macedonia and Achaia have seen fit to make a contribution for the poor among the saints in

Jerusalem. They were pleased to do it and they are their debtors. For if the Gentiles have become partakers of their spiritual goods, they should also minister to them in their bodily needs. Therefore, when I have accomplished this, and delivered to them this revenue, I shall go on by way of you to Spain. The Jews, who had learned the truth and turned toward him whom they had crucified partly out of envy, partly out of error, and who were mortifying the desires of the old man, burning with the newness of spiritual life, sold all that they had, as the Lord had enjoined in the gospel, and placed the price of their belongings at the feet of the apostles for them to distribute to each according to his need. And living harmoniously in christian love, they did not call anything their own, but all things were common to them, and there was one soul and one heart in the Lord.* They also suffered persecution from the carnal Jews, their own citizens, so that Christ might be preached more widely by their dispersion. The Apostle, in the course of setting up churches among all the nations where he sowed the gospel, urgently bade them to make contributions for the poor among the saints in Jerusalem, because coming from the worship of idols and new to the worship of the one true God, they could not easily attain the heights of this perfection. Thus he set up the saints in Judaea as soldiers, and the others as provincial contributors. The text continues:

Cf. Acts 4:32-35

Rm 15:29

VERSE TWENTY-NINE. I know that when I come to you I shall come in the abundance of the blessing of Christ. The whole world shares in the abundance of Christ's blessing which the Apostle brought to the Romans when he came.

Rm 15:30-32

VERSES THIRTY THROUGH THIRTY-TWO. I beseech you therefore, brethren, through our Lord Jesus Christ and by the charity of the Holy Spirit, that you help me in your prayers to God, that I may be delivered from the unbelievers in Judaea, that the offering of my service in Jerusalem may be acceptable

to the saints, and that I may come to you with joy,
by the will of God, and may be refreshed with you.
Concerning what he says about prayers, the Greek
seems to have more about the struggle of prayer,[20]
so that we may know that the onslaughts of our vices
and of wicked spirits are never lacking in our prayers.
Who could be sure about himself, when the Apostle
sought the help of prayer from the disciples? At the
same time notice how much care he has for the saints.
With what reverence is he, who is sure of himself and
of his salvation, solicitous about the offering of his
service that it might be brought there and be accepted
by the saints. And so it happened. When he had completed the service of his offering he was arrested by
the Jews, bound and handed over to the Gentiles.
Then he was brought to Rome because of his appeal
to Caesar.

Rm 15:33   VERSE THIRTY-THREE. **May the God of peace
              be with you all. Amen.** He ends in peace who began
Rm 1:7   with peace, saying, 'Grace to you and peace'.*

CHAPTER SIXTEEN

Rm 16:1-7   VERSES ONE THROUGH SEVEN. **And I commend
              to you Phoebe, our sister, who is in the ministry of the
              church that is in Cenchreae, that you receive her in the
              Lord as becomes saints; and that you assist her in
              whatever she may require of you. For she also has
              assisted many, including me. Greet Prisca and Aquila,
              my helpers in Christ Jesus, who have risked their
              necks for my life, to whom not only I give thanks, but
              also all the churches of the Gentiles, and greet the
              church in their house. Greet my beloved Epaenetus,
              who is the firstfruits of Asia in Christ Jesus. Greet
              Mary, who has labored much among you. Greet
              Adronicus and Junias, my kinsmen and fellow pri-
              soners, who are men of note among the apostles, who
              also were in Christ Jesus before me.** Perhaps the
              latter were bound to the Apostle by a closer tie of
              spiritual love, and for this reason he calls them

kinsmen; perhaps they were of higher merit and so he calls them fellow prisoners. He knew that they endured with difficulty the exile and troubles of this life because of their love for the heavenly homeland, and therefore for their consolation he calls himself their fellow prisoner.

Rm 16:8-16 VERSES EIGHT THROUGH SIXTEEN. **Greet Ampliatus, most beloved to me in the Lord. Greet Urban, our helper, and my beloved Stachys. Greet Apelles, approved in Christ. Greet those who are of Aristobulus' household. Greet Herodion, my kinsman. Greet those who are of Narcissus' household, who are in the Lord. Greet Tryphaena and Tryphosa, who labored in the Lord. Greet the dearly beloved Persis, who has labored much in the Lord. Greet Rufus, elect in the Lord, and his mother in the flesh, and mine in the spirit. Greet Asyncritus, Phlegon, Hermes, Patrobas, Hermas, and those who are with them. Greet Philologus and Julia, Nereus and his sister, and Olympias, and all the saints who are with them. Greet one another with a holy kiss. All the churches of Christ greet you.** As if he said, 'Why do I individually distinguish those who greet and those to be greeted? All the churches of Christ greet everyone who is in the church of Christ.'

Rm 16:17 VERSE SEVENTEEN. **Now I beseech you, brethren, to take note of those who make dissensions and offences contrary to the doctrine which you have learned, and to avoid them.** It is clear that dissensions come from offences, and divisions come from dissensions, and from division come heresies and schisms. If the Apostle enjoins that we should avoid those who cause offences, how much more those who divide the church with dissensions.

Rm 16:18 VERSE EIGHTEEN. **For such people do not serve Christ the Lord, but their own belly,** not caring whose heart they may empty as long as they can fill their own belly. He seems here to be touching some pestilential heresies already sprouting up in the church, as he says, by pleasing speeches and praise, seducing the hearts of the innocent, putting darkness for light and light for darkness, sweet for bitter and bitter for sweet, according to the prophet.* They speak in order to give pleasure and they fawn on vices, and all these things they seek only what pertains to the belly.

Is 5:20

Rm 16:19

VERSE NINETEEN. **For your obedience is published in every place.** This is what the teachers of the church most vehemently fear and seek to avert, lest the astuteness of the wicked abuse for an evil purpose the good of the simple. Behold the praiseworthy obedience of the Romans if it should encounter preachers of this kind who were secretive and deceptive, astute at persuading and clever at suggesting carnal things. What could be more dangerous? Therefore, he adds, **I rejoice in you.** I rejoice in you for your obedience, but I fear for you because of the astuteness of the enemy. **But I would have you wise in good, and simple in evil.** The one who is 'wise in good' relishes a good proposal immediately and, as it were, naturally. The one who is 'simple in evil' holds the form of good in his soul; the duplicity of the evil does not deceive him, because the form of evil, however adapted, cannot be adapted to the form which he carries within him.

Rm 16:20

VERSE TWENTY. **May the God of peace speedily crush Satan under your feet.** It was said to the woman, or rather to the serpent, when God was punishing the sin of the first man, 'She shall watch for your head, and you shall watch for her heel.'* The twisting serpent and Satan watch for your heel when you stumble from the way of the Lord, so that you fall and he can possess you as you fall. Watch for his first suggestion, that is, his head. If you despise the promised gain because of the damage to your soul, you have trampled on the head of the serpent. If you have acted that way frequently, the God of peace will be close to you, making peace, and the harmful serpent will be unable to raise up his head that has often been trampled upon. But you will crush Satan under your feet

Cf. Gen 3:15

Rm 7:7

completely when you obtain full victory over concupiscence so that you can totally fulfil the command of the law. It is a happy but rare conscience that merits in this life to accept fully what the law says, 'You shall not covet'.* The Apostle adds the way this can be done, **The grace of our Lord Jesus Christ be with you.**

Rm 16:21-27

VERSES TWENTY-ONE THROUGH TWENTY-SEVEN. **Timothy my fellow laborer greets you, and Lucius, and Jason and Sosipater, my kinsmen. I, Tertius, who wrote this epistle, greet you in the Lord. Gaius, my host, and the whole church greet you. Erastus, the city treasurer, greets you, and Quartus, our brother. The grace of God be with you all. Amen. Now to him who is able to strengthen you, according to my gospel and the preaching of Jesus Christ, according to the revelation of the mystery, which was kept secret for long ages, which is now made manifest by writings of the prophets, according to the precept of the eternal God, for the obedience of faith, known among all nations, to the only wise God, through Jesus Christ, to whom be honor and glory forever and ever. Amen.** The meaning is: to him who is able to strengthen you, to the only wise God be glory forever and ever. The intervening words 'through Jesus Christ' seem ambiguous. They might be taken as meaning 'to the only wise God through Jesus Christ', so that the only God, the wise Father, should be understood to be wise through Jesus Christ, not by participation, but by begetting the wisdom which is Jesus Christ. Or the text might be taken not as 'to the one who is wise through Jesus Christ', but 'glory through Jesus Christ to the only wise God'.* But who would dare say that it is through Jesus Christ that God the Father is wise, when it cannot be doubted that he is wise according to his own substance, and that the Son's substance exists through the begetting Father rather than the Father's substance through the begotten Son? It remains therefore that glory is to be given to the only wise one through Jesus Christ, 'glory' being clear knowledge with praise,[21] by which God the

See above on Rm 11:33-36

Trinity is made known to the nations. Glory is through Jesus Christ because, to omit other things, he commanded that all nations be baptized in the name of the Father and of the Son and of the Holy Spirit,* and here especially is the glory of this undivided Trinity mentioned. God who is that Trinity is therefore rightly called 'the only wise one', because he alone is wise according to his own substance, not according to accident or an adventitious sharing of wisdom as any rational creature is wise.

Mt 28:19

The additional words 'to whom' in the expression 'to whom be glory', when it would have sufficed to say 'to him be glory', form an unusual expression in our language. It does not convey the meaning we seek and about which we are in doubt. What is lost to the meaning if it is said, 'To him be glory, to whom there is glory through Jesus Christ'? It is the same to say, 'to him through Jesus Christ to whom be glory' as to say 'to whom be glory through Jesus Christ'. But one of these is a strange arrangement of the words and the other the usual order.

'Who can strengthen you, according to my gospel, and the preaching of Jesus Christ.' The gospel of Paul and the preaching of Christ have nothing in disagreement, nothing conflicting, since one proceeds from the other. 'According to the revelation of the mystery, which was kept secret for long ages.' What is this mystery except that the Word was made flesh and dwelt among us? His humiliation became our exaltation; by his weakness we were made strong. But we should inquire about the 'long ages'. If the Apostle meant eternity, certainly the mystery of Christ did not lie hidden for eternity; its reason and its mode were always in that eternity which is God, even before any time existed. For there was no time before creation, because time could not exist unless there was creation which something could alter by some change. For time would follow upon the shorter or longer periods of delay in this motion or change, when one thing ceases and a second thing succeeds it, because they cannot exist simultaneously. The Apostle says that the mystery was kept secret from others, but was known to God, who alone is wise, during those eternal ages; now it is made manifest through the writings of the prophets, according to the precept of the eternal God, for the obedience of faith among all the nations.

But what does the addition of 'eternal' to the noun 'God' signify here? Perhaps the eternal God commanded from eternity that what had been hidden from the other generations of the ages should be laid open through the prophetic writings now, that is, in the time of grace, when the Lord revealed the meaning to the disciples that they might understand the scriptures.* It is not absurd to understand that whole length of time before Christ's coming as the eternal times during which the mystery of Christ was kept secret from men. Even if during this time it was partly revealed to some patriarchs and prophets in an enigmatic and figurative way, still it was laid open to none of them as it is now, especially since the Apostle says elsewhere that the angels themselves progressed in their grasp of the truth through the gospel, and that the manifold wisdom of God was made known to principalities and powers in heavenly places through the Church.* What was known to God who alone is wise is made known through the preaching of the apostles in the time of grace, so that by their preaching the faith is obeyed in all nations.

Cf. Lk 24:45

Cf. Eph 3:10

NOTES

1. This entire paragraph is from Augustine, *City of God 10.6;* PL 41:283-284. Florus refers to it, PL 119:311.
2. On William's fondness for triads see note on Rm 8:26.
3. This sentence is taken word for word from Origen, *On Roms,* PG 14:1209-1210.
4. Migne, PL 180:672, gives σωφρονεῖν in parentheses. It does not occur in the text in MS 49, fol. 199ʳ. William's source here is Origen, *On Roms,* PG 14:1210-1211, where interestingly enough a Greek word does occur which William ignores in his discussion.
5. William contrasts the Christian assembly (*in ecclesia*) and the solitary monk (*in eremo*).
6. William's source here is Origen, *On Roms,* PG 14:1213. William makes no use of the Greek word ἀναλογία in Origen's discussion.
7. This distinction occurs as an interlinear gloss on fol. 13ʳ in MS 49, where it is attributed to Augustine.
8. This sentence is composed of three glosses on fol. 13ʳ of MS 49 on Rom 12; two are attributed to Basil, one to Origen. Other glosses attributed to Basil have been found in Rufinus' translation of Basil's *Rule,* but these have not yet been found.
9. Cf. Bernard, *On Consideration 4.III.6;* CF 37:116-117.
10. William paraphrases Augustine for the comparisons of day and night in this paragraph and the next one. See Augustine, *On Ps 76.4;* PL 36:973. Florus refers to this, PL 119:314.
11. From 'Hunger and thirst ... ' down to this point is Augustine, *Confessions, 10.31;* PL 32:797-98.
12. From here to the end of this paragraph is Augustine, *Tract 73 on Gospel of John;* PL 35:1824. Also, Florus, PL 119:315.
13. 'For deeds whose motives are unclear ... ' down to here is Bede, *On the Gospel of Luke;* PL 92:408.
14. In MS 49, fol. 208ʳ, William uses small capitals for the word which is meant to be SCANDALON. Origen's discussion of this verse offers no help on William's source here (PG 14:1241).
15. The expression 'liable to judgment and condemnation' is from a gloss on fol. 14ᵛ of MS 49.
16. This sentence is based on a marginal gloss on fol. 15ʳ of MS 49.
17. This sentence is based on a gloss on fol. 15ʳ of MS 49 and attributed to Basil.

18. The previous two sentences are Augustine, *Letter 140.17;* PL 33:557. Florus refers to this passage, PL 119.316.

19. William's source here is Origen, *On Roms,* PG 14:1268. The Rufinus translation gives the Greek word for *sanctificans,* ἱερουργοῦντα which William does not use in his discussion on fol. 212ʳ of MS 49.

20. William's source here is Origen, *On Roms,* PG 14:1276. William does not use the Greek word which occurs in Rufinus' translation of Origen's discussion at this point.

21. With William's definition of glory *clara cum laude notitia* compare Augustine, *On Gospel of John 100.1;* PL 35:1891. where glory is defined as *fama cum laude,* a definition gotten from Cicero.

INDEXES

Indexes have been prepared by the translator.

SCRIPTURAL INDEX
of William of St. Thierry's
Exposition on the Epistle to the Romans

	Book, Chapter, Verse	Page
Gen 1:26	VII; Rm 12: 1-3	231
Gen 2:9	III; Rm 6:5	116
Gen 2:17	IV; Rm 8: 2-3	151
Gen 3	VII; Rm 14:3	247
Gen 3:15	VII; Rm 16:20	265
Gen 3:19	V; Rm 8:20	166
Gen 3:19	VI; Rm 9:22-34	195
Gen 4:2	II; Rm 4:6	78
Gen 4:13	III; Rm 5:13	103
Gen 6:3	I; Rm 1: 20-21	40
Gen 6:8	II; Rm 4:17	84
Gen 9:25	III; Rm 5:13	103
Gen 12	II; Rm 4:5	76
Gen 15:6	II; Rm 4:9	78
Gen 15:16	VI; Rm 11: 26-27	217
Gen 18:10	V: Rm 9: 6-9	185 bis
Gen 21: 3-6	II; Rm 4: 10-12	80
Gen 22	II; Rm 4:5	76
Gen 22:2	II; Rm 4: 10-12	80
Gen 22: 16-17	II; Rm 4: 10-12	80
Gen 22:17	II; Rm 4: 18-19	86
Gen 22:17	VI; Rm 9:27	196
Gen 22:18	II; Rm 4:13	82
Gen 25:23	V; Rm 9: 10-13	185
Gen 25:34	VII; Rm 14:3	247
Gen 32: 26,31	VI; Rm 11: 28-29	218

	Book, Chapter, Verse	Page
Gen 49:27	I; Rm 1:1	19
Ex 3:14	II; Rm 4:17	85
Ex 3:14	VII; Rm 15: 10-12	258
Ex 9:16	V; Rm 9: 17-18	187
Ex 14-15	IV; Rm 7:12	137
Ex 20:7	I; Rm 1:9	27
Ex 20: 13-17	VII; Rm 13:9	241
Ex 20:17	IV; Rm 7: 8-9	135
Ex 33:19	V; Rm 9: 15-16	187
Ex 34:35	V; Rm 9: 1-5	183
Ex 40:21	I; Rm 1:4	23
Lev 18:5	VI; Rm 10:5	200
Lev 19:14	VII; Rm 14:13	251
Lev 19:18	VII; Rm 13:9	241 bis
Num 11	VII; Rm 14:3	246
Deut 5:31	III; Rm 5: 2-3	94
Deut 5:31	V; Rm 8:27	173
Deut 18:15	IV; Rm 7: 1-3	131
Deut 25:5	IV; Rm 7:4	133
Deut 28:66	VI; Rm 9:27	196
Deut 30: 11-13	VI; Rm 10: 6-7	201
Deut 30:14	VI; Rm 10: 8-9	201
Deut 32:9	VI; Rm 11:12	211
Deut 32:21	VI; Rm 10:19	205
Deut 32:35	VII; Rm 12:19	237
Deut 32:43	VII; Rm 15: 10-12	258
1 Sam 3:1	VII; Rm 15: 25-28	261
1 Sam 17	IV; Rm 7:12	137
2 Sam 7	II; Rm 3:4	64
1 Kgs 19:10	VI; Rm 11: 2-7	208
1 Kgs 19:18	VI; Rm 11: 2-7	208
1 Kgs 19:21	VII; Rm 12:6	234
2 Kgs 6:1	VII; Rm 12:6	234
Tob 4:16	II; Rm 2: 11-12	53
Jb 4:12	III; Rm 5: 5-6	96
Jb 14:1	VI; Rm 9: 22-24	193
Ps 1:1	VII; Rm 12:6	234
Ps 2: 11-12	V; Rm 8: 29-30	175 bis
Ps 4:2	I; Rm 2: 8-9	49
Ps 5:5	III; Rm 5: 2-3	94
Ps 5:13	V; Rm 8: 29-30	177
Ps 9:24	VI; Rm 9: 30-33	198
Ps 13:1	I; Rm 1:24	34
Ps 13:1	I; Rm 1: 20-21	39
Ps 13:1	II; Rm 3: 17-18	67
Ps 14: 2-3	III; Rm 6: 3-4	114
Ps 15:5	V; Rm 8:17	164
Ps 15:11	III; Rm 5: 5-6	95
Ps 16:2	V; Rm 8:27	173
Ps 17:4	I; Rm 1:8	24
Ps 17:50	VII; Rm 15: 8-9	258
Ps 18:5	VI; Rm 10:17	205
Ps 18:7	VII; Rm 14:11	250
Ps 18:8	V; Rm 8:26	173
Ps 20:13	I; Rm 1:1	20

	Book, Chapter, Verse	Page
Ps 21:1	III; Rm 6: 3-4	114
Ps 24:7	IV; Rm 7:7	135
Ps 24:10	VI; Rm 11: 33-36	220
Ps 25:11	IV; Rm 7: 14-15	140
Ps 26: 4, 8	V; Rm 8:27	173
Ps 29:7	V; Rm 8: 29-30	175
Ps 30:2	II; Rm 3: 24-25	71
Ps 30: 13	II; Rm 3:13	67
Ps 30: 20	V; Rm 8:18	165
Ps 30: 20	VI; Rm 11:32	220
Ps 30:21	III; Rm 5: 5-6	95
Ps 32:15	IV; Preface	129
Ps 35:7	VI; Rm 11: 33-36	220
Ps 35: 8-10	III; Rm 6: 3-4	111
Ps 36:27	II; Rm 2:25	59
Ps 38:7	VII; Rm 12: 1-3	231
Ps 40:5	III; Rm 5: 19-20	110
Ps 44: 2, 8	Preface	17
Ps 45:11	VII; Rm 12: 1-3	232
Ps 48: 13, 21	I; Rm 2: 6-7	48
Ps 49:2	VI; Rm 11: 26-27	216
Ps 49:2	VII; Rm 15: 8-9	258
Ps 50:1	III; Rm 5: 19-20	110
Ps 50:6	I; Rm 1: 25-28	41
Ps 50:6	II; Rm 3:4	64
Ps 50:7	III; Rm 5:13	103
Ps 53:3	V; Rm 8: 33, 31-32	177
Ps 58:11	VI; Rm 10:20	206
Ps 58:12	I; Rm 1:16	31
Ps 64:9	IV; Rm 7: 24-25	148
Ps 67:2	I; Rm 2:3	45
Ps 67:28	I; Rm 1:1	19
Ps 67:31	II; Rm 3:27	71
Ps 68:23	VI; Rm 11:9	210
Ps 70:2	IV; Rm 8: 2-3	153
Ps 70:5	IV; Rm 7: 24-25	148
Ps 70:5	VII; Rm 15: 5-6	256
Ps 71:14	Preface	17
Ps 72:28	VI; Rm 12: 1-3	232
Ps 75:2	II; Rm 2: 17-20	58
Ps 77:8	II; Rm 4:5	76
Ps 80:13	I; Rm 1:24	34
Ps 81:6	II; Rm 3:4	64
Ps 84:11	VI; Rm 11: 33-36	221
Ps 84:11	VII; Rm 15: 8-9	257
Ps 84:13	V; Rm 8:14	162
Ps 85:2	I; Rm 1:7	24
Ps 87:6	VII; Rm 14: 7-9	249
Ps 88:11	I; Rm 1:1	19
Ps 89:11	I; Rm 1:18	32
Ps 92:1	II; Rm 2: 17-20	58
Ps 93:19	V; Rm 8:18	165
Ps 97:2	II; Rm 3: 24-25	70
Ps 100:7	II; Rm 3:12	66
Ps 109:3	I; Rm 1:3	21

	Book, Chapter, Verse	Page
Ps 113:8	II; Rm 4:17	85
Ps 114:3	V; Rm 9:6	184
Ps 116:1	VII: Rm 15: 10-12	258
Ps 118:29	IV; Rm 8: 2-3	150
Ps 118:113	III; Rm 6:2	111
Ps 118:165	II; Rm 3: 17-18	67
Ps 131:9	VI; Rm 9: 30-33	199
Ps 132:1	VII; Rm 15: 5-6	256
Ps 136: 3-4	Preface	17
Ps 138:17	VII; Rm 15: 5-6	257
Ps 143:15	V; Rm 8:26	171
Ps 147:9	II; Rm 2: 17-20	58
Prov 24:16	VI; Rm 11:11	211
Qo 1: 2-3	V; Rm 8:20	166
Qo 3: 2-8	VI; Rm 10:11	203
Qo 7:30	I; Rm 2:1	44
Sg 1:1	IV; Rm 8: 3-4	153
Sg 1: 2-3	Preface	17
Sg 2:16, 1:12	I; Rm 1:8	26
Sg 5:8	V; Rm 9: 1-5	183
Wis 7: 24-25	VI; Rm 11: 33-36	221
Wis 8:21	VII; Rm 12: 1-3	231
Wis 13: 8-9	I; Rm 1:24	37
Si 7:40	III; Rm 6:12	119
Si 25:33	III; Rm 5:12	100
Si 30:24	VII; Rm 12: 1-3	232
Is 1:9	VI; Rm 9:29	197
Is 5:20	VII; Rm 16:18	265
Is 6: 9-10	VI; Rm 11:8	210
Is 7:9 (LXX)	VII; Rm 12: 1-3	232
Is 8:14	VI; Rm 9: 30-33	198
Is 8:14, 28:16	VI; Rm 9: 30-33	197
Is 10:22	VI; Rm 9:27	196
Is 11:10	VII; Rm 15: 10-12	258
Is 24:20	VI; Rm 11:11	211
Is 28:16	VI; Rm 9: 30-33	198
Is 28:16	VI; Rm 10:11	203
Is 37:31	III; Rm 6:5	116
Is 44: 7, 41:22	V; Rm 8: 29-30	174, 176
Is 45:5	I; Rm 1:24	35
Is 45:24	VII; Rm 14:11	250
Is 49:6	I; Rm 1:1	20
Is 52:7	VI; Rm 10: 14-15	204
Is 52:15	VII; Rm 15: 20-22	261
Is 53:1	VI; Rm 10:16	205
Is 54:13	VI; Rm 11: 28-29	218
Is 59:20	VI; Rm 11: 26-27	216
Is 65:1	VI; Rm 10:20	206
Is 65:2	VI; Rm 10:21	207
Jer 2:11	I; Rm 1:24	37
Ezek 18:4	III; Rm 5:12	101
Ezek 36: 20-23	II; Rm 2:21	59
Dan 5:13	I; Rm 1:4	22
Hos 1:10, 2:24	VI; Rm 9: 25-26	195
Hos 6:6	VII; Rm 12: 1-3	232

	Book, Chapter, Verse	Page
Hab 2:4	I; Rm 1:17	32
Hab 3:2	IV; Rm 8: 3-4	153
Zech 8:19	III; Rm 5:1	93
Zech 13:1	IV; Rm 7: 14-15	141
Mal 1: 2-3	V; Rm 9: 10-13	185
Mal 4:6	VI; Rm 11: 26-27	217
Mt 1:20	I; Rm 1:4	22
Mt 4:17	V; Rm 8:33, 31-32	177
Mt 4:18	Preface	17
Mt 5:3	Preface	16
Mt 5:6	V; Rm 8:15	163
Mt 5:10	VII; Rm 12: 20-21	237
Mt 5:16	III; Rm 6: 3-4	116
Mt 5:16	VII; Rm 15: 5-6	257
Mt 5:17	II; Rm 2: 26-27	60
Mt 5:17	IV; Rm 8: 3-4	154
Mt 5:37	I; Rm 1:9	27
Mt 6:12	II; Rm 4:6	78
Mt 6:13	IV; Rm 8: 2-3	150
Mt 7:5	VII; Rm 14:5	248
Mt 7: 7-8	V; Rm 8:15	163
Mt 7:12	II; Rm 2: 11-12	53
Mt 7:20	VII; Rm 14:10	249
Mt 7:23	IV; Rm 7:14-15	141
Mt 8: 8-12	VI; Rm 11: 17-18	213-214
Mt 8:10	II; Rm 3: 1-2	63
Mt 9:9	Preface	17
Mt 9:18	I; Rm 1:4	22
Mt 10:12	I; Rm 1:15	30
Mt 10:20	VII; Rm 12: 1-3	232
Mt 10:39	III; Rm 6:19	124
Mt 11:13	III; Rm 5:13	103
Mt 11:27	VI; Rm 11: 33-36	223
Mt 11:30	I; Rm 1:1	20
Mt 12:33	VI; Rm 11: 22-24	215
Mt 12:40	II; Rm 4: 10-12	81
Mt 15:14	II; Rm 2: 17-20	58
Mt 15:24	VI; Rm 10:21	207
Mt 15:24	VII; Rm 15: 8-9	258
Mt 15: 26-27	VII; Rm 15: 8-9	258
Mt 17:25	VII; Rm 13:6	239
Mt 18:28	II; Rm 4:6	78
Mt 20: 14-15	V; Rm 9: 20-21	188
Mt 20:16	VI; Rm 11:28-29	218
Mt 22:21	VII; Rm 13:8	240
Mt 22:30	VII; Rm 14:17	253
Mt 22:37	VII; Rm 12: 1-3	231
Mt 22: 37, 40	VI; Rm 9:28	196
Mt 22:40	II; Rm 2: 11-12	54
Mt 22:40	VII; Rm 13:10	242
Mt 23:13	VI; Rm 9: 30-33	198
Mt 25:21	I; Rm 2:4	46
Mt 26:39	VII; Rm 15: 2-3	255
Mt 26:41	V; Rm 8:23	168
Mt 27:43	VII; Rm 15: 2-3	256

		Book, Chapter, Verse	Page
Mt 27:53	. . . .	I; Rm 1:4	22
Mt 28:19	. . . .	III; Rm 6: 3-4	116
Mt 28:19	. . . .	VII; Rm 16: 21-27 . . .	267
Mk 7:27	. . . .	VI; Rm 10:21	207
Mk 16:16	. . . .	II; Rm 4: 14-15	83
Lk 1:28	. . . .	Preface	16
Lk 1:35	. . . .	I; Rm 1:4	22
Lk 1:35	. . . .	IV; Rm 8: 3-4	154
Lk 5:34	. . . .	V; Rm 8:17	164
Lk 7:43	. . . .	IV; Rm 7: 14-15 . . .	141
Lk 7:47	. . . .	III; Rm 5: 19-20 . . .	110
Lk 8:10	. . . .	III; Rm 6:17	122
Lk 8:15	. . . .	I; Rm 2: 6-7	48
Lk 8:15	. . . .	II; Rm 3: 1-2	62
Lk 10: 5-6	. . .	I; Rm 1:7	24
Lk 11:7	. . . .	V; Rm 8:26	171
Lk 11:26	. . . .	V; Rm 8:9	159
Lk 12:20	. . . .	I; Rm 2:5	47
Lk 12:21	. . . .	I; Rm 2:5	47
Lk 12: 47-48	. . .	I; Rm 2: 8-9	49
Lk 13:27	. . . .	II; Rm 4:6	78
Lk 13:32	. . . .	V; Rm 8:33, 31-32 . . .	178
Lk 15:28	. . . .	VI; Rm 10:19	206
Lk 16:16	. . . .	III; Rm 5:13	103
Lk 16:16	. . . .	VII; Rm 12:6	234
Lk 16: 19-31	. . .	IV; Rm 7:24	147
Lk 17:5	. . . .	II; Rm 4: 14-15	83
Lk 17: 21	. . .	VII; Rm 14:17	253
Lk 18:19	. . . .	II; Rm 3:12	67
Lk 21:31	. . . .	VII; Rm 13:11	243
Lk 24:45	. . . .	VII; Rm 16:20	268
Jn 1: 3-4	. . . .	I; Rm 1:24	35
Jn 1:12	. . . .	V; Rm 8:15	163
Jn 1:14	. . . .	Preface	16
Jn 1:14	. . . .	IV; Rm 8: 3-4	152
Jn 1:17	. . . .	IV; Rm 7: 1-3	132
Jn 1:17	. . . .	IV; Rm 7: 14-15 . . .	139
Jn 4:22	. . . .	I; Rm 1:16	31
Jn 6	. . . . .	VII; Rm 14:21	254
Jn 6:29	. . . .	VI; Rm 10:4	200
Jn 6:45	. . . .	VI; Rm 11: 28-29 . . .	219
Jn 8:28	. . . .	V; Rm 8:27	173
Jn 8: 33, 39, 41	. . .	VI; Rm 11: 17-18 . . .	213
Jn 8:36	. . . .	III; Rm 6:20	124
Jn 8:36	. . . .	IV; Rm 7: 22-23	146
Jn 8:56	. . . .	II; Rm 4:5	76
Jn 10:18	. . . .	III; Rm 5:12	101
Jn 10:35	. . . .	II; Rm 3:4	64
Jn 12:25	. . . .	III; Rm 6:19	124
Jn 12:25	. . . .	VI; Rm 9:29	197
Jn 13:35	. . . .	VII; Rm 14:16	252
Jn 14:1	. . . .	III; Rm 5:18	108
Jn 14:6	. . . .	VI; Rm 9: 30-33 . . .	198
Jn 14:9	. . . .	V; Rm 9:6	185
Jn 14:12	. . . .	II; Rm 4:5	76

	Book, Chapter, Verse	Page
Jn 14: 15, 23	V; Rm 8:16	163
Jn 14:27	V; Rm 8:17	164
Jn 14:30	IV; Rm 8: 3-4	152
Jn 15:5	III; Rm 6: 21-22	125
Jn 15:5	VI; Rm 9: 30-33	197
Jn 15:12	VII; Rm 13:10	242
Jn 15:12	VII; Rm 15: 5-6	256
Jn 15:15	IV; Rm 7:6	134
Jn 15:16	VI; Rm 11: 28-29	219
Jn 16:21	V; Rm 8: 21-22	168
Jn 16:33	III; Rm 5:1	93
Jn 17:3	I; Rm 2: 6-7	48
Jn 17:3	VI; Rm 11: 33-36	223
Jn 17:5	I; Rm 1:4	22
Jn 17: 12, 18:9	VI; Rm 11: 28-29	219
Jn 17: 21, 24	III; Rm 5: 5-6	95
Ac 4: 27-28	VI; Rm 11: 28-29	218
Ac 4: 32-35	VII; Rm 15: 25-28	262
Ac 9	I; Rm 1:1	19
Ac 13:2	I; Rm 1:1	20
Ac 13:9	I; Rm 1:1	20
Ac 16:7	I; Rm 1:13	29
Ac 20:10	I; Rm 1:14	30
Ac 28:8	I; Rm 1:4	30
Rm 1:7	VII; Rm 15:33	263
Rm 1:8	III; Rm 6:17	122
Rm 1:9	I; Rm 1:1	20
Rm 1:9	IV; Preface	129
Rm 1:9	V; Rm 8:23	168
Rm 1:9	V; Rm 9:2	184
Rm 1:9	I; Rm 1:8	26
Rm 1:17	VII; Rm 12: 1-3	233
Rm 1:18	I; Rm 1:24	37
Rm 1:18	I; Rm 1:24	37
Rm 1: 18-19	I; Rm 1:24	35
Rm 1:19	I; Rm 1:24	38
Rm 1:20	I; Rm 1:24	38
Rm 1:23	I; Rm 1:24	37
Rm 1:24	I; Rm 1: 20-21	40
Rm 1: 26-27	I; Rm 1: 20-21	41
Rm 1:27	I; Rm 1: 20-21	41
Rm 1:28	V; Rm 8: 29-30	176
Rm 2:6	I; Rm 2:5	47
Rm 2:7	II; Rm 3: 1-2	62
Rm 2:8	VI; Rm 11:8	209
Rm 2:11	I; Rm 2: 6-7	48
Rm 2:11	II; Rm 3: 1-2	62
Rm 2:12	II; Rm 2: 28-29	61
Rm 2:14	II; Rm 2: 28-29	61
Rm 2:14	II; Rm 3: 1-2	62
Rm 2:17	II; Rm 2: 28-29	61
Rm 2:17	II; Rm 3: 1-2	62
Rm 2:25	II; Rm 2: 28-29	61
Rm 2: 26-27	II; Rm 2: 28-29	61
Rm 3:3	II; Rm 3:4	63

	Book, Chapter, Verse	Page
Rm 3:9	II; Rm 3: 1-2	62
Rm 3:19	VI; Rm 9: 22-24	192
Rm 3:21	II; Rm 3: 1-2	62
Rm 3:23	V; Rm 8: 29-30	176
Rm 3:24	II; Rm 3:23	69
Rm 3:28	II; Rm 3: 1-2	62
Rm 3:28	VI; Rm 10:4	200
Rm 3:29	VI; Rm 10:12	203
Rm 4:3	II; Rm 4:9	78
Rm 4: 4-5	II; Rm 4:6	77
Rm 4:5	III; Rm 5:18	108
Rm 4:15	III; Rm 5: 19-20	109
Rm 4:15	IV; Rm 7: 1-3	131
Rm 4:15	IV; Rm 7:13	138
Rm 4:16	II; Rm 4:17	84
Rm 4:17	Preface	17
Rm 4:17	VI; Rm 11: 33-36	225
Rm 4: 20-21	II; Rm 4: 14-15	83
Rm 5:1	III; Preface	92
Rm 5:5	III; Rm 5: 19-20	110
Rm 5:5	IV; Rm 8: 3-4	152
Rm 5:5	VI; Rm 9: 30-33	198
Rm 5:5	VII; Rm 12: 1-3	231
Rm 5:5, 8:14	VI; Rm 9: 25-26	196
Rm 5:6	III; Rm 5: 2-3	94
Rm 5: 6, 8	III; Rm 5: 7-11	97
Rm 5: 10, 9	V; Rm 8:33, 31-32	177
Rm 5:15	III; Rm 6: 3-4	115
Rm 5: 17-21	III; Rm 5:15	106
Rm 5:18	III; Rm 5: 7-11	99
Rm 5:19	III; Rm 5:14	105
Rm 5:19	III; Rm 6: 3-4	114
Rm 5:20	III; Rm 6:2	111 bis
Rm 5:20	II; Rm 2:17	56
Rm 5:20	III; Rm 5:13	102
Rm 5:20	III; Rm 6: 3-4	115
Rm 5:20	III; Rm 6:5	116
Rm 6:1	III; Rm 6: 3-4	115
Rm 6:1	III; Rm 6:15	121
Rm 6:2	III; Rm 6: 3-4	115 bis
Rm 6:6	III; Rm 6: 3-4	114
Rm 6:9	III; Rm 6:14	120
Rm 6:11	III; Rm 6: 3-4	113
Rm 6:13	III; Rm 6: 3-4	114
Rm 6:14	IV; Rm 7: 1-3	132
Rm 6:19	VII; Rm 12: 1-3	231
Rm 7:6	IV; Rm 7: 1-3	132
Rm 7:7	II; Rm 3:27	72
Rm 7:7	IV; Rm 7:12	137
Rm 7:7	IV; Rm 7:13	138
Rm 7:7	VII; Rm 12: 1-3	231
Rm 7:7	VII; Rm 16:20	266
Rm 7:8	IV; Rm 7:13	138

	Book, Chapter, Verse	Page
Rm 7: 8-9	III; Rm 5:13	103
Rm 7: 10-11	IV; Rm 7:13	138
Rm 7: 11	IV; Rm 7:7	135
Rm 7:12	II; Rm 3:27	73
Rm 7:12	IV; Rm 7: 1-3	132
Rm 7:13	IV; Rm 7: 1-3	131 bis
Rm 7:13	IV; Rm 7: 1-3	132 bis
Rm 7:23	III; Rm 5: 19-20	109
Rm 7:23	III; Rm 6:12	119
Rm 7:24	V; Rm 8:23	168
Rm 7:25	V; Rm 8:23	168
Rm 8:1	IV; Rm 7: 24-25	149
Rm 8:3	III; Rm 5:12	101
Rm 8: 6-7	III; Rm 6:12	119
Rm 8:9	I; Rm 1: 20-21	40
Rm 8:11	V; Rm 8:23	169
Rm 8:11	IV; Rm 7: 14-15	139
Rm 8: 18-25	VII; Rm 13:7	239
Rm 8:23	IV; Rm 7: 14-15	140
Rm 8:27	V; Rm 8:26	171
Rm 8:28	V; Rm 8: 29-30	175
Rm 8:30	V; Rm 8:33, 31-32	177
Rm 8:32	III; Rm 5: 7-11	97
Rm 8: 35-39	V; Rm 8: 33-34	180
Rm 8:39	V; Rm 8: 33-34	180
Rm 9:4	VI; Rm 11: 2-7	208
Rm 9:18	VI; Rm 11: 33-36	221
Rm 9: 31-32	VI; Rm 11: 2-7	209
Rm 10: 9-10	III; Rm 6:9	118
Rm 10:10	IV; Rm 8: 3-4	153
Rm 10:10	VII; Rm 15: 5-6	257 bis
Rm 11:5	V; Rm 9: 1-5	183
Rm 11:6	I; Rm 1:7	23
Rm 11:6	II; Rm 2:13	55
Rm 11:20	VII; Rm 12: 1-3	232
Rm 11: 25-26	II; Rm 4: 10-12	81
Rm 11:26	V; Rm 9: 1-5	183
Rm 12:2	V; Rm 8: 29-30	176
Rm 12:16	VI; Rm 11: 17-18	214
Rm 13:10	II; Rm 3:28	74
Rm 13:10	VI; Rm 9: 30-33	198
Rm 14:23	Preface	17
Rm 14:23	II; Rm 3:27	72
Rm 14:23	VII; Rm 12: 1-3	233
1 Cor 1:4	I; Rm 1:8	26
1 Cor 1:13	VI; Rm 9: 22-24	192
1 Cor 1: 23-24	I; Rm 1:16	31
1 Cor 1: 23-24	I; Rm 1:24	38
1 Cor 1:24	I; Rm 1:4	21
1 Cor 1:30	III; Rm 6:11	118
1 Cor 2:2	I; Rm 1:14	29
1 Cor 2:8	VI; Rm 9:27	196
1 Cor 2:12	VI; Rm 9: 22-24	195

281

	Book, Chapter, Verse	Page
1 Cor 2:13	I; Rm 1: 11-12	28
1 Cor 2:15	VI; Rm 9: 22-24	194
1 Cor 3:4	I; Rm 1:18	33
1 Cor 3:7	VI; Rm 10: 14-15	204
1 Cor 3:12	I; Rm 2:5	47
1 Cor 4:5	VII; Rm 13:11	243
1 Cor 4:5	VII; Rm 14:10	250
1 Cor 4:7	II; Rm 3:27	72
1 Cor 4:7	III, Preface	93
1 Cor 4:7	VI; Rm 11:18	214
1 Cor 5:12	VII; Rm 14:10	249
1 Cor 6: 2-3	VII; Rm 14:4	247
1 Cor 7:21	VII; Rm 13:7	239
1 Cor 7:25	II; Rm 3:27	72
1 Cor 7:40	I; Rm 1:7	24
1 Cor 9:14	VII; Rm 13:6	239
1 Cor 9:17	I; Rm 1:15	30
1 Cor 10: 25-27	VII; Rm 14:14	252
1 Cor 11:1	III; Rm 5:18	108
1 Cor 12:4	VII; Rm 12: 1-3	233
1 Cor 12:8	VII; Rm 12: 1-3	232
1 Cor 12:11	V; Rm 8:26	171
1 Cor 13:2	II; Rm 3:28	74
1 Cor 13: 4-6	III; Rm 5:1	93
1 Cor 13:9	VII; Rm 15: 15-17	259
1 Cor 13:12	III; Rm 6:17	122
1 Cor 13:12	V; Rm 8:17	164
1 Cor 14:3	VII; Rm 12:6	234
1 Cor 15:10	II; Rm 4:17	84
1 Cor 15:22	IV; Rm 7:24-25	148
1 Cor 15:28	VII; Rm 13:10	242
1 Cor 15:43	V; Rm 8: 29-30	176
1 Cor 15: 44, 53	V; Rm 8: 10-11	160
1 Cor 15: 46	V; Rm 9:3	184
1 Cor 15:55	V; Rm 8:23	169
1 Cor 15:56	IV; Rm 7: 1-3	132
2 Cor 3:5	III; Rm 5: 5-6	95
2 Cor 3:6	IV; Rm 7:6	134
2 Cor 4:10	III; Rm 6:12	119
2 Cor 5:16	III; Rm 5: 7-11	96
2 Cor 5:21	III; Rm 5:12	101
2 Cor 6:15	II; Rm 4:20, 22-25	87
2 Cor 11:6	IV: Preface	129
2 Cor 11:6	VII; Rm 12: 1-3	232
2 Cor 11: 28-29	VII; Rm 12: 7-16	235
2 Cor 11:29	I; Rm 1:29	42
2 Cor 12:4	I; Rm 1:1	19
2 Cor 12:9	Preface	17
2 Cor 13:3	I; Rm 1:7	24
Gal 5:6	II; Rm 2:13	55
Gal 5:6	II; Rm 3:28	73
Gal 5:6	VI; Rm 10:4	200
Gal 5:6	VII; Rm 12: 1-3	233
Gal 5:19	I; Rm 1:13	29
Gal 5: 19-21	III; Rm 6:12	118

	Book, Chapter, Verse	Page
Gal 5:22	I; Rm 1:13	29
Gal 5:24	III; Rm 6: 3-4	113
Eph 1:4	III; Rm 5: 7-11	98
Eph 2:3	IV; Rm 7:24	147
Eph 2:10	Preface	16
Eph 2:12	I; Rm 1:5	23
Eph 2: 14-16	III; Rm 5:1	93
Eph 2: 14, 20	VI; Rm 9: 25-26	195
Eph 2: 14-20	VII; Rm 15: 8-9	257
Eph 3:10	VII; Rm 16:20	268
Eph 4: 22-24	II; Rm 4:20, 22-25	87
Eph 4:25	III; Rm 6: 3-4	114
Eph 5:2	III; Rm 5: 7-11	97
Eph 5:5	I; Rm 1: 20-21	41
Eph 5:19	VII; Rm 15: 8-9	258
Eph 5:27	IV; Rm 7: 1-3	131
Eph 5:29	IV; Rm 7:17	144
Phil 1: 23-24	IV; Rm 7: 24-25	148
Phil 2: 12-13	V; Rm 8: 29-30	175
Phil 2:15	II; Rm 4: 18-19	86
Phil 3:8	II; Rm 4: 18-19	85
Phil 4:12	VII; Rm 14:3	246
Col 1:3	I; Rm 1:8	26
Col 1:13	V; Rm 8: 33-34	180
Col 1:18	V; Rm 8: 29-30	176
Col 2:9	VII; Rm 12: 1-3	233
Col 3: 1-3	III; Rm 6: 3-4	114
Col 3:4	V; Rm 8: 29-30	174
Col 3:5	III; Rm 6:12	119
Col 3:9	III; Rm 6: 3-4	114
1 Th 2:18	I; Rm 1:13	29
1 Th 5:8	II; Rm 4: 10-12	80
1 Th 5:17	I; Rm 1:9	27
1 Th 5:23	I; Rm 1: 20-21	40
1 Tim 1:5	I; Rm 1:24	37
1 Tim 4:4	VII; Rm 14:14	252
1 Tim 5:23	I; Rm 1:14	30
1 Tim 6:16	I; Rm 2:4	46
2 Tim 1:12	IV; Rm 7: 24-25	148
2 Tim 4:20	I; Rm 1:14	30
Heb 2:18	V; Rm 8:17	165
Heb 3: 3-6	V; Rm 8:15	162
Heb 5:4	I; Rm 1:1	20
Heb 7:10	III; Rm 5:12	102
Heb 9: 13-14	IV; Rm 8: 3-4	152
Heb 9: 14	IV; Rm 8: 3-4	153
Heb 11:1	VI; Rm 8:26	173
Heb 11:1	VI; Rm 10: 8-9	202
Heb 11:6	VII; Rm 12: 1-3	233
Heb 11:19	II; Rm 4: 20, 22-25	86
Jm 1:17	II; Rm 3:27	73
Jm 1:22	III; Rm 6:14	121
Jm 4:6	VI; Rm 10: 8-9	202
Jm 4:6	VI; Rm 11: 20-21	215
Jm 4:6	VI; Rm 11: 33-36	221

	Book, Chapter, Verse	Page
1 Pet 4:8	III; Rm 5: 5-6	95
1 Jn 3:2	V; Rm 8:17	164
1 Jn 3:2	V; Rm 8:19	166
1 Jn 3:9	IV; Rm 7:17	143
1 Jn 3:17	VII; Rm 15:7	257
1 Jn 4:18	VI; Rm 11: 19-20	214
1 Jn 5:19	IV; Rm 7: 24-25	148
Rev 5: 3-5	IV; Rm 8: 3-4	151
Unknown source	I; Rm 1:15	30

TABULATION OF SCRIPTURAL CITATIONS

Gen	28 citations	Mt	52 citations
Ex	10	Mk	2
Lev	4	Lk	26
Num	1	Jn	40
Deut	11	Ac	8
1 Sam	2	Rm	133
2 Sam	1	1 Cor	45
1 Kgs	3	2 Cor	13
2 Kgs	1	Gal	8
Tob	1	Eph	15
Jb	2	Phil	5
Ps	87	Col	8
Prov	1	1 Th	4
Qo	3	1 Tim	4
Sg	4	2 Tim	2
Wis	3	Heb	10
Si	3	Jm	5
Is	24	1 Pet	1
Jer	1	1 Jn	6
Ezek	2	Rev	1
Dan	1		------
Hos	2		388
Hab	2		
Zech	2	Unknown source	1
Mal	2		

	201		
		OT	201
		NT	388

		Total	589

INDEX OF PATRISTIC AND OTHER ANCIENT SOURCES NAMED, QUOTED OR USED BY WILLIAM OF ST. THIERRY, OR REFERRED TO BY THE EDITOR IN HIS NOTES

The asterisk attached to many texts of St Augustine indicates that these texts are to be found in the 'Exposition on Paul's Letters' by Florus of Lyons, one of Williams chief sources (PL 119).

	Book, Chapter, Verse	*Page*
Ambrose, merely named	Preface	15
Augustine, merely named	Preface	15 bis
*Confessions 8:4	I, note 2; Rm 1:1	20
Confessions 10:29:40	II; Rm 3:27	73
Confessions 10:31:43-44	VII, note 11; Rm 13:14	244
Confessions 10:37:60	II; Rm 3:27	73
Letter 92 (PL 33:319)	I, note 25; Rm 1:24	37
Letter 98:9-10	III, note 14; Rm 6:3-4	113
Letter 130 (PL 33:498)	III, note 1; Preface	92
Letter 130 (PL 33:498)	III, note 2; Rm 5:1	93
Letter 130 (PL 33:503)	V, note 6; Rm 8:26	171
Letter 130:28 (PL 33:505)	V, note 8; Rm 8:27	173
*Letter 140:17	VII, note 18; Rm 15:8-9	258
*Letter 153 (PL 33:655)	I, note 35; Rm 2:4	46
Letter 157:3:15-17	III, note 13; Rm 5:19-20	110
Letter 157:3:19	III, note 10; Rm 5:12	102
Letter 157:3:19-29	III, note 12; Rm 5:15	106
Letter 170:5	VI, note 7; Rm 11:33-36	222
Letter 170:5	VI, note 8; Rm 11:33-36	223
*Letter 190:3	VI, note 1; Rm 9:22-24	194

	Book, Chapter, Verse	Page
Letter 194:4:20-21	III, note 23; Rm 6:23	125
*Letter 194:16-18	V, note 4; Rm 8:26	171
City of God, 4:23	Preface, note 4	16
*City of God, 8:6	I, note 22; Rm 1:24	36
City of God, 10:1	Preface, note 4	16
*City of God, 10:6	VII, note 1; Rm 12:1-3	230
*City of God, 22:16	V, note 12; Rm 8:29-30	176
True Religion (PL 34:172)	VI, note 12; Rm 11:33-36	226
Catholic & Manichaean Ways of Life I,11,19	V, note 17; Rm 8:38-39	182
Against Faustus 19, 13	II, note 8: Rm 3:27	73
On the Spirit and Letter 11:18	Preface, note 4	16
On the Spirit and Letter 11:18	I, note 21; Rm 1:18	33
On the Spirit and Letter 11:18	II, note 6, Rm 3:27	71
On the Spirit and Letter 11:18	II, note 7; Rm 3:27	71
*Grace and Free-Will 17:33	V, note 9: Rm 8:29-30	175
*Grace and Free-Will 21:43	I, note 28; Rm 1:20-21	40
(This is William's sole explicit citation of a patristic text)		
*Predestination of the Saints 10:19 (PL 44:974-975)	V, note 10; Rm 8:29-30	176
*Predestination of the Saints (PL 44:981)	I, note 4; Rm 1:4	21
*Predestination of the Saints (PL 44:983)	I, note 5; Rm 1:4	21
*Gift of Perseverance 14:35 (PL 45:1014)	V, note 11; Rm 8:29-30	176
*Gift of Perseverance (PL 45:1034)	I, note 8; Rm 1:4	21
*Gift of Perseverance (PL 45:1034)	I, note 9; Rm 1:4	22
*Christian Doctrine 1:5	VI, note 13; Rm 11:33-36	226
*Christian Doctrine 3:3:6	V, note 16; Rm 8:33-34	179
*Enarr. on Psalm 5:17 (PL 36:89)	V, note 14; Rm 3:33, 31-32	177
*Enarr. on Psalm 9 (PL 36:126)	I, note 36; Rm 2:4	46
*Enarr. on Psalm 34 (PL 36:335)	IV, note 5; Rm 8:3-4	154
*Enarr. on Psalm 55 (PL 36:650-651)	I, note 34; Rm 1:29	42
*Enarr. on Psalm 67 (PL 36:820)	I, note 10; Rm 1:4	23
Enarr. on Psalm 67, 39 (PL 36:836)	II, note 5; Rm 3:27	71
Enarr. on Psalm 72 (PL 36:916)	I, note 1; Rm 1:1	20
*Enarr. on Psalm 76:4 (PL 36:973)	VII, note 10; Rm 13:11	243
*Enarr. on Psalm 150:3 (PL 36:1962-1963)	V, note 15; Rm 8:33, 31-32	178
Gospel of St. John, Tract 26:2	I, note 31; Rm 1:20-21	40
*Gospel of St. John, Tract 73 (PL 35:1824)	VII, note 12; Rm 14:3	247
Gospel of St. John, Tract 100,1	VII, note 21; Rm 16:21-27	266
*First Epistle of St. John, Sermon III, ch. 2	I, note 3; Rm 1:1	20
*First Epistle of St. John, Sermon VI, ch. 8	V, note 5; Rm 8:26	171
Propositions on Romans (PL 35:2065 ffl.)	II, note 3; Rm 2:17	56
Propositions on Romans (PL 35:2074)	V, note 3; Rm 8:21-22	167

	Book, Chapter, Verse	Page
*Exposition on Epistle to the		
Galatians (PL 35:2117)	II, note 1; Rm 2:11-12	54
Trinity 5:11 and 6:5	I, note 27; Rm 1:24	38
*Trinity 6:10:11	VI, note 10; Rm 11:33-36	224
*Trinity 13:16:21	III, note 8; Rm 5:7-11	98
*Trinity 14:18:24	V, note 13; Rm 8:29-30	176
Trinity 7:1:2	VI, note 6; Rm 11:33-36	222
Sermon 71:12:18	III, note 4; Rm 5:5-6	95
Sermon 71:12:18	III, note 5; Rm 5:5-6	95
Sermon 71:12:18	III, note 6; Rm 5:5-6	95
*Sermon 158:2:2	VI, note 11; Rm 11:33-36	224
Basil		
Unknown place	VII, note 8; Rm 12:20-21	237
Unknown place	VII, note 17; Rm 15:1	255
Bede		
Gospel of Luke (PL 92:408)	VII, note 13; Rm 14:10	250
Benedict		
Rule, chapter 1	I, note 17; Rm 1:11-12	28
Bernard		
Letter 174	IV, note 4	156
Sermon 85 on Canticle, 8-9	V, note 1; Rm 8:5-7	157
Consideration 4:111:6	VII, note 9; Rm 13:3-4	238
Cassian		
Conference 23, title and ch. 7	IV, note 1; Preface	129
Conference 7:12	I, note 32	51
Cicero		
De Officiis 2:25	I, note 26; Rm 1:24	38
———	VII, note 21	270
Gregory the Great		
Homily 37 on Gospel (PL 76:1275)	V, note 7; Rm 8:26	172
Unknown place	VI, note 5; Rm 11:33-36	220
Florus		
(PL 119:296-297)	IV, note 6; Rm 8:3-4	154
Horace		
Epistle 1:3:19	Preface, note 3	15
Satire 2:3:21	III, note 7; Rm 5:5-6	95
Isidore		
Etymologies 1:34:5	I, note 33	52
(Mansi)		
Councils of Elvira and of Orange	I, note 32	51
Origen		
(merely named)	Preface	15
———	I, note 13; Rm 1:7	24
On Romans PG 14:555	I, note 19; Rm 1:11-12	28
On Romans PG 14:585	II, note 13; Rm 4:10-12	81
On Romans PG 14:849	I, note 6; Rm 1:4	21
On Romans PG 14:852	I, note 11; Rm 1:5	23
On Romans PG 14:853	I, note 12; Rm 1:5	23
On Romans PG 14:853	I, note 14; Rm 1:7	24
On Romans PG 14:854	I, note 15; Rm 1:8	26
On Romans PG 14:857	I, note 16; Rm 1:10	28
On Romans PG 14:857	I, note 18: Rm 1:11-12	28
On Romans PG 14:861	I, note 20; Rm 1:16	31

	Book, Chapter, Verse	Page
On Romans PG 14:865	I, note 29; Rm 1:20-21	40
On Romans PG 14:866	I, note 30; Rm 1:20-21	40
On Romans PG 14:866	V, note 3; Rm 8:21-22	167
On Romans PG 14:875	I, note 38; Rm 2:5	47
On Romans PG 14:879-880	I, note 39; Rm 2:6-7	48
On Romans PG 14:883-886	I, note 40; Rm 2:8-9	49
On Romans PG 14:884	I, note 41; Rm 2:8-9	49
On Romans PG 14:885	I, note 42; Rm 2:8-9	49
On Romans PG 14:886	I, note 43; Rm 2:8-9	49
On Romans PG 14:944	II, note 4; Rm 3:21-22	69
On Romans PG 14:966	II, note 9; Rm 4:6	77
On Romans PG 14:966	II, note 10; Rm 4:9	78
On Romans PG 14:967	II, note 11; Rm 4:10-12	79
On Romans PG 14:967	II, note 12; Rm 4:10-12	79
On Romans PG 14:968-969	II, note 14; Rm 4:10-12	81
On Romans PG 14:975-978	II, note 15; Rm 4:17	85
On Romans PG 14:981	II, note 16; Rm 4:18-19	85
On Romans PG 14:1009-1010	III, note 11; Rm 5:12	102
On Romans PG 14:1012-1013	III, note 9; Rm 5:12	100
On Romans PG 14:1043	III, note 15; Rm 6:5	116
On Romans PG 14:1043	III, note 16; Rm 6:6	117
On Romans PG 14:1054	III, note 17; Rm 6:11	118
On Romans PG 14:1056	III, note 18; Rm 6:11	118
On Romans PG 14:1058	III, note 19; Rm 6:14	120
On Romans PG 14:1059	III, note 20; Rm 6:15	121
On Romans PG 14:1059	III, note 21; Rm 6:16	121
On Romans PG 14:1061	III, note 22; Rm 6:17	122
On Romans PG 14:1142-1143	V, note 18; Rm 9:10-13	186
On Romans PG 14:1155	VI, note 2; Rm 9:30-33	199
On Romans PG 14:1190	VI, note 4; Rm 11:15	212
On Romans PG 14:1209-1210	VII, note 3; Rm 12:1-3	232
On Romans PG 14:1210-1211	VII, note 4; Rm 12:1-3	232
On Romans PG 14:1213	VII, note 6; Rm 12:6	234
On Romans PG 14:1241	VII, note 14; Rm 14:13	251
On Romans PG 14:1268	VII, note 19; Rm 15:15-17	259
On Romans PG 14:1276	VII, note 20; Rm 15:30-32	263

Peter Lombard
   On Romans 2:15 (PL 191:1346 BC) II, note 2; Rm 2:14-16 . . 55

Plotinus
   Enneads 1:6:8 . . . . I, note 24; Rm 1:24 . . 37

Quintilian
   ———   I, note 33 52

TABULATION OF PATRISTIC CITATIONS

Ambrose	1
Augustine	68
(Those contained in Florus	33)
Basil	2
Bede	1
Benedict	1
Bernard	3
Cassian	2
Cicero	2
Councils (Mansi)	1
Florus	1
Gregory the Great	2
Horace	2
Isidore	1
Origen	48
Peter Lombard	1
Plotinus	1
Quintilian	1
Total	138

TOPICAL INDEX
for the Exposition of the Epistle to the Romans
by William of St. Thierry

	Book, Chapter, Verse	Page
Abraham	Preface	16
	II; Rm 4:1-25	75-86
	V; Rm 9:6-9	185
Adam	I; Rm 2:6-7	48
Adam, the two Adams	III; Rm 5:7-20	98-109
	III; Rm 6:3-4	114
Baptism	III; Rm 5:12	101
	III; Rm 6:3-4	113-115
	IV; Rm 7:19-20	144-145
Baptismal formula, question about	III; Rm 6:3-4	116
Baptism, infant	III; Rm 6:3-4	112-113
Baptized: social and sexual differences remain in the baptized	VII; Rm 13:8	240
Beatitude, definition	III; Rm 5:1	93
	V; Rm 8:26	171
Blindness of heart	I; Rm 1:21-22	34
	I; Rm 2:4	46
	VI; Rm 10:16	205
	VI; Rm 11:2-8	209-210
	VI; Rm 11:25	216
Body will be spiritual in heaven	IV; Rm 7:14-15	139
Carnal, animal, spiritual man, three types (See Faith: doctrine of faith)	I; Rm 2:5	47
Charity, fraternal	I; Rm 1:8	25
	I; Rm 1:11-12	28
	II; Rm 2:11-12	54
	VII; Rm 12:7-21	235-237

	Book, Chapter, Verse	Page
Charity, fraternal (continued)	VII; Rm 13:8-9	240-241
	VII; Rm 14:13	251
	VII; Rm 14:16	252
	VII; Rm 14:18-23	253-255
	VII; Rm 15:1-3	255
	VII; Rm 15:7	257
Christ, his constitution (hypostatic union)	I; Rm 1:3	21
Christ, the cornerstone	VII; Rm 15:8-9	257
Christ, full of grace	IV; Rm 8:3-4	152
Christ's historic mysteries shape Christians now	III; Rm 6:3-9	113-118
Christ, the mystery of his name	I; Rm 1:1	20
Christ, not the son of the Holy Spirit	I; Rm 1:4	22
Christ, memory of the passion of	IV; Rm 8:3-4	153
	V; Rm 8:17	165
Christ, predestination of	I; Rm 1:4	21
Circumcision	II; Rm 2:25	59-61
(see Abraham, and Sacraments	II; Rm 4:10-12	79-82
of the Old Law)	III; Rm 5:13	103
Civil authority	VII; Rm 13:1-7	237-239
Combat, spiritual	III; Rm 5:2	101
	III; Rm 6:12	118-119
	IV; Rm 7:19-20	144
	IV; Rm 8:2-3	149-150
	IV; Rm 8:3-4	155
	V; Rm 8:12-13	161
	V; Rm 8:19	165-166
	V; Rm 8:35-37	180
	VII; Rm 15:30-32	263
Concupiscence	I; Rm 1:20-21	40
	III; Rm 5:12-13	101-103
	III; Rm 6:12	119
	IV; Rm 7:5-25	133-148
	IV; Rm 8:2-3	150
	VII; Rm 13:12-14	244
	VII; Rm 14:21	253
	VII; Rm 16:20	266
Contemplation, theory and description (see Prayer)	V; Rm 8:26	171-173
David	II; Rm 3:4	64
	IV; Rm 7:12	137
Death, Kingdom of	III; Rm 5:12-17	101-107
	III; Rm 6:23	125
	IV; Rm 7:22-23	147
	VII; Rm 14:7-9	249
Delight in the Law of God	III; Rm 6:19	123-124
	IV; Rm 7:10-24	136-147
	V; Rm 8:9	159
	V; Rm 8:14	162
	VII; Rm 14:3	247
The devil (Satan)	I; Rm 1:13	29
	I; Rm 1:20-21	40
	VII; Rm 16:20	265
Elias, the coming of	VI; Rm 11:26-27	217
Envy	I; Rm 1:29	41

		Book, Chapter, Verse	Page
Envy (continued)		VI; Rm 10:19	205-206
		VI; Rm 11:2-7	209
		VII; Rm 14:13	251
Eremitical life		VII; Rm 12:6	234
Evil: God's use of the wicked		V; Rm 8:5-7	158
		V; Rm 9:17-18	187
		VI; Rm 9:22-24	191-193
		VI; Rm 11:28-29	218
		VII; Rm 13:1	238
Faith, the nature of		I; Rm 1:17	32
		III; Rm 6:3-4	112
		VI; Rm 9:30-33	197
		VI; Rm 10:6-7	201
Faith is a free gift of God, not merited		Preface	17
		I; Rm 1:17	32
		II; Rm 3:27	72
		II; Rm 4:5	76
		VI; Rm 10:4	200
Faith: the doctrine of faith has three forms: rational, spiritual, intellectual (see Carnal, animal, spiritual man)		III; Rm 6:17	122-123
Faith, hope, charity		II; Rm 4:10-12	79
		II; Rm 4:18-19	85
		IV; Rm 8:3-4	152-153
		VII; Rm 15:13	259
Faith is sterile without good works (see Good Works)			
Faith: open confession of faith is necessary		VI; Rm 10:6-10	201-203
Fear: chaste, servile and vicious fearlessness		V; Rm 8:15	162
		VI; Rm 11:19-20	214-215
		VII; Rm 13:3-4	238
		VII; Rm 13:7	239
The flesh is not to be hated, but disciplined		IV; Rm 7:17	144
		VII; Rm 13:14	244
Freedom in regard to sin and to justice		III; Rm 6:16-23	121-126
Gentile Christians rebuked		II; Rm 2:17	57
		II; Rm 2:28-29	61
		VI; Rm 11:17-20	214
		VI; Rm 11:25	216
Gluttony (see Temperance)		VII; Rm 13:14	244
		VII; Rm 14:21	253
God the Trinity		VI; Rm 11:33-36	221-226
		VII; Rm 12:1-3	233
		VII; Rm 16:21-27	266-268
God the Father is wise by himself, not by generating his Son, the Word		VI; Rm 11:33-36	221-222
		VII; Rm 16:21-27	266-267
God: the justice of God		I; Rm 1:17	31
		II; Rm 3:21-22	68-69
		VI; Rm 9:30-33	197-199
God's knowledge of the world		VI; Rm 11:33-36	223-224
God knows future sins but does not cause them		V; Rm 8:29-30	176
		VI; Rm 10:20	206
God: likeness and unlikeness to him		I; Rm 1:24	37
		V; Rm 8:24-25	170

	Book, Chapter, Verse	Page
God: likeness and unlikeness (continued)	VII; Rm 12:1-3	231
God: the love of God for men	III; Rm 5:2-3	95
	III; Rm 5:7-11	98
	V; Rm 8:35-37	181
God: the love of men for God	I; Rm 1:8	26
	III; Rm 5:2-3	95
	III; Rm 5:7-11	96
God: the love of God, of self, of neighbor	VII; Rm 13:9-10	241-242
: the nature of God as seen by true philosophy	I; Rm 1:24	35-36
(see Philosophers, heathen, approved)	I; Rm 1:20-21	38-39
God: the wrath of God	I; Rm 1:16	31
	I; Rm 1:18	32
	I; Rm 1:24	37
	III; Rm 5:7-11	97
	VI; Rm 9:22-24	193
Good works necessary for salvation	II; Rm 3:28	74
(see Merit)	II; Rm 4:5	76
	II; Rm 4:10-12	79
Grace: the praise and primacy of grace	Preface	16-17
	II; Rm 2:13	55
	V; Rm 9:15-16	187
	VI; Rm 9:22-24	192
	VI; Rm 9:30-33	197
	VI; Rm 10:20	207
	VI; Rm 11:2-7	209
	VI; Rm 11:28-29	218-219
	VI; Rm 11:33-36	224-225
	VII; Rm 15:18-19	260
Grace in general	Preface	16-17
	I; Rm 1:5-7	23-24
	II; Rm 3:1-2	62-63
	III; Rm 5, Preface	92
	III; Rm 6:23	125
	IV; Rm 7:14-15	138-141
	IV; Rm 7:24-25	148
Grace and gratitude	Preface	16
(see Gratitude to God)	I; Rm 1:8	25-26
	III; Rm 5, Preface	92
	VI; Rm 10:13	203
	VI; Rm 10:20	207
	VI; Rm 11:33-36	225
Grace excludes sin	III; Rm 6:2	111
	III; Rm 6:3-5	115-116
Grace: operating and cooperating grace	Preface	16
	V; Rm 8:29-30	175
Grace: the distinction of graces	I; Rm 1:11-12	28
Grace in the Saints of the Old Law	Preface	16
(see Abraham, David)	II; Rm 4:10-12	80
	II; Rm 4:17	84
	III; Rm 5:14	104
Grammatical science used	V; Rm 8:33-34	179
Gratitude to God	II; Rm 3:24-25	71
(see Grace and Gratitude)	III; Rm 6:17	122
	VI; Rm 11:33-36	225
Greek text or words referred to	I; Rm 1:4	21

	Book, Chapter, Verse	Page
Greek text or words referred to (continued)	I; Rm 1:20-21	41
	II; Rm 2:13	55
	II; Rm 3:21-22	68
	II; Rm 3:27	71
	II; Rm 4:6	77
	III; Rm 5:5-6	95
	III; Rm 6:11	118
	IV; Rm 7, Preface	129
	VII; Rm 12:1-3	232
	VII; Rm 12:6	234
	VII; Rm 14:13	251
	VII; Rm 15:15-17	259
	VII; Rm 15:30-32	263
Growth, spiritual	I; Rm 1:20-21	39
(see Justice, how to grow in it)	II; Rm 4:6	77
	III; Rm 5, Preface	91
	III; Rm 5:5-6	95
	VII; Rm 12:1-3	230-231
Heavenly state described	V; Rm 8:18	165
	V; Rm 8:33,31-32	178-179
	VII; Rm 14:17	253
Hell fire	I; Rm 2:5	47
Holy Spirit	I; Rm 1:4	22
	I; Rm 1:24	38
	II; Rm 4:10-12	80
	II; Rm 4:17	84
	V; Rm 8:9	159
	V; Rm 8:35-37	181
	VI; Rm 11:33-36	223-224
	VII; Rm 12:1-3	233
Hope	II; Rm 4:5	76
(see Faith, hope, charity)	II; Rm 4:18-19	85
	IV; Rm 7:5	133
	V; Rm 8:10-11	160
	V; Rm 8:24-25	169-170
Infants in regard to grace and	VI; Rm 9:22-24	193-194
predestination (see Infant baptism)		
Jews or Jewish Christians rebuked	I; Rm 2:1	44
	II; Rm 2:17	57
	II; Rm 2:21	59
	II; Rm 2:28-29	61
	II; Rm 3:17-18	67
Jewish Christians praised	VII; Rm 15:25-28	262
Jewish people, the honor of	II; Rm 3:2-3	63
	V; Rm 9:4-5	184
	VI; Rm 11:2-7	208
	VII; Rm 15:8-9	258
Justice and faith closely connected	I; Rm 1:17	31-32
	II; Rm 3:21-22	69
Justice, how to grow in it	II; Rm 2:17	56-57
(see Spiritual growth)		
Law: four degrees of obeying the divine law	II; Rm 2:17	56-57
	III; Rm 5 Preface and 5:1	91-93
	IV; Rm 7, Preface	129
	IV; Rm 7:14-15	139

	Book, Chapter, Verse	Page
Law, Mosaic	II; Rm 2:11-12	53-54
	III; Rm 5:19-20	109
	III; Rm 6:14	120
	IV; Rm 7:6-16	134-143
	IV; Rm 8:3-4	152
Logical science used	III; Rm 6:2-4	114
	V; Rm 8:33-34	179
Man is a summary of the universe	V; Rm 8:21-22	167-168
Mary	Preface	16
	I; Rm 1:4	22
	IV; Rm 8:3-4	154
Medical terms and practices referred to	I; Rm 1:24	35
	I; Rm 2:8-9	49
	II; Rm 2:17	57-58
	III; Rm 6:2	111
	III; Rm 6:17	122
	IV; Rm 7:14-15	142
	IV; Rm 7:22-23	147
	VII; Rm 15:1	255
Merit exists	Preface	16
(see Good works)	II; Rm 3:27	72
	VI; Rm 11:33-36	221
Natural law	I; Rm 1:24	35
	I; Rm 1:24	38
	I; Rm 1:29	42
	II; Rm 2:11-12	53-54
	III; Rm 5:13-20	103-109
	V; Rm 8:16	163
Oaths, necessary, useful, but because of evil	I; Rm 1:9	27
Obscure passages with several interpretations	III; Rm 5:7-11	98-99
(see Philological interests)	III; Rm 5:12	102
	IV; Rm 7:1-3	130-132
	V; Rm 8:29-30	176
	VII; Rm 16:21-27	266
Obscure passages left undecided	II; Rm 3:30	75
(see Philological interests)	III; Rm 5:13	104
Olive-tree, natural lore about	VI; Rm 11:17-18	213
Original sin	III; Rm 5:12-20	100-110
	III; Rm 6:3-4	113
	III; Rm 6:6	117
	IV; Rm 7:14-15	142
	V; Rm 9:10-13	180
	VI; Rm 9:22-24	194
Orthodoxy, concern for	Preface	15
	VII; Rm 16:18-19	264-265
Parables invented or used by William	II; Rm 3:12	66
	III; Rm 5:7-11	97
	IV; Rm 7:1-3	131-132
	V; Rm 8:19	166
	VI; Rm 10:5-9	200-202
	VII; Rm 14:13	251
	VII; Rm 15:14	259
Passions of sin	IV; Rm 7:1-5	131-133
Patience and holy impatience*	I; Rm 2:1	44
	I; Rm 2:4	46

	Book, Chapter, Verse	Page
Patience and holy impatience (continued)	I; Rm 2:6-7	48
	II; Rm 3:1	62
	III; Rm 5:2-3	94
	*IV; Rm 7:24-25	148
	IV, Rm 7:24-25	149
	*V, Rm 8:24-25	169
	V; Rm 8:28-29	175
	VII; Rm 12:19	237
	VII; Rm 15:5-6	256
Pauline mannerisms noted	I; Rm 1:4	23
	II; Rm 2:28-29	60
	II; Rm 3:9-11	66
	III; Rm 5:12	99
	III; Rm 6:3-4	116
Peace towards God	III; Rm 5, Preface	92-93
	V; Rm 8:17	164
Philological interests	I; Rm 1:1	19-20
(see Obscure passages)	II; Rm 2:14-16	55
	II; Rm 3:21	68-69
	II; Rm 3:30	74
	V; Rm 8:17	165
Philosophers, heathen, approved	I; Rm 1:13	29
(see God, nature)	I; Rm 1:24	35-36
	II; Rm 4:10-12	79
	VII; Rm 12:1-3	233
Philosophers, heathen, blamed	I; Rm 1:18	33-34
	V; Rm 8:38-39	182
Prayer addressed directly to God or to Jesus	Preface	17
	I; Rm 1:1	22
	III; Rm 5:2-3	94-95
	IV; Rm 7:14-15	141
	IV; Rm 7:24-25	148
	IV; Rm 8:3-4	151
	IV; Rm 8:3-4	153
Prayer is among the gifts of grace	Preface	16
(see Contemplation)	II; Rm 3:27	72
	V; Rm 8:26	170-171
Prayer of petition	V; Rm 8:26	171
Predestination of Christians	I; Rm 1:4	21
(see Predestination of Christ)	II; Rm 4:14-15	83
	II; Rm 4:17	84
	V; Rm 8:28-33	174-178
	V; Rm 9:10-13	186
	VI; Rm 9:22-24	191-194
	VI; Rm 11:28-29	219
Pride	I; Rm 1:21-22	34
	I; Rm 1:29	42-43
	II; Rm 2:17	57
	II; Rm 3:12	66
	II; Rm 3:27	71-72
Prophecy, nature of Christian	VII; Rm 12:6	234
Prudence of the flesh	V; Rm 8:5-7	157-158
Punishment, temporal, of sin	V; Rm 8:24-25	169-170
Purgatory	I; Rm 2:5	47
Rash judgement	I; Rm 2:2	45

	Book, Chapter, Verse	Page
Rash judgement (continued)	II; Rm 3:4	64
	VII; Rm 14:1	245
	VII; Rm 14:4-10	247-250
Reading, spiritual	II; Rm 2:11-12	54
	III; Rm 6:17	122
	VII; Rm 15:4	256
Redemption through the blood of Jesus	II; Rm 3:23	70
	IV; Rm 7:14-15	140-141
	IV; Rm 8:3-4	153
	V; Rm 8:17	165
Resurrection, the general	V; Rm 8:10-11	160
	VI; Rm 11:15	212
Resurrection of Jesus Christ	II; Rm 4:20,22-25	86-87
	III; Rm 6:9-10	117-118
Rome and the Romans, devotion to	I; Rm 1:8	26-27
	VII; Rm 15:29	262
	VII; Rm 16:19	265
Sacraments of the New Law	II; Rm 3:27	73
(see Baptism)	III; Rm 5:7-11	96
	III; Rm 6:3-4	112
Sacraments of the Old Law	II; Rm 2:11-12	54
(see Circumcision)	VII; Rm 12:1-3	229-230
Sin	I; Rm 1:4	21
	I; Rm 2:1	44
	II; Rm 4:14-15	82
	II; Rm 4:20,22-25	87
	III; Rm 5:7-11	96
	III; Rm 6:12	118-119
	III; Rm 6:16	121
	IV; Rm 7:7-23	134-145
	IV; Rm 8:3-4	154
	VII; Rm 12:1-3	232-233
	VII; Rm 14:23	255
Sin as lying latent before the time	IV; Rm 7:8-9	135
	IV; Rm 7:13	138
Soul, Christian, as spouse	IV; Rm 7:1-4	131-133
	IV; Rm 8:3-4	153
Soul, structure of, bipartite	I; Rm 1:20-21	40
	IV; Rm 7:14-15	139
Soul, structure of, tripartite	I; Rm 1:20-21	40
Temperance in eating, rules for	VII; Rm 14:3	246-247
(see Gluttony)		
Time, nature of	VII; Rm 16:21-27	267
Virtues are mutually inclusive	I; Rm 1:13	29
	II; Rm 4:10-12	79
Wisdom	I; Rm 1:5	23
(see Prudence of the flesh; God the	I; Rm 1:24	37
Father is wise by himself)	I; Rm 1:29	41
	II; Rm 3:27	71
	V; Rm 8:5-7	157
	VI; Rm 11:33-36	221-223
	VII; Rm 12:1-3	232
	VII; Rm 16:19	265
	VII; Rm 16:21-27	266-267

A SELECTED BIBLIOGRAPHY

TEXTS

Charleville Ms 49, ff. 103-216
Migne, J.P., *Patrologia latina*, vol. 180 (Paris, 1855) cols. 547-694
Tissier, Bertrand, *Bibliotheca patrum cisterciensium*, vol. 4 (Bonnefontaine, 1662) pp. 174-237.

WORKS ABOUT THE EXPOSITION ON ROMANS

Adam, André, *Guillaume de Saint-Thierry sa vie et ses oeuvres* (Bourg, 1923).

Anderson, John D., 'William of Saint Thierry's *Exposition on the Epistle to the Romans*', (CS 60) *Cistercian Ideals and Reality*, John R. Sommerfeldt, editor, pp. 136-151.

Bouyer, Louis, *The Cistercian Heritage* (London: Mowbrays—Philadelphia: Westminster, 1958).

Ceglar, Stanislaus, *William of Saint Thierry the Chronology of His Life With a Study of His Treatise 'On the Nature of Love,' His Authorship of the Brevis commentatio, the* In lacu, *and the 'Reply to Cardinal Matthew'* (Diss., Washington, D.C., 1971).

Déchanet, Jean–Marie, *Aux sources de la spiritualité de Guillaume de Saint-Thierry* (Bruges, 1940).

———, *Guillaume de Saint-Thierry l'homme et son oeuvre* (Bruges, 1942). Translated by Richard Strachan as *William of St Thierry, the Man and his Work* (CS 10) (Cistercian Publications, 1972).

Wilmart, André, 'La série et la date des ouvrages de Guillaume de Saint-Thierry,' *Revue Mabillon* 14 (1924) pp. 157-167.

ABBREVIATIONS

Aug., *Enarr. on Ps*   Augustine of Hippo, *Enarration on Psalms*

Origen, *On Roms*   Origen, *On Romans*

William, *Enigma*   William of St Thierry, *The Enigma of Faith*

CF   Cistercian Fathers Series

CS   Cistercian Studies Series

PL   J.-P. Migne, *Patrologia Latina*

Marginal scriptural references have been made according to the nomenclature and enumeration of The Jerusalem Bible.

www.ingramcontent.com/pod-product-compliance
Lightning Source LLC
Chambersburg PA
CBHW031235290426
44109CB00012B/299